JOHN WESLEY'S
MISSION TO SCOTLAND,
1751-1790

John Wesley at Forty.

(Reproduced from N. Curnock's edition of John Wesley's *Journal*)

JOHN WESLEY'S MISSION TO SCOTLAND, 1751-1790

Samuel J. Rogal

Studies in the History of Missions
Volume 3

The Edwin Mellen Press
Lewiston/Queenston
Lampeter

Library of Congress Cataloging-in-Publication Data

Rogal, Samuel J.
  John Wesley's mission to Scotland, 1751-1790.

  (Studies in the history of missions ; v. 3)
  Bibliography: p.
  Includes indexes.
  1. Wesley, John, 1703-1791--Journeys--Scotland.
  2. Methodist Church--Scotland--History--18th century.
  3. Scotland--Church history--18th century.
  4. Scotland--Description and travel--To 1800.
  I. Title. II. Series.
  BX8495.W5R595 1989   287' .09411   87-31371
  ISBN 0-88946-070-1

> This is volume 3 in the continuing series
> Studies in the History of Missions
> Volume 3 ISBN 0-88946-070-1
> SHM Series ISBN 0-88946-068-X

For information contact: **The Edwin Mellen Press**
Box 450   Box 67
Lewiston, New York   Queenston, Ontario
U.S.A. 14092   CANADA L0S 1L0
                     Mellen House
                 Lampeter, Dyfed, Wales
            UNITED KINGDOM SA48 7DY

Printed in the United States of America

CONTENTS

ii

PREFATORY NOTE

    <u>John Wesley's Mission to Scotland</u> has originated
from my attempts to summarize, centralize, and relate
the experiences and the activities of John Wesley
during his various journeys into Scotland--beginning
April 1751 and ending in early June 1790. In
fulfilling my purpose, I have relied principally upon
Wesley's own observations of and reactions to the
people and the places north of the River Tweed.
Further, I have consulted with and cited from Wesley's
own letters, diaries, and journals--those very
documents essential to the study of the rise and the
growth of Methodism in Great Britain during the
eighteenth century. Nonetheless, I also determined
that the accounts of selected contemporaries--
particularly James Boswell (1740-1795) and Samuel
Johnson (1709-1784), as well as the reactions of the
Scottish novelist, Tobias George Smollett (1721-1771)--
would function well to present to the reader different
points of view upon similar persons and the same
locales.
    Therefore, by bringing together, wherever
possible, a number and variety of observations,
experiences, and recreations, a fairly balanced and
certainly full awareness of Scotland during the
eighteenth century can be produced. In addition, the
observations and the opinions of an earlier traveler,
Daniel Defoe (1660-1731), allow the twentieth-century
reader to imagine Scotland during the formative years
of the Union and, basically, to appreciate conditions
within the country approximately a generation prior to
the period of Wesley's regular visits.

The principal focus for this project, however, remains upon John Wesley as the founder, leader and spiritual patriarch of British Methodism. As such, the details presented herein underscore his attempts to establish Methodism in the northernmost parts of Great Britain. Thus, this study discusses and analyzes not only the specific and varied efforts of John Wesley and his Methodist preachers to convert the Scots and then organize them into effective bands, classes, and societies, but it also casts some light upon those persons who opposed such conversion and organization. Or, from another point of view, the substance of this discussion helps the reader to understand the various reasons for what amounts to the inability of John Wesley to establish firmly the idea of Methodism north of the River Tweed.

In the end, then, <u>John Wesley's Mission to Scotland</u> unfolds what I believe to be small but necessary chapter in the overall history of religious attitude and opinion in both England and Scotland during the major portion of the Hanoverian period. That period proved to be, according to one Scottish historian, "the century which in England saw the rise of Methodism, and John Wesley, its founder, himself paid many visits to Scotland. Methodism as a separate sect did not gain many followers among the Scots, but it encouraged, within the Church of Scotland itself, a new type of evangelicalism, spontaneous and emotional and quite at variance with the Moderate distrust of 'enthusiasm.'" (Mackie 259).

S.J.R.   Division of Humanities and
                                   Fine Arts
                                Illinois Valley Community
                                   College   1988

A Note on Documentation

To avoid the oftentimes inconvenience of footnotes and endnotes, I have placed short title references, with appropriate volume and page identifications, directly in the text and enclosed by parentheses. The reader need only check those against the full citations listed in Appendix D.

Chapter One

WHITEFIELD AND WESLEY IN SCOTLAND

--What right has such a fellow as you to set
up for a reformer? [asks Bramble] "Begging
your honour's pardon, (replied Clinker) may
not the new light of God's grace shine upon
the poor and ignorant in their humility, as
well as upon the wealthy, and the philosopher
in all his pride of human learning?" "What
you imagine to be the new light of grace,
(said his master) I take to be a deceitful
vapour, glimmering through a crack in your
upper story--In a word, Mr. Clinker, I will
have no light in my family but what pays the
king's taxes, unless it be the light of
reason, which you don't pretend to follow."
    (Smollett, Humphrey Clinker 127)

"I am now just entered Scotland," wrote Daniel
Defoe in late 1725, "and by that ordinary way from
Berwick. We tread upon Scots ground, after about three
miles riding beyond Berwick; the little district
between, they say, is neither in England or Scotland,
and is called Berwickshire, as being formerly a
dependent upon the town of Berwick; but we find no
towns in it, only straggling farm-houses; and one sees
the Tweed on one side, which fetches a reach northward,
the sea on the other, and the land between lies so
high, that in stormy weather 'tis very black and

unpleasant; however, the land is good, and . . . we
ought to think very well of it" (Tour, Letter 11, 563).

In all probability, two men on horseback traversed
the same route on Wednesday, 24 April 1751. However,
John Wesley and his companion, Christopher Hopper, had
left Berwick-upon-Tweed between 3:00 and 4:00 a.m.
Thus, "Whether the country was good or bad we could not
see, having a thick mist all the way" (Journal 3:522).
Such a combination of mist and darkness may well have
been a significant sign to mark the entrance of
Wesleyan methodism into Scotland. Its founder and
leader, then in the forty-eighth year of his life, and
marking the twelfth year of his own form of religious
and social reformation, had tramped the length and
breadth of England, had visited the British colony of
Georgia, and had spent time among Nicholas von
Zinzendorf's Moravian Brethren in Germany. However,
until that moment in late April 1751, he had never set
foot across the River Tweed! Thus, he knew not what to
expect from Scotland's land or from Scotland's people.
He possessed little in the way of insight regarding
their character or their attitudes. Forty years later,
John Wesley still sought to comprehend the mind and
the heart of Scotland.

Methodism north of the River Tweed actually did
not begin with John Wesley's departure from Berwick in
the early spring of 1751. Rather, that event took
place approximately twelve years earlier, on 23 July
1739. On that date, George Whitefield (1714-1770)
communicated with Ralph Erskine (1685-1752), praising
that Scottish cleric's sermons and stating that his
(Whitefield's) tenderest affections lay with the newly
formed Associated Presbytery. Erskine--no doubt at the
urgence of his more recognized brother, Ebenezer

Erskine (1680-1754)--then wrote from Dunfermline to Whitefield in London on 10 April 1741, entreating the English field preacher to visit Scotland. Ebenezer Erskine, the founder of the Secession Church in Scotland, had been, from 1703 until 1731, an extremely popular preacher in Portmoak, Kinross-shire; from there he transferred, in 1731, to Stirling. As a result of his participation in a conservative-evangelical dispute known as the Marrow Controversy (1733), in which he advocated the right of the people to choose their own pastors, the Established Presbytery suspended and then deposed him almost in a single stroke.

Although the General Assembly of the Church of Scotland recalled Erskine's sentence in 1734, the minister declined to return to Stirling unless the reforms that he advocated were put into practice. The Kirk continued to invite him to return until 1740, at which time the General Assembly finalized the deposition. During the interim, Erskine and his adherents met on 6 December 1733, at Gairney Bridge, near Kinross, where they formed themselves into the Associate Presbytery of the Church of Scotland (the "Secession Church"). Ebenezer Erskine's younger brother, Ralph, joined the secessionists in 1737. By 1740, the members of the Associate Presbytery had been formally excluded from the ministry by the General Assembly of the Church of Scotland; no doubt the Erskines wanted George Whitefield leveling his rhetorical cannonades from their pulpits rather than from those of the establishment. In fact, that idea became a strict condition attached to the Erskines' invitation to Whitefield.

Despite his differences with the Church of England and his personal disagreements with John Wesley, George

Whitefield had no real commitment to administrative responsibility, nor did he particularly incline himself toward political dispute. He wanted only to preach to as many persons who would hear him. Thus, he replied to the Erskines, expressing dissatisfaction over their restriction upon his visit and declaring his desire to remain neutral regarding their controversy over the reformation of church government. The elder Erskine settled the matter by not seeking to identify Whitefield with the seceding faction. Instead, he suggested that the Methodist field preacher come to Scotland at the invitation of all the Scottish people, rather than of the so-called "corrupt" Scottish clergy. Whitefield returned the courtesy by coming to Dunfermline on 30 July 1741 and preaching, first, at Ralph Erskine's meeting-house. According to one source, the room appeared filled beyond capacity, and when the orator announced his text, all the members of the congregation fell at once to rustling the pages of their Bibles in an effort to find the proper place. Such a practice surprised him, since he had never before been exposed to it (Southey 391).

On 5 August of that year, Whitefield met with the Associate Presbytery, whose leaders attempted to secure from him a commitment to their cause. When he reiterated his desire to remain neutral, the Presbyters simply chose a more indirect route. They demanded that he preach for them exclusively until the new light from their solemn league and covenant took hold of him. However, Whitefield refused to bend to the pressures from the Erskines and their followers; he would have absolutely nothing to do with what he considered the governmental (or non-essential) aspects of religion. "I believe there is no church perfect under heaven; but as God, by His providence, is pleased to send me forth simply to preach the gospel to all, I think there is no need of casting myself out [of the Church of England]" (Southey 393).

In all, George Whitefield spent thirteen weeks in Scotland, visiting approximately thirty towns and addressing large audiences in the open fields. His detractors rose indignantly against his habit of collecting money, forgetting to consider or even to observe that all funds went directly to more than a dozen charitable causes throughout Great Britain. One of the Associate Presbyters, the Rev. Adam Gib (1713-1788)--a native of Perthshire and a leader of the division of the Associate Presbyters known as "Antiburghers"-- published, in 1742, a pamphlet ominously entitled A Warning against countenancing the ministrations of Mr. George Whitefield, wherein is shown that Mr. Whitefield is no minister of Jesus Christ; that his call and coming to Scotland are scandalous; that his practice is disorderly and fertile of disorder. Indeed, in the true spirit of Thomas B. Macaulay, the title of Gib's piece almost serves as its preface! At any rate, in that sixty-five page tract, the author maintained that George Whitefield's entire doctrine and method, and thus his popularity in Scotland, constituted the fundamental work of the devil. Gib triumphantly claimed that "in raking through this dunghill of Mr. Whitefield's doctrine, we have raised as much stink as will suffocate all his followers, that shall venture to draw near without stopping their noses" (Tyerman, Life of Wesley 1:374).

Yet, George Whitefield had no real political purpose for visiting Scotland--either during his initial journey in 1741 or on at least four other

occasions: June 1742, September-October 1748, July-
August 1753, and Spring 1757.   He expected nothing
beyond the enthusiasms generated by his voice and by
his Calvinism, although he did receive a certain degree
of notoriety.   On 23 December 1743, the Associate
Presbytery declared a public fast in atonement for "the
fond reception given to Mr. George Whitefield,
notwithstanding it is notoriously known that he has
sworn the Oath of Supremacy, abjured the solemn League
and Covenant, and endeavours by his lax toleration and
principles to pull down the hedges of government and
discipline which the Lord hath planted about His
vineyard in this land."   Included in the pronouncement
came forth a "Declaration, Protestation, and Testimony
of the suffering remnant of the anti-Popish, anti-
Lutheran,   anti-Prelate,   anti-Whifieldian,   anti-
Erastian, anti-Sectarian true Presbyterian Church of
Scotland . . . ."   (Tyerman, Life of Whitefield
1:509-514;   2:10-11).   Whitefield encountered that
attack with his usual weapon--by ignoring it
completely.   He had not the slightest intention of
entering into polemic exercises with the Associate
Presbytery; he had never intended to join them, oppose
them, or even to counter their principles by organizing
his own body of rival followers.   Thus, Scottish
Methodism proved a dead issue at least eight years
prior to John Wesley's arrival in that kingdom.

One reasonable conclusion to be drawn from
studying the career of John Wesley focuses upon the
founder and leader of Methodism having experienced two
major setbacks during his lifetime.   The first concerns
his relations with women; the second concerns the
relative impotency of his mission to Scotland.   In both
cases, failure (or lack of significant success)

resulted because of people's insensitivity to Wesley's character and to his ideals. Of course, he, himself, might well have manufactured some adjustments to and within his own personality, modified somewhat his ideals of womanhood, and found a partner with whom he could have been satisfied--and, perhaps, even happy. However, John Wesley had, too early in his life, wed himself to social and religious reform, and one must doubt seriously if he would have been willing to spare significant amounts of his time from his grand commitment in order to devote himself to a partner, a home, or a family. For that reason, his marriage to Mrs. Molly Vazielle, widow of a London merchant, ended in disaster. The woman who, initially, seemed to resemble the mother of the Wesleys turned out, instead, to be a shrew!

But then, shrews are made, not born. Few women of any era would thrill to the idea of a marriage to a man who spent eighteen hours a day traveling throughout the island-kindgom, preaching, organizing, praying, reading, and writing. Even fewer women would generate high levels of excitement toward a man who traveled in excess of 4500 miles each year--a considerable accumulation by eighteenth-century standards. In Scotland, unfortunately, there existed little Wesley could do to solidify even his "marriage" to Methodism. He found himself almost totally unable to change the characteristics, beliefs, and traditions of the people whom he attempted to convert. Even had he managed to do so, to alter his own attitudes and thus re-direct his efforts, the effects would hardly have been noticed.

Essentially, Wesleyan Methodism met with no hard opposition in Scotland, merely insurmountable

obstacles. Had those who worked with Wesley north of
the Tweed been hotly opposed, as they had been in
England, by a band of self-appointed defenders of
tradition and stagnation, the movement would have
received some impetus from a direct cause. Opposition
would have aroused, them, enflamed their zeal. But
Wesley met only with coolness and with insensibility
from a people whom he classified as decent, serious,
and totally unconcerned. Thus, the real cause of his
inability to achieve a high level of success in
Scotland stemmed from the simple fact that the majority
of Scots could have cared less about Methodism--they
saw no need for it, and therefore refused to consider
it seriously. And who could have blamed them for that
attitude? Scotland had its own Church, a disciplined
organization in which clerics wielded considerable
influence over their parishioners. The Scots reared
their children in piety, dedicated themselves to the
Church establishment, and regarded the Church of
England with the same contempt as they extended to the
Church at Rome. How, then, was one to convert the
converted? How could one spread frugality, industry,
and religion among a people generally esteemed as being
frugal, industrious, and religious? Certainly, such a
dilemma would have caused a lesser man to abandon hope
of even initiating an evangelical mission to Scotland.
Instead, John Wesley persisted--and even managed, as we
shall observe later in this discussion--to achieve
slight indentation in the theological and social armor
of Scotland.

By October 1742, the split between John Wesley and
George Whitefield had healed somewhat. Both decided to
renew and to maintain the friendship that dated from
1732, when the latter entered Pembroke College, Oxford,

and then joined the Wesleys' Oxford Holy Club. Nonetheless, both men also, in 1742, determined to travel their separate routes on the road to the eighteenth-century evangelical revival. Whitefield informed Wesley, in a letter dated 1 September 1748, that he would leave to others the responsibility for forming Methodist societies and devote himself to general preaching. When the famous field-preacher heard that Wesley intended to visit Scotland, he attempted to dissuade him. "You have no business in Scotland; for your principles are so well known, that if you spoke like an angel, none would hear you; and if they did, you would have nothing to do but to dispute with one another from morning to night." Wesley's response to this warning proved typical of his nature and of his purpose. "If God sends me, people will hear. And I will give them no provocation to dispute; for I will studiously avoid all controverted points, and keep to the fundamental truths of Christianity. And if any still begin to dispute, they may; but I will not dispute with them" (Wesley, Works 10:356). Obviously, Whitefield was not to be impressed--either by his friend's convictions or by what he had already observed of the religious character of the Scots. On 30 July 1751, in a letter to his patroness, Selina Shirley, Countess of Huntingdon (1707-1791), he noted that "I have been to Musselburgh to see Captain Gallatin [Wesley's friend; see below, Chapter 5, under "Musselburgh"] and his lady. They hold on. Mr. Wesley has been there, and intends setting up societies, which I think imprudent" (Whitefield, Works, 2:420). Even Charles Wesley possessed serious doubts as to his brother's chances for success in Scotland. Writing from Newcastle-upon-Tyne in August 1751, he claimed to have "had much discourse from a brother [Methodist] from Scotland, who had preached there many weeks, and not converted one soul.   You may just as well preach to the stones,' he added, as to the Scots.'"   (from Tyerman, Life of Wesley 2:118)

Reactions to the Methodist venture into Scotland proved not to have been limited to those especially close to John Wesley. Nevertheless, the conclusions tended to have been about the same. John Pawson, one of Wesley's erratic veterans, for a time a principal force in the endeavor north of the Tweed and eventually superintendent of the London Methodist circuit, pointed to the significant differences between the English and the Scots. He viewed the latter as having early been accustomed to hearing the fundamentals of the Gospel, combined with doses of Calvinism, constantly from the pulpits, with the results that the Gospel truths had become totally familiar to them. However, he accused the Scots of knowing little or nothing of Christian experience; thus, Pawson viewed genuine religion ("the life and power of godliness") as being in a considerably low state in Scotland. "I am fully satisfied that it required a far higher degree of the Divine influence. . .to awaken a Scotsman out of the dead sleep of sin, than an Englishman. So greatly are they [the Scots] bigoted to their own opinions, their mode of church government, and way of worship, that it does not appear probable, that our preachers will ever be of much use to that people: and, in my opinion, except those that are sent to Scotland exceed their own ministers in heart-searching, experimental preaching, closely applying the truth to the consciences of the hearers, they may as well never go hither" (quoted in Southey, Life of Wesley 406).

Another commentator, Dr. Adam Clarke (1762-1832), the Wesleyan divine and commentator on the Scriptures who once maintained the tempter of Eve was actually a baboon, placed the issue on a more succinct and practical level. Writing in 1826, Clarke considered "Methodism as having no hold of Scotland, but in Glasgow and Edinburgh. If all the other chapels were disposed of, it would be little loss to Methodism; and a great saving of money, which might be much better employed" (see Clarke, Works 13:242). Twentieth-century researchers have substantiated Clarke's generalizations: in 1767, the number of Methodists in England stood at 22,410, while only 468 resided in Scotland, in 1791, the year of John Wesley's death, there existed 56,605 Methodists in England and 1079 in Scotland; in 1826, the year in which Clarke set down his statement (see above), England housed 217,486 Wesleyan Methodists and another 10,233 belonging to the Methodist new Connexion (or a total of 227,710 English Methodists), while the Methodist rolls in Scotland had risen to only 3428 (Currie, Gilbert, Horsley 139-140).

Certainly, John Wesley never met with nearly the success or the popularity in Scotland that he had achieved in England, Wales, or even Ireland. In Wales, for example, the changes affected by the Methodist itinerant preachers resulted in detaching a majority of the population from the Church of England--an institution to which Welshmen had very little ties to begin with. The Welsh Dissenters immediately welcomed the new ideas of social and institutional reform, and Nonconformity in general rose there at a steady and rapid pace. The complete severance of the Calvinistic Methodists from Anglicanism came about in 1811, while the number of Nonconformist congregations in Wales increased form 105 in 1742 to 2927 in 1861 (Lecky, England in the Eighteenth Century, 2:606). Ireland provided Wesley with little opposition during the years he journeyed there. He viewed the people as significantly teachable and extremely civil. In fact, he always maintained that had he been permitted to spend long periods of time in Dublin, he might have established in that city a society far more numerous than the one in London: one set of figures for 1767 reveals a total of 2250 members in the London Methodist societies, while--in that same year, there resided approximately 2801 methodists throughout the whole of Ireland (see Tyerman, Life of Wesley 2:608). Wesley preached in the streets and the public market-places throughout Ireland, often addressing large congregations consisting chiefly of Roman Catholics. In spite of the obvious opposition of parish priests, those commoners thronged to hear him. Finally, the leader of the Methodists observed that the Irish required nothing beyond rigorous discipline, both in matters of church and civil government, in order to be converted into useful Christians.

However, to contrast Wesley's efforts in Scotland to those in England, Wales, and Ireland does not necessarily mean that Methodism in the land of kilt and kirk proved a complete failure--especially in Wesley's own mind. Simply, there existed problems in Scotland that made Wesley's task--or the task of any eighteenth-century Evangelical, for that matter--terribly difficult. In England, for instance, the Methodist leaders found the people basically ignorant, yet willing to learn and to be spiritually and economically uplifted. The Scots, on the other hand, appeared at least partially enlightened but not in the least heavily prejudiced. A majority of English commoners had, since the seventeenth century, endured without a creed; they stood as outstanding examples of Milton's complaint, more than a hundred years prior to Wesley's mission, that

> The hungry Sheep look up, and are not fed,
> But swoln with wind, and the rank mist they
>   draw,
> Rot inwardly, and foul contagion spread:
>   (Lycidas lls. 125-127)

Thus, in Wesley's view, the English stood ready to receive the light from the new love.

In Scotland, however, John Wesley viewed the populace as firmly anchored to set theological principles from which most refused to drift or stray. Further, his scheme of itinerant ministers and lay preachers, which had met with almost instant success in England, found rejection from the Scots--who refused to consider either the concept for the procedure. "I have written," the Methodist patriarch stated on 16 October 1774, ". . .that Edinburgh and Dunbar must be supplied by one preacher. While I live, itinerant preachers shall be itinerant: I mean, if they choose to remain in connection with me. The society at Greenock are entirely at their own disposal: they may either have a preacher between them and Glasgow, or none at all. But more than one between them they cannot have. I have too much regard both for the bodies and souls of our preachers, to let them be confined to one place any more. I have weighed the matter, and will serve the Scots as we do the English, or leave them" (Wesley, Works 13:395). Thus we may understand why, for example, no less a personage as Dr. Adam Clarke, who presided over the Methodist conferences on three

separate occasions (1806, 1814, 1822), nonetheless had
to be stationed at a number of places: Ireland,
Scotland, the Channel Islands, and the Shetlands.

In any event, John Wesley chose not to abandon his
mission to Scotland. Rather, he determined to accept
for himself the responsibility to continue his labors
among the Scots. He went forth neither to condemn nor
oppose,   in   public,   Calvinistic   principles   and
Calvinistic practices. He went forth to preach the
same fundamental truths he had developed (but had never
been permitted to practice) during his earlier mission
to Georgia. He strove to convert men, women, and
children to those truths. Once they had been
converted, he needed (or so he thought) only to
organize them into those heralded evangelical divisions
known as Methodist bands, classes, and societies. When
on one occasion during a moment of self-inquiry, Wesley
asked, rhetorically, what could be done to intensify
Methodist efforts in Scotland, he provided himself with
these answers: "Preach abroad as much as possible.
Try every town and village. Visit every member of the
society at home" (Wesley, Works 8:316).

On 25 January 1782, the seventy-eight year-old
patriarch summarized his entire scheme for his mission
to Scotland. In a brief letter (a field order from the
commanding general to one of his subordinates) to
Samuel Bardsley, a preacher in the Aberdeen circuit who
had left Sheffield in August 1781, Wesley directed,
"The way to do them good in Scotland is to observe all
our rules at Inverness, just as you would at Sheffield;
yea, and to preach the whole Methodist doctrine, as
plainly and simply as you would in Yorkshire" (Telford,
Letters 7:103). And, for nearly forty years, Wesley
did indeed practice what he had preached to others--

which may provide us with a clue as to why Methodism in
Scotland did not meet with significant success.

Chapter Two

JOHN WESLEY'S READINGS ON SCOTLAND

If you would, in compliance with your
father's advice, enquire into the old tenures
and old charters of Scotland, you would
certainly open to yourself many striking
scenes of the manners of the middle ages.
The feudal system, in a country half-
barbarous, is naturally productive of great
anomalies in civil life. The knowledge of
past times is naturally growing less in all
cases not of publick record; and the past
time of Scotland is so unlike the present,
that it is already difficult for a Scotchman
to image the oeconomy of his grandfather. Do
not be tardy nor negligent; but gather up
eagerly what can yet be found.
(Boswell, Life of Johnson 1042)

The volumes comprising the journals, diaries, and
letters of John Wesley originate from Christ Church and
Lincoln colleges, Oxford; cross the ocean to the
Georgia colony; traverse the paths, roads, and highways
of England, Ireland, Scotland, Wales, and the islands
of Britain; and continue through the greater part of
their author's final week of life. Those same volumes
also contain the record of one of the most notable
commitments to learning in all of eighteenth-century
literary and theological history. Hundreds of popular
and scholarly essays have been devoted to Wesley's

travels, missionary work, sermon addresses, scholarly
activities, and tireless energy. All mention directly
or at least allude to the length of a typical John
Wesley day: from 4:00 in the morning until 9:00 or
10:00 in the evening. And, everywhere he went, by
whatever means he traveled, he read: works on
medicine, natural and physical science; philosophy,
theology; letters, biography, autobiography; volumes of
poetry; history and accounts of ocean voyages and
overland travels. His quest for knowledge and ideas
knew practically no bounds and only occasional
preference in terms of chronology, discipline, genre,
writer, language, purpose, or even (on occasion of
accident) literary quality and logic of argument.

Wesley's purpose for consuming everything he could
get his hands on--or everything that was handed to
him--became, essentially, twofold. First, he placed
the pursuit and attainment of knowledge high on the
list of priorities for those who would embrace
Methodism. Thus, as founder and leader of the
movement, he felt compelled to set an example; he
viewed himself not only as one dedicated to the
assimilation of knowledge and ideas, but as a
communicator and (more important) interpreter of
knowledge and ideas to his followers. Second, although
Wesley derived considerable pleasure from study and
scholarship, he managed a large portion of his reading
during the "fragments" of his time. Simply, reading
provided him with necessary relief throughout those
tedious journeys on horseback, in his chaise, or on
board a ship. Interestingly enough, as the journals
and diaries clearly indicate, Wesley seemed always to
prepare for this tedium: in the hours before a journey
and prior to evening prayer, he devoted himself to

meditation and study; he stuffed pockets and saddlebags with books when he traveled by horse; a small but fully stocked bookcase he had neatly fitted into the famous yellow chaise.

Wesley's program of self-examination and self-education into the areas of Scottish studies appears to have been confined to eight works that he read principally during his periodic travels through Scotland. As five of the titles would indicate, he sought, essentially, attempts to familiarize himself with the history of the land, particularly its people and their religious background. Note, first, the titles of those volumes (listed in chronological order, according to date of publication), in addition to the dates upon which and the locales where Wesley read them:

> John Knox. <u>The History of the Reformation of</u>
> <u>Religion within the Realm of Scotland</u>.
> Edinburgh, 1584. Monday, 23 June 1776,
> at Thornhill (60 miles from Glasgow)
>
> Robert Wodrow. <u>The History of the Suffering</u>
> <u>of the Church of Scotland, from the</u>
> <u>Restoration to the Revolution</u>.
> Edinburgh, 1721-1722. 2 vols. Monday,
> 11 January-Sunday, 17 January 1768, at
> London
>
> William Tytler. <u>An Historical and Critical</u>
> <u>Inquiry into the Evidence, &c. against</u>
> <u>Mary, Queen of Scots</u>. Edinburgh, 1760.
> Tuesday, 26 April 1768, at Aberdeen
>
> William Guthrie. <u>A History of Scotland</u>.
> 10 vols. London, 1767-1768. Friday,
> 10 November 1769, enroute from Norwich
> and Yarmouth to London

Thomas Pennant. A Tour in Scotland in 1769.
    Chester, 1771. Thursday, 23 May 1776,
    at Aberdeen; Tuesday, 12 June 1781, on
    board a boat from Scotland to Whitehaven
Samuel Johnson. A Journey to the Western
    Islands of Scotland. London, 1775.
    Saturday, 18 May 1776, at Aberdeen;
    Monday 11 June 1781, on board a boat
    from Scotland to Whitehaven
Gilbert Stuart. A History of Scotland from
    the Establishment of the Reformation
    till the Death of Queen Mary. 2 vols.
    London, 1782. Sunday, 5 February-
    Wednesday, 8 February 1786, at London
Dr. James Anderson. An Account of the
    Hebrides, and West Coasts of Scotland,
    with hints for encouraging the
    fisheries. Edinburgh, 1785. Thursday,
    11 May 1786, enroute to Penrith

Before looking at the specifics of those works, as well
as Wesley's reaction to them in some detail, one may
note with interest that the founder and leader of the
Methodists seemed not to have engaged in any reading on
Scotland until after 1751, the year in which he
initially entered that land. However, one cannot
always be certain of such matters, since Wesley
obviously did not record everything he did, saw, or
read upon the pages of his journals, diaries, and
letters. And, of course, one would have difficulty,
based upon pure speculation, attempting to determine
what titles were or were not available to Wesley
between 1751 and 1776, as well as why he did or did not
read them and why he did not record his reactions in
his various narratives.

Knox's History of the Reformation of Religion, published twelve years after the writer's death, may well have been the most significant literary achievement of the Scottish theologian. Certainly the most dramatic section (Book IV) contains the notable account of the return of Mary Stuart to Scotland in August 1561, the details of Knox's interviews with Mary, and his fiery denunciations from the pulpit of St. Giles. Wesley's reaction to the History focused not so much upon John Knox or the Reformation itself, but upon the leaders of the movement. Simply, he could not comprehend the reasons behind their excessive zeal, passion, and bitter spirit. ". . .the work of God," he noted, "does not, cannot need the work of the devil to forward it. And a calm, even spirit goes through rough work far better than a furious one. Although, therefore, God did use, at the time of the Reformation, some sour, overbearing, passionate men, yet He did not use them because they were such, but notwithstanding they were so. And there is no doubt he would have used them much more had they been of a humbler and milder spirit" (Journal, 5:171).

Robert Wodrow's qualifications for writing his two-volume History of the Suffering of the Church of Scotland had gained respect beyond question. Educated at the University of Glasgow, he returned to that institution as University Librarian; in addition, he served as minister of Eastwood, near Glasgow, from his ordination on 28 October 1703 until his death on 21 March 1734. No less a statesman than Charles James Fox, an historian in his own right, claimed Wodrow's accounts to be beyond challenge for their authenticity, while David Hume believed the entire History to have been far superior to the treatment extended to the subject by Bishop Gilbert Burnet in his <u>History of the</u> <u>Reformation in England</u> (Volume I, 1679; Volume II, 1681; Volume III, 1714). Wesley, too, expressed the opinion that Wodrow's evidence appeared too authentic to admit doubt; he spent a week reading the two volumes, exclaiming, "Oh what a blessed governor was the <u>good</u>-<u>natured</u> man, so called, King Charles the Second! Bloody Queen Mary was a lamb, a mere dove, in comparison to him!" (<u>Journal</u>, 5:248).

A writer who obviously contributed significantly to Wesley's understanding of Scottish history, William Tytler (1711-1792), earned a degree from the University of Edinburgh and became a successful lawyer. In his <u>Historical and Critical Inquiry</u>, Tytler endeavored to prove that James Murray and James Douglas, Earl of Morton, with their confederates, brought about the murder of Henry Stewart, Lord Darnley. Thus, the act could not be attributed to Mary, Queen of Scots, as had always been supposed. Samuel Johnson reviewed the book in the <u>The Gentleman's Magazine</u> for October 1760 (pp. 453-456), concluding, "It has now been fashionable, for near half a century, to defame and vilify the house of Stuart, and to exalt and magnify the reign of Elizabeth. The Stuarts have found few apologists, for the dead cannot pay for praise; and who will, without reward, oppose the tide of popularity? Yet there remains still among us, not wholly extinguished, a zeal for truth, a desire of establishing right in opposition to fashion" (Boswell, <u>Life of Johnson</u>, p. 250). The work also received favorable reviews from Tobias George Smollett and from Lord Henry Brougham, in his <u>Historical Sketches of Statesmen in the Time of George</u> <u>III</u> (1839-1843). The Scot legislator labeled Tytler's book as the ablest of all the studies focusing upon the controversies over Mary Stuart.

Tytler's arguments obviously produced serious second thoughts for John Wesley, since, no doubt, his readings in Elizabethan history--first at Charterhouse and then at Christ Church, Oxford--had presented to the young scholar the fashionable interpretations attacked by Johnson in his review. Notice, therefore, that Wesley's journal entry for Friday, 29 April 1768, reads almost as though he had just recently transcribed a set of lecture notes:

> By means of original papers, he [Tytler] has made it more clear than one would imagine it possible at this distance (1) that she [Mary] was altogether innocent of the murder of Lord Darnley, and no way privy to it; (2) that she married Lord Bothwell (then near seventy years old, herself but four and twenty) from the pressing instance of the nobility in a body, who at the same time assured her he was innocent of the king's murder; (3) that Murray, Morton, and Lethington themselves contrived that murder in order to charge it upon her, as well as forged those vile letters and sonnets which they palmed upon the world for hers.

> (Journal, 5:257)

Wesley then raised the question as to how one could account for the heretofore accepted versions of the episode, those which place the murder squarely in the hands of Mary. "Most easily," he concluded. "It [the anti-Stuart version] was penned and published in French, English, and Latin (by Queen Elizabeth's order), by George Buchanan, who was secretary to Lord Murray, and in Queen Elizabeth's pay; so he was sure to

throw dirt enough. Nor was she [Mary] at liberty to
answer for herself. 'But what, then, was Queen
Elizabeth?' As just and merciful as Nero, and as good
a Christian as Mahomet" (Journal, 5:257). Thus, after
assimilating these reflections, it becomes a simple
matter to determine the source for Wesley's new-found
conviction that Queen Mary had absolutely no part in
the crimes of which she eventually stood accused.

Eighteen months later, during the week of 6
November 1769, Wesley again confronted the memory of
Mary Queen of Scots when he read "several" of the ten
volumes from William Guthrie's History of Scotland. A
native of Brechin, in Angus, and one-time Aberdeen
schoolmaster, Guthrie (1708-1770) came to London and
established a fair reputation as a contributor of
political pieces to The Gentleman's Magazine and The
Critical Review--the latter founded in 1756 by
Archibald Hamilton in support of Tory and Anglican
policies, edited for a time (1756-1759) by Tobias
George Smollett, and generally supported by Samuel
Johnson and the historian William Robertson. In fact,
Guthrie had the responsibility to digest and compile
the Parliamentary debates and send his notes to Edward
Cave (editor of The Gentleman's Magazine). Prior to
November 1740, Cave sent this material on to Samuel
Johnson, who re-wrote it for publication. James
Boswell thought that Guthrie's "writing's in history,
criticism, and politicks, had considerable merit";
Johnson was somewhat less enthusiastic: "Sir, he
[Guthrie] is a man of parts. He has no great regular
fund of knowledge; but by reading so long, and writing
so long, he no doubt has picked up a good deal"
(Boswell, Life of Johnson, pp. 85, 391).

Wesley thought Guthrie's History impartial, and thus considered it a text upon which the reader might rely. "I never read any writer before," he noted as his initial reaction, "who gave me so much light into the real character of that odd mixture, King James the First; nor into that of Mary Queen of Scots, so totally misrepresented by Buchanan, Queen Elizabeth's pensioner, and her other hireling writers. . . ." (Journal, 5:348). George Buchanan (1506-1582), the Scottish historian, psalmodist, and classical tutor to Mary, abandoned his pupil after the death of Darnley; in his Detectio Mariae Reginae of 1571 and also in his Rerum Scoticarum Historia (1582), Buchanan stated, with undue violence, the case of the insurgent lords against Mary. At any rate, Wesley concluded his evaluation of Guthrie's volumes by re-enforcing, in his own mind, his recently acquired respect for Mary Queen of Scots; "Upon the whole, that much-injured Queen appears to have been far the greatest woman of that age, exquisitely beautiful in her person, of a fine address, of a deep, unaffected piety, and of a stronger understanding even in youth than Queen Elizabeth had at threescore. And probably the despair wherein Queen Elizabeth died was owing to her death, rather than that of Lord Essex" (Journal, 5:348). Unfortunately, Wesley permitted his emotions to distort historical truth here, since no evidence exists to suggest that a guilty conscience emerged as the principal contributor to Elizabeth's death. What might be suggested instead, however, concerns the notion that Methodism's leader had formed in his own mind an overly idealized image of Mary Stuart--a romantic dream, as it were, in which his young heroine had been cut down by a jealous sovereign and her scheming henchmen. In the end, the villainous,

anti-Christian Queen of England received her just
punishment from God.

To this point, the discussion of John Wesley's
readings on Scotland has confined itself to historical
speculation. The first evidence of his having
consulted a travel book on Scotland comes forward
twenty-five years after he first ventured north of the
River Tweed. While in Aberdeen on 23 May 1776, he read
Thomas Pennant's Tour in Scotland in 1769, published in
1771--a work that went through five editions to 1790.
In addition, the writer published A Tour in Scotland
and Voyage to the Hebrides in 1772, in Two Parts
(Chester, 1774). Pennant (1726-1798) was perhaps, next
to Wesley, one of eighteenth-century England's most
habitual travelers--that is, when not pursuing his
research into various aspects of zoology, orinthology,
geology, and history. If, for some reason, he was not
traveling, reading, or observing nature, he devoted his
hours to writing about what he had seen or read: at
least twenty-two volumes in all between 1750 and 1798,
not including a series of lengthy essays on these
subjects. Horace Walpole thought him "a superficial
man, and knows little of history or antiquity: but he
has a violent rage for being an author. He set out
with Ornithology, and a little Natural History, and
picks up his knowledge as he rides. I have a still
lower idea of Mr. [Richard] Gough: for Mr. Pennant, at
least, is very civil: the other is a hog" (Walpole,
Correspondence, 3:441). However, civility alone seemed
not sufficient to obscure from Samuel Johnson what he
believed to be a major deficiency in Pennant's
political ideology. For instance, on Monday, 6
September 1773, Boswell and Johnson came to a farm
about a mile beyond Broadfoot, on the Isle of Skye.

"Mr. Pennant," wrote Boswell, "in the course of his tour to the Hebrides, passed two nights at this. . . house. On it being mentioned, that a present had here been made to him of a curious specimen of Highland antiquity, Dr. Johnson said, 'Sir, it was more than he deserved: the dog is a whig.'" (Boswell, Tour to the Hebrides, p. 261). As we shall observe, though, Johnson could hardly be termed unkind in his overall estimation of Thomas Pennant.

Naturally, Pennant's Tour in Scotland formed a basis for some interesting commentary from Johnson and Boswell as they traveled through the country from August to November 1773. Boswell noted, for instance, that prior to visiting Fort George, Inverness-shire (on Saturday, 28 August 1773), he had consulted Pennant's volume. "He says nothing of this fort; but that 'the barracks, &c. form several streets.' This is aggrandising. Mr. [George] Ferne [master of the stores at Fort George] observed, if he had said they form a square, with a row of buildings before it, he would have given a juster description." As usual, Johnson had the last work on the subject: ". . .how seldom descriptions correspond with realities; and the reason is, that people do not write them until some time after, and then their imagination has added circumstances" (Boswell, Tour to the Hebrides, p.238). Three weeks later (17 September) at Dunvegan, Isle of Skye, Johnson found himself engaged in the first of two defences of Thomas Pennant. He countered the criticisms set forth by Boswell, Colonel John Macleod, and the Reverend Donald M'Queen of Skye to the effect that the traveler-writer was too superficial. "Pennent has great variety of enquiry than almost any man," maintained Johnson, "and has told us more than perhaps

one in ten thousand could have done, in the time that
he took. He has not said what he was to tell; so you
cannot find fault with him, for what he has not told.
If a man comes to look for fishes, you cannot blame him
if he does not attend to fowls." After listening to
all arguments, mostly upon the issue of truth in
Pennant's account, Boswell could only conclude "that he
[Pennant] had better have given more attention to fewer
things, than have thrown together such a number of
imperfect accounts" (Boswell, Tour to the Hebrides,
pp. 307-308). Almost five years later, on Sunday, 12
April 1778, Pennant became the battleground for a
spirited verbal skirmish in which Johnson again assumed
the role of defender; on this occasion, London was the
setting and the Earl of Percy stood forth in the role
of the attacker. The argument reached its zenith when
Percy exclaimed, "Pennant does not describe well; a
carrier who goes along the side of Lock-lomand would
describe it better." To this, Johnson merely responded
with, "I think he describes very well." Then
followed--

> Percy: I traveled after him
> Johnson: And I traveled after him.
> Percy: But, my good friend, you are short-
>   sighted, and do not see so well as I
>   do.

After further exchanges of rude remarks, Johnson
brought the issue to a close by maintaining Pennant to
be "the best traveller I ever read; he observes more
things than anyone else does" (Boswell, Life of
Johnson, pp. 932-933). Boswell, who probably knew more
about Scotland than Pennant, Percy, or Johnson, was
never impressed by the Tour, although he did praise its
author for his scientific studies and writings.

The most interesting aspect of Wesley's reactions
to Pennant's Tour in Scotland is that he never seems to
have been concerned with the work as a piece of travel
literature, or even as a guide that would provide him
with some useful information about Scotland and its
inhabitants. Instead, Wesley focused upon a bit of
minute detail that appears to have escaped the eyes of
Boswell, Johnson, and their fellow voyagers (actual or
critical). At one point in his narrative, Pennant
labels witchcraft "an imaginary crime"; such
observation challenged one of John Wesley's long-time
convictions. ". . .I cannot give up to all the Deists
in Great Britain the existence of witchcraft till I
give up the credit of all history, sacred and profane.
And at the present time I have not only as strong, but
stronger proofs of this, from eye and ear witnesses,
than I have of murder; so that I cannot rationally
doubt of one any more than the other" (Journal, 6:109).
The preceding statement does not mean to imply that
Wesley's belief in ghosts and in witchcraft somehow
affected his power of thought and reason. Essentially,
such beliefs were by-products of his intense religious
conviction of the dread realities contained within an
unseen world. The witches and ghosts that he saw and
heard (or thought he saw and heard), combined with
references from history and contemporary testimony,
provided him with the single significant proof of the
invisible state, wherein men might mingle with separate
spirits. Further, this spiritual world would prove to
be the most powerful weapon for Christians against the
false teachings spread by deism, atheism, and
materialism. At any rate, despite Pennant's one
"mistake," Wesley still thought him, generally, a
"lively as well as judicious writer." But then, five

years later, on 12 June 1781, he discovered another
defect in Thomas Pennant's Tour. "He is doubtless a
man of sense and learning. Why has he then bad English
in almost every page? No man should be above writing
correctly" (Journal, 6:322).

Perhaps the most notable of the travel books on
Scotland that Wesley read is Samuel Johnson's A Journey
to the Western Islands of Scotland (London, 1775). Dr.
Johnson made this celebrated tour with James Boswell in
1773, arriving on 18 August and departing for England
on 22 November. During this period, the two visited
the Hebrides, the three principal cities of Scotland
(Glasgow,   Edinburgh,   and   Aberdeen),   the   four
universities (Edinburgh, Glasgow, Aberdeen, and St.
Andrews), and a considerable section of the Highlands.
In addition, they spent time in company with the great
and the learned of the country, as well as enjoying the
hospitality of persons of lower--and even humble--rank.
Negative reaction to the Journey came mostly from
Scots, who misinterpreted Johnson's frank observations
on the country and its inhabitants, believing the
account to be little more than an on-the-spot
reiteration of ancient British prejudice.

In essence, the writer expressed fairly liberal
attitudes toward Scottish society--its members as well
as   its   institutions.   However,   Johnson's   rigid
adherence to the Church of England and to Tory
principles allowed him little or no room for favor
toward the religious and political practices of the
area. Presbyterianism and John Knox were simply alien
to his own beliefs and traditions; he refused to attend
service in a Scottish kirk, and every ruined church he
came upon seemed to conceal the ghost of Knox's
sixteenth-century reformation. In regard to politics,

Johnson simply distrusted the tendency toward mob rule
and revolution. Thus, he believed that the flames
which sparked the Jacobite uprisings of 1715 and 1745
had not been extinguished entirely, accounting
principally for the radical Whig strongholds still (in
the 1770's) lodged in the northern Highlands.

Wesley, who read the Journey to the Western
Islands on at least two occasions, thought highly of it
and seemed to capture the essence of Johnson's attitude
toward Scotland. "It is a very curious book," he noted
in his journal for Saturday, 18 May 1776, "wrote with
admirable sense, and, I think, great fidelity; although
in some respects, he is thought to bear hard on the
nation, which I am satisfied he never intended"
(Journal, 6:106). Five years later, on Monday, 11 May
1781, neither Wesley's view nor even his language
concerning the Journey seem to have changed. "I had
heard that he [Johnson] was severe upon the whole
nation; but I could find nothing of it. He simply
mentions (without any bitterness) what he approved or
disapproved; and many of the reflections are extremely
judicious; some of them are very affecting" (Journal,
6:322). The companion piece to Johnson's account,
Boswell's Journal of a Tour to the Hebrides, with
Samuel Johnson, LL.D., did not reach publication until
1785 (the "Dedication" bears the date 20 September
1785), but there exists no evidence that Wesley read
it.

Wesley's final encounter with the controversy over
the reputation of Mary Queen of Scots came during the
week of 6 February 1786. While in London, he took time
to read Gilbert Stuart's A History of Scotland from the
Establishment of the Reformation till the Death of
Queen Mary, a two-volume work published in London in

1782. Stuart (1742-1786), originally an Edinburgh lawyer who never actually practiced his profession, devoted the greater part part of his adult life to literary journalism, the study of constitutional law, and history. In addition, he edited the English Review (1783), The Political Herald and Review (1785), and The Edinburgh Magazine and Review--the last in association with William Smellie. Apparently, Stuart's primary purpose in writing the 1782 History of Scotland was to convince British readers of Mary's innocence and to depict the Queen of the Scots as both an amiable and a respectable personage. By 1786, as a result of having already read William Tytler's Inquiry and William Guthrie's History of Scotland, John Wesley hardly needed to be convinced of Mary's innocence; he had, by this time, indeed found his idea of woman. Stuart proved to him "beyond all possibility of doubt that the charges against Queen Mary were totally groundless; that she was betrayed basely by her own servants from the beginning to the end; and that she was not only one of the best Princesses then in Europe, but one of the most blameless, yea, and the most pious women!" (Journal, 7:139-140).

The last of the travel books with which John Wesley came in contact focused primarily upon a specific area of eighteenth-century Scotland's economy. James Anderson (1739-1808) developed his theories on agriculture principally from experiments carried on at his own farm in Aberdeenshire, where he had more than 1300 acres under cultivation. Early in 1785, Anderson, under the direction of the Committee on the State of the British Fisheries, set out on an extensive journey through the Highlands, recording his observations in a work entitled An Account of the Hebrides, and West

Coasts of Scotland, with hints for encouraging the fisheries, published in 1785 at Edinburgh. The traveler suggested the development of fishing communities at Dunvegan, Stornoway, Loch Boisdale, Tobermory, and Bowmore, indicating that such establishments were necessary for the future development and prosperity of the industry. Further, he advanced the ideas that the western coast of Scotland be divided into districts, and that all fishing boats be registered and marked boldly for easy identification (see Hamilton, Economic History, pp. 118-119). Wesley thought Anderson an accurate reporter and a sensible writer. "But how clearly does he show that, through the ill-judged salt [duty], the herring-fishery there, which might be of great advantage, is so effectually destroyed that the King's revenue therefrom is annihilated; yea, that it generally, at least frequently, turns out some thousand pounds worse than nothing" (Journal, 7:162). Unfortunately, Scottish salt, produced by distillation from sea water, was unfit for curing herring, which meant that foreign salt had to be imported. According to terms of the Union 1707), the Scots could import salt without paying excise duty; yet, they had to pay a customs charge of 7s. 4d. per fifty bushels for curing that herring intended for export. Also, under provisions of the Union, foreign salt had to be registered at a customs house at a fee of 7s. 6d. per shipment, and there were other fees and registration costs that exceeded fifty shillings for a single shipment (Hamilton, Economic History, pp. 114-115). Obviously, such severe restrictions hardly benefitted the promotion and expansion of the industry, which was one of the motivations for Anderson's journey and subsequent publication.

Certainly the most interesting aspect of the
discussions set forth in the study of the eight books
on Scottish history and travel is John Wesley's
reaction to the material he read. Indeed, the remarks,
as they exist in the journals, appear as fragments from
the notes of a professional reviewer. No matter what
the general subject or substance of a particular
volume, Wesley always seems to get caught up in a
particular phase of a presentation, something that ran
either parallel or counter to strong personal beliefs
and prejudices. Thus, Mary Queen of Scots, witchcraft,
or even the difficult state of the Scottish fishing
industry reached out and isolated his thoughts from the
larger themes or more comprehensive areas of
discussion. Of course, a major cause for this type of
reaction and eventual notation in the journals stemmed
from Wesley's habit of reducing broad, complex issues
of life and thought to simple but practical solutions.
If people were ignorant, then schools and books could
educate them; if they were hungry, food would provide
them nourishment; if they were poor, Christian charity,
followed by employment, would enrich them; if they had
lost faith, God would replenish and uplift their
spirits. He always sought evidence of this philosophy
in his readings--or, from another view, he became quick
to identify the instances wherein the philosophy was
lacking. Many suffered from those who would abuse
their power, only deists and materialist misunderstood
the real meaning of witchcraft, and the salt duties
were attempts by the wealthy in England to undermine
the efforts of the poor and the industrious in
Scotland. Yes, John Wesley read books on Scottish
history and on Scottish life in order to acquaint

himself with those whom he sought to uplift and, perhaps, even convert; but he also read these volumes for the same general purpose as every other book to which he had access: to familiarize himself with the fundamental strengths and weaknesses, past and present, of men from all ranks and nations. His readings on Scotland constitute one example of a deeply committed eighteenth-century reformer striving terribly hard to append the intellectual and practical qualities of life to the strictest requirements of evangelical Christianity.

Chapter Three

THE CITIES

The city swarms intense. The public haunt,
Full of each theme and warm with mixed discourse,
Hums indistinct. The sons of riot flow
Down the the loose stream of false enchanted joy
To swift destruction. On the rankled soul
The gaming fury falls; and in one gulf
Of total ruin, honor, virtue, peace,
Friends, families, and fortune headlong sink.
Upsprings the dance along the lighted dome,
Mixed and evolved a thousand sprightly ways.
The glittering court effuses every pomp;
The circle deepens; beamed from gaudy robes,
Tapers, and sparkling gems, and radiant eyes,
A soft effulgence o'er the palace waves--
While, a gay insect in his summer shine,
The fop, light-fluttering, spreads his mealy wings.
            (James Thomson, <u>Winter</u>, ll. 630-645)

Glasgow
The city of Glasgow, in Lanark, with a present
population of approximately 1,054,913 and situated at
the entrance of what has now become the Clyde coast
resorts, serves as a prime example of the growth and
development of Scottish industry. In 1708, according
to a census carried out under the magistrates' orders,
the number of its inhabitants stood at 12,766; by 1740,
the population increased to 17,034, to 23,546 by 1755,

to 42,832 (including the suburbs) in 1780, and then to
83,769 at the beginning of the nineteenth century
(Cleland, Statistical and Population Tables, pp.2-3).
The tobacco trade with America existed as the principal
contributor to the wealth and growth of the city,
followed closely by the linen and cotton industries
during the mid and late eighteenth century. As a
result of expanding labor markets, considerable numbers
of Scots moved to Glasgow from nearby counties and from
as far away as the West Highlands; naturally, such an
influx created a need for substantial building, an
activity that continued in Glasgow throughout the
century.

Crossing the River Clyde in the latter part of
1725, Daniel Defoe came upon what he believed "a very
fine city; the four principal streets are the fairest
for breadth, and the finest built that I have ever seen
in one city together" (Defoe, Tour through Great
Britain, Letter 12, pp. 604, 605). He observed the
houses to be all of stone, uniform in size; "the lower
story generally stands on vast square Doric columns,
not round pillars, and arches between give passage into
the shops, adding to the strength as well as beauty of
the building; in a word, 'tis the cleanest and
beautifullest, and best built city in Britain, London
excepted" (Defoe, Tour, p. 605). Further, Defoe noted
that Glasgow stood on the side of a hill that sloped to
the Clyde; where the four streets joined, he looked
upon a square or spacious market-place. "As you come
down the hill, from the north gate to the said cross
[or square], the Tolbooth, with the Stadhouse, or
Guild-hall, make the northeast angle, or, in English,
the right-hand corner of the street, the building very
noble and very strong, ascending by large stone steps,

with an iron balustrade. Here the town-council sit,
and the magistrates try causes, such as come within
their cognizance, and do all their public business"
(Defoe, Tour, p. 605). Finally, he realized full well
the activity in trade and commerce going on within the
city, placing the major cause for this upon the Union.
Aside from the tobacco trade, he observed some four or
five principal areas of domestic activity: sugar,
baking houses; a large distillery that produced
"Glasgow brandy," made from molasses; a mill that
manufactured "plaiding, a stiff cross-striped with
yellow and red, and other mixtures for the plaids or
veils, which the ladies in Scotland wear;" and the
manufacture of muslin and linen (Defoe, Tour, p. 607).

   Another view of eighteenth-century Glasgow may be
gleaned from the novelist Tobias George Smollett
(1721-1771), who returned to his native Scotland in the
spring of 1766. He relates his observations in The
Expedition of Humphry Clinker (1771), through the
epistles of his characters: Matthew and Tabitha
Bramble, Jeremy and Lydia Melford, and Winifred
Jenkins. Thus, when Jeremy Melford relates that "My
uncle is in rapture with Glasgow" (Humphry Clinker p.
217), the latter provides concrete evidence of his
euphoric state in a letter to Dr. Richard Lewis:
". . .to the best of my recollection and judgment,
[Glasgow] is one of the prettiest towns in Europe; and,
without all doubt, it is one of the most flourishing in
Great Britain. It stands partly on a gentle declivity;
but the greatest part of it is in a plain, watered by
the river Clyde. The streets are straight, open, airy,
and well paved; and the houses lifty and well built of
hewn stone" (Humphry Clinker, p. 224). According to
the population figures cited above, Glasgow probably

contained 15,000 inhabitants when Defoe visited there
around 1725; Smollett's Matt Bramble viewed a city of
upward of 30,000. Although by comparing the two
accounts we perceive similar physical and topographical
descriptions and become aware of the affluence from
commerce and industry, only the irritable hypochondriac
Bramble points out the defects of the town. "The water
of their public pumps is generally hard and brackish,
and imperfection the less excusable, as the river Clyde
runs by their doors, in the lower part of the town; and
there are rivulets and springs above the cathedral,
sufficient to fill a large reservoir with excellent
water, which might be thence distributed to all the
different parts of the city. It is of more consequence
to consult the health of the inhabitants in this
article, than to employ so much attention to
beautifying their town with new streets, squares, and
churches" (Humphry Clinker, p. 224).

Fortunately for Bramble's disposition, his stay in
Glasgow came about, really, at the beginning of the
city's expansion and development. The building boom
reached its height almost twenty-five years later and
remained in evidence until well into the next century.
For example, during the ten years following the
American Revolution, Dugald Bannatyne's Glasgow
Building Company invested at least £120,000 in the
construction of new streets and houses (Hamilton,
Economic History, p. 20). Yet, Smollett's Welsh squire
seemed to believe that the growth of the city, even at
its outset, could not atone for such drawbacks as "the
shallowness of the river, which will not float vessels
of any burthen within ten or twelve miles of the city;
so that the merchants are obliged to load and unload
their ships at Greenock and Port Glasgow, situated

about fourteen miles nearer the mouth of the Firth, where it is about two miles broad" (Humphry Clinker, p. 224). However, despite such inconveniences to health and commerce, Bramble was quick to acknowledge his respect for the citizens of Glasgow--especially the merchants, whom he believed possessed "a noble spirit of enterprise. . ." (Humphry Clinker, p. 224).

If eighteenth-century Glasgow appears to have earned the laurel for its growth, development, and industry--all of which produced considerable affluence--it seems to have failed miserably in providing both natives and visitors with anything close to cultural and social activity. True, the city could claim one of Scotland's major universities; but when Alexander Boswell ordered his son James to spend the 1759-1760 academic year at the University of Glasgow, the young scholar felt as though he had been sent into exile--a scholastic St. Helena only forty miles away from his home in Auchinleck! In contrast to the opportunities for amusement and diversion discovered during the previous term at Edinburgh, James Boswell found only a collection of persons whose primary concerns focused upon the commerce and trade, whose manner of living seemed to him coarse and vulgar. Few families, even from among the wealthy, hosted dinners for anyone other than commercial travelers or relatives; hardly more than six households in all of Glasgow employed manservants. According to Alexander Carlyle, who spent two winter terms (1743-1745) at the University, the city was without chaises or hackney coaches; he saw but three or four sedan chairs-- reserved mostly for old ladies and midwives. Also, Carlyle noticed but one concert in two years, and that given by a University student.

Finally, during Boswell's tenure there (and
certainly even before), Glasgow lacked a theatre--or,
more accurately, the strength of the Kirk and its
leaders had successfully prevented anything close to
the establishment of a stage in or near the town.
When, in 1752, a theatre of sorts had begun to take
hold and even hosted the Edinburgh Company at the end
of the season, the Kirk mustered its forces and brought
in fresh opposition. In the following year, George
Whitefield appeared upon the scene; preaching from an
open-air pulpit in the Cathedral churchyard, Whitefield
denounced the theatre, thus causing the proprietor to
order it demolished. Another attempt at a playhouse
occurred in 1764, but a mob put the torch to the
building on the opening night (see Boswell: The
Earlier Years, pp. 43-44). Obviously, the citizens of
Glasgow were content to remain entertained by the more
realistic and practical performances of masons,
carpenters, and street pavers.

At approximately 8:00 on the evening of Tuesday
17, April 1753, John Wesley rode into Glasgow; he had
come at the invitation of the Reverend John Gillies,
D.D. (1712-1796), minister of the New College Church,
Glasgow, from 1742 until his death. At this time
Gillies must still have been working on his two-volume
Historical Collections of the Success of the Gospel,
which he published at Glasgow in 1754. Eighteen years
later he would produce The Life of the Reverend George
Whitefield (1772). During the maiden visit, Wesley was
a guest in Gillies' house, where he helped his host
with his literary project; the two thus commenced a
long friendship. "I bless the Lord for the benefit of
your acquaintance." wrote Gillies after his guest had
departed; "for your important assistance in my

Historical Collections; and for your edifying conversation and sermons in Glasgow" (Tyerman, Life of Wesley, 2:165). Consider, then, the following summary of Wesley's stay in Glasgow, from Wednesday, 18 April, through Sunday, the 22nd:

Wednesday, 18 April. At 7:00 P.M., he attended service at the New College Church. "It was so full before I came that I could not get in without a good deal of difficulty. After singing and prayer he [Mr. Gillies] explained a part of the Catechism, which he strongly and affectionately applied. After sermon he prayed and sung again, and concluded with the blessing. He then gave out, one after another, four hymns, which about a dozen young men sung. He had before desired those who were so minded to go away; but scarce any stirred till all was ended" (Journal, 4:62). Reverend Gillies explained the situation to his Methodist friend and colleague: "The singing of hymns here meets with greater opposition than I expected. Serious people are much divided. Those of better understanding and education are silent; but many others are so prejudiced, that they speak openly against it, and look upon me as doing a very sinful thing. I beg your advice, whether to answer them only by continuing to practice of the thing, or whether I should also publish a sheet of arguments from reason, and Scripture, and the example of the godly. Your experience in dealing with people's prejudice, makes your advice of the greater importance" (Tyerman, Life of Wesley, 2:165).

Thursday, 19 April. Wesley conducted an early morning service, at 7:00, in an open field about a quarter of a mile from Glasgow. ". . .it was an extremely rough and blustering morning, and few people came either at the time or place of my preaching: the

natural consequence of which was that I had but a small
congregation." However, by 4:00 P.M., improvements had
been made, something of an innovation for Wesley:
". . .a tent, as they term it, was prepared: a kind of
moving pulpit, covered with canvas at the top, behind,
and on the sides. In this I preached near the place
where I was in the morning, to near six times as many
people as before; and I am persuaded what was spoken
came to some of their hearts, 'not in word only, but in
power.'" (Journal, 4:62-63).

Friday, 20 April. Although scheduled to speak
again in the open fields outside Glasgow, Wesley had to
cancel the service because of the heavy rains.
However, John Gillies extended an invitation to preach
at new College Church, between 7:00 and 8:00 A.M. No
doubt this pleased Wesley, who, during these years, had
not many opportunities to preach from Establishment
pulpits--either Anglican or Scots Presbyterian.
"Surely with God, nothing is impossible!" he exclaimed.
"Who would have believed, five and twenty years ago,
either that the minister would have desired it or that
I should have consented to preach in a Scotch kirk?"
What made the occasion even more remarkable was that
Gillies had committed a double heresy; he had turned
over his service not only to the leader of the
Methodists, but to an ordained minister of the Church
of England as well. His guest also delivered the
sermon at 4:00 P.M. to "a far larger congregation. . .
than the church could have contained"; Reverend Gillies
then resumed his duties for the 7:00 P.M. service. The
day's end found Wesley most pleased by what had
transpired: "Has not God still a favour in this city?
It was long eminent for serious religion; and He is
able to repair what is now decayed, and to build up the

waste places" (Journal, 4:63).

Saturday, 21 April. Originally, Wesley had intended to leave Glasgow on this day and ride east to Edinburgh. However, the citizens persuaded him to remain two days longer. He had found "an open effectual door, and not many adversaries." Only one member of the Associate Presbytery walked among those gathered in the field, one who "did not see much fruit of his labour; the people would come and hear for themselves, both in the morning, when I explained (without touching the controversy), 'Who shall lay anything to the charge of God's elect?' and in the afternoon, when I enforced 'Seek ye the Lord while He may be found.'" (Journal, 4:63)

Sunday, 22 April. On this, the last day of his first visit to Glasgow, the rains attempted to dampen the spirits of Wesley's early morning open-air service. Nevertheless, he estimated more than a thousand people in attendance (although his crowd estimates always tended to be in excess of the exact figures). At 9:00 A. M., he preached at the Glasgow prison, where the "felons, as well as debtors, behaved with such reverence as I never saw at any prison in England. It may be some even of these sinners will occasion joy in heaven." He still had time in the morning, and again in the afternoon, to attend service at New College Church, where he found opportunity to react to the behavior of the congregation: "None bowed or courtsied to each other, either before or after the service; from the beginning to the end of which none talked or looked at any but the minister. Surely much of the power of godliness was here, when there is so much of the form still" (Journal, 4:63-64). Finally, Wesley returned to the meadow in the late afternoon, where he addressed a throng that included soldiers and students.

John Wesley's second visit to Glasgow did not come
about until four years later, on 1 June 1757. Again,
his stay was of five days' duration, and again he
lodged with the Reverend John Gillies, who rode out to
meet his friend and guest when he reached within a mile
of the city. We may observe this summary account of
Wesley's activities:

Wednesday, 1 June. In the evening, his followers
placed the protective tent (see above, under 19 April
1753) in the yard of the poorhouse at Glasgow, an
institution which Wesley described as "a very large and
commodious place. Fronting the pulpit was the
infirmary, with most of the patients at or near the
windows. Adjoining to this was the hospital for
lunatics; several of them gave deep attention. And
cannot God give them also the spirit of a sound mind?"
(Journal, 4:216) Even here in Glasgow, Wesley sought
out those whom everyone else seemed to have abandoned--
the poor and the mentally depraved. After the sermon,
he baptized four children of the asylum according to
the method of the Church of Scotland. These events
occurred at the Toun's Hospital, a combination hospital
and poorhouse, opened in 1733; it would remain, until
1787, the only infirmary within the city of Glasgow.

Friday, 3 June. Wesley preached at New College
Church at 7:00 A.M., noticing that "the congregation
was increased [over that of the previous evening], and
earnest attention sat on every face" (Journal,
4:216-217).

Saturday, 4 June. Again, Wesley preached at New
College Church, this time at evening service; once more
he expressed his pleasure at the seriousness of the
worshipers. However, "still I prefer the English

congregation. I cannot be reconciled to men sitting in prayer or covering their heads while they are singing praise to God" (Journal, 4:217). The entire matter of worship in the Scottish Kirk was a phenomenon to which John Wesley would never become accustomed.

Sunday, 5 June. At seven in the morning, then again in the late afternoon, Wesley addressed large gatherings in the open field outside Glasgow. He estimated that for the afternoon service, "two thousand at least went away not being able to hear, but several thousands heard very distinctly, the evening being calm and still." After the later sermon, he advised those in attendance to meet weekly with John Gillies and "to examine each other's hearts and lives!" (Journal, 4:217). It must have been during this second visit that Wesley actually organized a praying society in Glasgow; although Reverend Gillies certainly did not become a member, he may well have served as the unofficial counselor of the small band.

Two more years passed before Wesley again spent some time in Glasgow, arriving on Wednesday, 23 May 1759 and remaining through Sunday, the 27th. At 7:00 P.M. on the 23rd and at 7:00 A.M. on the 24th, he preached at the poorhouse; Thursday evening found him addressing a gathering at an open-air service. On Saturday, 26 May, he discovered that "the little society which I had joined here two years since [1-5 June 1757] had split in pieces." Thus, later in the day he met "several members of the praying societies and showed them what Christian fellowship was, and what need they had of it." The next morning, Sunday the 27th, at 7:00, he preached to "a numerous congregation" at New College Church; "I spoke very plain on 'Ye must be born again.' Now I am clear of the blood of these

people. I have delivered my own soul." That evening,
following the service at New College Church, Wesley met
with about forty members of his society and repeated
the instructions of two years earlier: to meet weekly
with John Gillies. His final remark in the journal
concerning this praying society demonstrates the
frustrations arising out of the entire mission to
Scotland. "If this [the weekly meeting with Gillies]
be done, I shall try to see Glasgow again; if not, I
can employ my time better" (Journal, 4:316-317).

Although Wesley had no real intent to abandon
Glasgow, he did not return to the city until six years
later, arriving on Saturday afternoon, 27 April 1765.
In the evening, he preached in the hall of the hospital
at Glasgow, and the following day--his last for this
particular visit--delivered three sermons in the
hospital yard. His spirits must certainly have
improved during this two-day stay, for he observed that
"So much of the form of religion is here still as is
scarce to be found in any town in England. There was
once the power too. And shall it not be again? Surely
the time is at hand" (Journal, 6:112). The journal
entries provide no indication of meetings with the
praying societies or with Reverend Gillies. However,
during this particular year Wesley was to receive some
needed assistance in his attempts to pump some life
into Methodist activities in Glasgow.

Upon returning to England, the leader of the
Methodists dispatched Thomas Taylor, one of his
preachers, to Glasgow for the purpose of organizing a
full-fledged Methodist society in the city. According
to a combination of heresay and related reports,
Taylor's first congregation consisted of two baker's
apprentices and an equal number of ancient ladies!

Also, because of insufficient funds, the society had little difficulty in observing almost every fast-day known to Christendom. Still, Taylor pressed forward and eventually obtained a preaching-room and enough converts to term the attendance as respectable. At one point, he even contracted for the services of a precentor at the rate of 4d. per service, although he had to abandon this luxury when his funds became too meagre to pay the man. Nevertheless, when Thomas Taylor left Glasgow, the Methodist society there numbered in excess of seventy members (Tyerman, Life of Wesley, 3:9-10). The society's rooms were located in the Barber's Hall in Stockwell Street, at the corner of Howard Street; in 1787, a new chapel was opened in John Street.

Apparently, the abbreviated visit of 1765 had been planned as such, for John Wesley returned to Glasgow the very next year and remained for the normal period of five days--from Wednesday, 18 June, through Sunday the 22nd. On Thursday, Friday, and Saturday, he took his services to the open fields; for the Saturday sermon he "enlarged upon communion with God, as the only real, scriptural religion; and I believe many felt that, with all their orthodoxy, they had no religion still." Obviously, Wesley's work was beginning to take hold in Glasgow. He estimated his society there at "seventy-four members, and near thirty among them lively, zealous believers; one of whom was justified thirty years ago and another of them two-and-forty, and several of them have been for many years rejoicing in God their Saviour" (Journal, 5:171).

Sunday, 22 June 1766. Wesley preached outdoors at 7:00 A.M., attended service at New College Church in the early afternoon, and preached at 5:00 P.M. His

reaction to the congregation in attendance at the 5:00
service conveys an obvious tone of encouragement and
general positivism: "I almost despaired of making the
whole congregation hear, but by their behaviour it seems
they did. In the close [of the sermon] I enlarged upon
their prejudices, and explained myself with regard to
most of them. Shame, concern, and a mixture of various
passions were painted on most faces; and I perceived
the Scots, if you touch by the right key, receive as
lively impressions as the English" (Journal, 5:171).

The following summer, Wesley came once more to
Glasgow, but his visit lasted less than twenty-four
hours. He arrived at 2:00 P.M. on Friday, 31 July
1767, preached that evening and again at 5:00 the next
morning, and then boarded an early morning coach for
Edinburgh. He returned, though, on Tuesday, 19 April
1768, riding from Drumlanrig through a heavy rain.
During the two days following, he addressed the members
of his society, remarking, "I doubt we have few
societies in Scotland like this. The greater part of
those I saw not only have found peace with God, but
continue to walk in the light of His countenance."
Further, there exists strong evidence that John Gillies
had been doing more than his share to aid the cause of
Methodism in Glasgow, for Wesley found him "encouraging
them [the Methodists], by all possible means, to abide
in the grace of God" (Journal, 5:255).

An additional word relative to John Gillies may be
in order here, since, obviously, he had something to do
with Wesley's sporadic moments of modest success in
Glasgow. One must note that Gillies' association with
New College Church dated from 29 July 1742; thus he had
entrenched himself among his flock for a full decade
prior to Wesley's arrival. He preached three services

each Sunday, lectured to his congregation three times
each week (apparently to large audiences), published a
weekly news sheet, and regularly moved about throughout
his parish in response to his parishoners' spiritual
needs (see DNB). Actually, Wesley's mission to Glasgow
appears to have served merely as a complement to the
evangelical mission that John Gillies had already
established, one that would continue for five years
beyond the death of John Wesley.

With the exception of a brief period of two days
in 1770--Tuesday, 16 April and Wednesday the 17th--
Wesley did not spend much of his time in Glasgow until
April 1772, when he arrived on Saturday evening the
18th and departed on Friday morning the 24th. He had
ridden over from Edinburgh, imagining "it was the
middle of January than the middle of April. The snow
covered the mountains on either hand, and the frost was
exceeding sharp. . ." (Journal, 5:454). Thus, he
preached indoors both in the evening and the next
morning (Sunday, the 19th). However, the large
attendance for the Sunday evening service forced him
outside in the street, where he preached on "'What God
hath cleansed, that call not thou common.' Hence I
took occasion to fall upon their miserable bigotry for
opinions and modes of worship. Many seemed to be not a
little convinced; but how long will the impression
continue?" (Journal, 5:454). Wesley then spent all
day Monday (the 20th) and Tuesday, and a considerable
part of Wednesday (the 22nd) at Port Glasgow and
Greenock (see under Chapter 5), returning to Glasgow on
the evening of the 22nd. Upon his arrival he met the
society there, a small congregation, and spoke to them
upon "a subject fit for experienced Christians; but
soon after a heap of fine gay people came in. Yet I

could not decently break off what I was about, though
they gaped and started abundantly. I could only give a
short exhortation in the close more suited to their
capacity" (Journal, 5:455). Here, at least, is an
indication that the citizens of the city were beginning
to take note of Wesley and his activities there.

Thursday, 23 April 1772. This being the fast
before the Lord's Supper, the shops of Glasgow closed
for the day and the conduct of business came to a halt.
Three ministers of the Scottish Kirk arrived to assist
Reverend Gillies at New College Church. Wesley, who
termed these men pious and sensible, took the
opportunity to engage them in conversation. In the
evening, rain forced him to meet the Methodist society
in the Grammar School, apparently a room of
considerable size. "I know not that ever I spoke more
plain, nor perhaps with more effect," he noted in
regard to that service (Journal, 5:455).

Friday, 24 April. At 5:00 A.M., Wesley addressed
a "large congregation. . .and many of the rich and gay
among them. I was aware of them now, and they seemed
to comprehend perfectly well what it is to be 'ashamed
of the gospel of Christ.'" (Journal, 5:455) The
obvious reference, of course, is to the encounter of 22
April mentioned above.

Two years passed before John Wesley found another
opportunity to visit the society of Glasgow. Taking
the stage from Edinburgh on Thursday, 12 May 1774, he
arrived in the city on the same day; the next day, the
13th, and also on Saturday the 14th, he preached on the
old Green "to a people the greatest part of whom hear
much, know everything, and feel nothing" (Journal,
6:19). He attended both morning and afternoon services
on Sunday, 15 May, either at Glasgow Cathedral or New

College Church; the sermons that he heard "contained much truth, but were no more likely to awaken one soul than an Italian opera." That evening he preached on the old Green to a large crowd: his sermon text, "Though I have all knowledge. . .though I have all faith. . .that I give all my goods to feed the poor . . .and have not love, I am nothing" (Journal, 6:19).

Monday, the 16th, found Wesley at Port Glasgow and Greenock; by Tuesday evening he was back at Glasgow, delivering a sermon on the Green and bearing up well under severe wind and cold. Yet, although Wesley had learned to accept the harsh spring climate of Scotland, he still had serious reservations about the effect of his mission in this land, especially since the Methodist society in Glasgow showed no signs of adding to its numbers. "One preacher stays here two or three months at a time," he lamented, "preaching on Sunday mornings and three or four evenings a week. Can a Methodist preacher preserve either bodily health or spiritual life with this exercise? And if he is but half alive, what will the people be?" (Journal, 6:105-106).

Evidently, the sight of the Clyde injected new enthusiasm and hope into Wesley's sagging spirits, for when he returned to Glasgow in the spring of 1779, he noticed fresh signs of life, both in the small Methodist society and in the general population. On Friday, 28 May, Wesley preached at the society's meeting-house; the next evening found him delivering a sermon to an attentive throng assembled by the riverbank. At 7:00 A.M. on Sunday, 30 May, he addressed the society, speaking "exceeding strong words in applying the parable of the Sower." That afternoon he attended service at the Anglican chapel and, as he

had done three years previously, expressed surprise at
the decorum of the congregation. "Such decency have I
seen even at West Street [Chapel, London] or the new-
room in Bristol. (1) All, both men and women, were
dressed plain: I did not see one high head; (2) no one
took notice of any one at coming in, but, after a short
ejaculation, sat quite still; (3) none spoke to any one
during the service, nor looked either on one side or
the other; (4) all stood, every man, woman, and child,
while the Psalms were sung; (5) instead of an unmeaning
voluntary was an anthem, and one of the sweetest I ever
hear; (6) the prayers, preceding a sound, useful
sermon, were seriously and devoutly read; (7) after
service, none bowed or courtsied or spoke, but went
quietly and silently away" (Journal, 6:235-236). In
reference to Wesley's comment that he did not see a
"high head," one is reminded of a report on the first
sermon preached at the New Chapel in City Road, London,
on Sunday, 1 November 1778. "The first quarter of an
hour of his [John Wesley's] sermon was addressed to his
numerous female auditory on the absurdity of the
enormous dressing of their heads; and his religious
labours have so much converted the women who attended
at that place of worship that widows, wives, and young
ladies appeared on Sunday without curls, without flying
caps, and without feathers; and. . .the female sex
never made a more pleasing appearance" (Journal, 6:216,
note 1).

After the service (of 30 May 1779) at the Church
of England Chapel, Wesley conducted his own assembly by
the banks of the Clyde. He described those in
attendance as "a large multitude of serious people
. . . ." Thus, he left for Edinburgh on Monday, the
31st, in extremely high spirits about the future of

Methodism in Glasgow: "Surely we shall not lose all our labour here" (Journal, 6:236). Obviously, however, the one drawback to this optimism was Wesley's age; although still in reasonably good health for a man of seventy-six, the demands from his other societies throughout Scotland--not to mention those in England, Ireland, and Wales--must have taken their toll upon his time and energy. He would not pay another visit to Glasgow until almost five years later.

On Monday, 26 April 1784, John Wesley preached in the evening to the Glasgow society on Luke 16:31, afterward dining and conversing with John Gillies. The next morning he preached on Luke 1:72, noting the large congregation, "although the morning preaching had been long discontinued [by the itinerants] both here and at Edinburgh" (Journal, 6:499). No doubt the preaching-room at Barber's Hall was becoming too small for the growing society in Glasgow; at the services on Tuesday the 27th, Wednesday the 28th, and Thursday morning, the 29th, people had to be turned away.

During his next visit (13 - 17 May 1786), nothing of note occurred, Wesley remarking that, throughout his stay, he was "fully employed." To comprehend the full meaning of that term, we may do well to examine his schedule, as outlined in the diaries:

Saturday, 13 May 1786. Up at 3:30 A.M.; prayer; 4:00 A.M., chaise for Elvanfoot, arriving at 6:30 A.M.; 7:30 A.M., chaise for Douglas Mills; 12:15 P.M., chaise for Mauchlan; 4:45, chaise for Glasgow, arriving at 6:15; sermon at 7:00; bed at 9:30. Length of day: 18 hours.

Sunday, 14 May. Up at 4:00 A.M.; sermon at 10:30 A.M.; visits, dinner, prayer, and a short nap--all between 1:00 and 2:00 P.M.; sermon at 2:00; tea and conversation between 4:30 and 5:00; sermon at 6:00; society meeting supper, and prayer after service; bed at 9;30. <u>Length of day: 17 hours, 30 minutes</u>.

Monday, 15 May. Up at 4:00 A.M.; sermon at 5:00 A.M.; tea, conversation, prayer between 8:00 and 9:00 A.M.; read over journal, walk, conversation from 9:00 to 11:30 A.M.; 1:00 P.M., dinner, conversation, prayer; 2:00 write letters and read 4:00, tea, conversation, prayer; service at 5:00; retired at 9:30. <u>Length of day: 17 hours, 30 minutes</u>.

Tuesday, 16 May. Up at 4:00 A.M.; service at 5:00 A.M.; 2:00 P.M., at Dr. Gillies' house for dinner; conversation, and prayer; service at 6:00; bed at 9:30. <u>Length of day: 17 hours, 30 minutes</u>.

Wednesday, 17 May. Up at 4:00 A.M.; departure for Edinburgh shortly after 5:00 P.M.

If this most recent visit proved barren of major incidents, the next, exactly two years later, was marked by two occurrences of note. Prior to Wesley's arrival, certain Scottish ministers circulated a rumor that he stood ready to publish a new edition of Scriptures, one that omitted parts of the Epistle to the Romans, St. John's Apocalypse, and other portions of the inspired writings. Yet, despite this venomous gossip, Wesley "was far better received in Glasgow than ever," according to Charles Atmore, one of the Wesleyan Methodist ministers to Scotland (Tyerman, <u>Life of Wesley</u>, 3:533). When Methodism's founder reached the city at 10:30 A.M., Friday 16 May 1788, he must have been elated by what he saw. A year earlier, 27 May 1787, Atmore had opened a new preaching-house in Glasgow, situated at the corner of John Street and Cochrane Street. This structure, rebuilt in 1854, served the cause of Methodism until the watch-night service on 31 December 1881; on the next day (1 January 1882), St. John's Chapel was opened. Wesley described the new preaching-house as having "the pulpit on one side, and has exactly the look of a Presbyterian meeting-house" (Journal, 7:388). He preached there at 7:00 P.M. on the 16th "to a tolerably large congregation" on Romans 3:22, and again at 5:00 A.M. on Saturday the 17th, his text being Matthew 5:6. At the 6:00 P.M. Saturday service, the congregation was "increased fourfold, but still I could not find the way to their hearts" (Journal, 7:389).

On Sunday, the 18th, the final day of this current visit, Wesley preached at 11:00 A.M. on Mark 4:3, at 2:30 P.M. on Psalms 50:23, and again at 6:00 on Isaiah 57:1-2. Also, during the evening service, he addressed the congregation on the matter of Methodism with these words:

> There is no other religious society under heaven which requires nothing of men in order to their admission into it but a desire to save their souls. Look all round you: you cannot be admitted into the Church, or society of the Presbyterians, Anabaptists, Quakers, or any others, unless you hold the same opinions with them, and adhere to the same mode of worship.
>
> The methodists alone do not insist on your holding this or that opinion; but they think and let think. Neither do they impose any particular mode of worship; but you may continue to worship in your former manner, be it what it may. Now, I do not know any other religious society, either ancient or modern, wherein such liberty of conscience is now

allowed, or has been allowed, since the age
of the apostles. Here is a glorying peculiar
to us. What society shares it with us?

(_Journal_, 7:389)

Two years later, on Thursday, 27 May 1790, Wesley
came to Glasgow for the final time. Unfortunately, the
visit (he left on Monday, the 31st) was not especially
pleasant or heartening. On Friday, the 28th, he noted
that "The congregation was miserably small; verifying
what I had often heard before, that the Scots dearly
love the word of the Lord--on the Lord's day. If I
live to come again, I will care to spend only the
Lord's day at Glasgow" (_Journal_, 8:67). No matter, for
he was never to see another spring in this city; within
nine months, John Wesley would be dead.

Glasgow Cathedral

Glasgow can boast of the only complete medieval
cathedral (twelfth century) surviving on the Scottish
mainland. It is remarkable for the ambulatory that
runs all round the building, thus providing for the
traffic of pilgrims to the shrine of St. Mungo's
(Kentigern), placed in a crypt or lower church under
the eastern limb, where the ground falls. Located in
Cathedral Square, off Castle Street, Glasgow Cathedral
comprises an aisled nave, aisled choir and presbytery,
dwarf transepts, and a central tower crowned with a
lofty stone spire. The two western towers have,
unfortunately, been removed, which gives the building
somewhat of an austere exterior appearance; however,
the interior more than compensates for this failure.
The presbytery dates from the thirteenth century, the
nave was built about 1300, and the tower perhaps a
century later. In 1484, the Blacader aisle was

attached to the south transept. Other notable features
of this cathedral include the elaborate vaulting in the
crypt, the fourteenth-century timber roof, and the
stone screen, or pulpitum, dating from the fifteenth
century. At the northeast corner is the sacristy,
completed in the fifteenth century in the manner of a
castle.

Daniel Defoe described Glasgow Cathedral as "an
ancient building, and has a square tower in the middle
of the cross, with a very handsome spire upon it, the
highest that I saw in Scotland, and, indeed, the only
one that is to be called high" (Defoe, Tour, p.605).
He observed, also, that the Cathedral was divided into
three churches. Smollett's Matthew Bramble termed the
structure a "venerable cathedral, that may be compared
with York minster or Westminster. . ." (Humphry
Clinker, p. 224). Less enthusiastic than Defoe or
Matthew Bramble, Samuel Johnson saw the Cathedral as a
symbol, rather than as a building. Glasgow, he
commented with his usual authority, "is the only
episcopal city whose cathedral was left standing in the
rage of Reformation. It is now divided into many
separate places of worship, which, taken all together,
compose a great pile, that had been some centuries in
building, but was never finished; for the change of
religion intercepted its progress, before the cross
aisle was added, which seems essential to a Gothick
cathedral" (Journey to the Western Islands, p. 145).

John Wesley, who tended to view churches more
carefully and critically than did any of the three
preceding travelers, toured Glasgow Cathedral first on
Wednesday, 18 April 1753. From the outside, he thought
it a fine building, equal to most cathedrals in
England. However, "it is miserably defaced within,

having no form, beauty, or symmetry left" (<u>Journal</u>,
4:62). Nonetheless, four years later--Saturday, 4 June
1757--he found that the building did have one quality
to recommend it: "I walked through all parts of the
old cathedral, a very large and once beautiful
structure--I think more lofty than that at Canterbury,
and nearly the same length and breadth. We then went
up the main steeple, which gave us a fine prospect
both of the city and the adjacent country. A more
fruitful and better cultivated plain is scarce to be
seen in England. Indeed, nothing is wanting but more
trade (which would naturally bring more people) to make
a great part of Scotland no way inferior to the best
counties in England" (<u>Journal</u>, 4:217). One may indeed
wonder at the relationship between the steeple of
Glasgow Cathedral and Wesley's simple cure for
Scotland's economic ills.

Glasgow University

Founded in 1451 by William Turnbull (d. 1454),
Bishop of Glasgow from 1447 to his death, the
University of Glasgow had undergone considerable
rebuilding during the late seventeenth century: two
handsome and commodious quadrangles, spacious
classrooms, and a court of comfortable houses for the
professors. The students wore red gowns, and a goodly
number of them lived and took their meals at the
University; thus, by the eighteenth century, the
institution presented a pleasantly collegiate
appearance. Defoe described the exterior as "of
freestone, very high and very august" (<u>Tour</u>, p. 605),
while Tobias George Smollett provides his readers with
a view of "a respectable pile of building, with all
manner of accommodation for the professors and

students, including an elegant library, and an observatory well provided with astronomical instruments" (Humphry Clinker, p. 224). Aside from James Boswell, whose forced tenure at Glasgow lasted hardly a single term, the University's most notable eighteenth-century scholar and don was Adam Smith (1723-1790); he studied there from 1737 to 1740, became Professor of Logic (1751-1752) and later of Moral Philosophy (1752-1763), and finally was elected Rector of the University in 1787. Two of his principal works, The Theory of Moral Sentiments (1759) and the Inquiry into the Nature and Causes of the Wealth of Nations (1776), were, essentially, the products of his lectures on moral philosophy. Professor Frederick A. Pottle strongly suggests that Adam Smith's lectures on rhetoric and belles-lettres had a profound effect upon the nineteen year-old Boswell, since they emphasized the value of "characteristic detail in biography" and the "marks of good style," illustrated with references to English authors (Pottle, The Earlier Years, p. 42).

John Wesley toured the University of Glasgow some six years before Alexander Boswell exiled his son to that institution. Methodism's leader was not impressed by what he saw, perhaps, in part, because of his deep loyalty to and fondness for his own Oxford. As with practically everything with which he came into contact the first time, he tended toward comparisons: "The University (like that of Dublin) is only one college, consisting of two small squares; I think not larger, nor at all handsomer, than those of Lincoln College [where Wesley served as a tutor from 1729 to 1735] in Oxford. The habit of the students gave me surprise. They wear scarlet gowns, reaching only to their knees. Most I saw were very dirty, some very ragged, and all

of very coarse cloth" (<u>Journal</u>, 4:62). On another
visit to Glasgow--Friday, 3 June 1757--he walked about
the University and examined the paintings in the new
library. "Many of them are by Raphael, Rubens, Van
Dyck, and other eminent hands; but they have not room
to place them to advantage, their whole building being
very small" (<u>Journal</u>, 4:217).

<u>Edinburgh</u>

By the middle of the eighteenth century,
inhabitants of the old town of Edinburgh found
themselves confronted with the one problem that
eventually bears down upon every significant urban
century during its history--growth! According to an
account in the <u>Scots Magazine</u> (14 [August 1752], 370-
371), "The narrow lanes leading to the north and south
from the main street [principally Castle Hill Street
and the High Street] by reason of their steepness,
narrowness, and dirtiness can only be considered as so
many unavoidable nuisances. Confined by the small
compass of the walls, and the narrow limits of the
royalty, which scarcely extends beyond the walls, the
houses stand more crowded than in any other town in
Europe and are built to a height that is almost
incredible. Hence necessarily follows a great want of
free air, light, cleanliness and every other
comfortable accommodation." The population had grown
from roughly 4,000 in 1722 to upward of 57,000 by 1755;
the city stood, without rival, as the largest in
Scotland. In the spring of 1752, however, there
appeared a pamphlet entitled <u>Proposals for Carrying on
Certain Public Works in the City of Edinburgh</u>; the next
year saw the passage of the first Act for expansion and
improvement. Finally, beginning in 1763, proposals for

a new town created in Edinburgh a degree of activity rarely before witnessed in all of Britain.

To describe or even attempt to summarize that grand project within the pages of the present study would, indeed, be both foolhardy and superfluous. Such a volume as A. J. Youngson's The Making of Classical Edinburgh, 1750-1840 tells the story completely and graphically, while Henry Hamilton's An Economic History of Scotland in the Eighteenth Century presents the essential details from such points of view as population, industry, trade, banking, and labor. For the purposes of this discussion, the eyes of selected eighteenth-century men of letters will serve splendidly to supplement and support the observations and reactions of John Wesley as he tried to establish a firm foothold for Methodism within Edinburgh. Whenever necessary, the fruits harvested by Professors Youngson and Hamilton will be sampled to clarify certain matters and, generally, to bring the total image of Edinburgh during the mid and late eighteenth century into focus.

John Wesley's initial visit to the former capital of the Scottish kingdom occurred on his second day north of the River Tweed--Thursday, 25 April 1751. He must have stayed there only for several hours at most, for he rode back to Musselburgh in time for dinner and evening service. ". . .one of the dirtiest cities I had ever seen, not excepting Cologne in Germany," is all he can set down in his journal (3:523). Obviously, few individuals who gazed for the first time upon Edinburgh could ignore this condition. Earlier in the century, Daniel Defoe took note of the problems arising from the topography, the area, and the proximity (as well as necessity) of the town to its Castle:

. . .regarding immediate safety, [the early

inhabitants] fixed on the place as above [the
Castle Rock] as a sure strength, formed by
Nature, and ready at their hand. By this
means   the   city   suffers   infinite
disadvantages, and lies under such scandalous
inconveniences as are, by its enemies, made a
subject of scorn and reproach; as if the
people were not as willing to live sweet and
clean as other nations, but delighted in
stench and nastiness; whereas, were any other
people to live under the same unhappiness, I
mean as well of a rocky and mountainous
situation, thronged buildings, from seven to
twelve story high, a scarcity of water, and
that little they have difficult to be had,
and to the uppermost lodgings, for to fetch;
we should find a London or a Bristol as dirty
as Edinburgh, and, perhaps, less able to make
their dwelling tolerable, at least in so
sorrow a compass; for, though many cities
have more people in them, yet, I believe,
this may be said with truth, that in no city
in the world so many people live in so little
room as Edinburgh.

(Defoe, Tour, p. 577)

Forty years later, the congestion, filth, and problems
with the water had not improved to any extent.   In
fact, according to Tobias George Smollett--who last
visited Scotland in 1766 and presented his observations
in 1771 through the epistles of Matthew Bramble--the
situation had even deteriorated since the time of
Defoe's account:

. . .the water is excellent [remarks
Bramble], though I'm afraid not in sufficient

quantity to answer all the purposes of cleanliness and convenience. . . . The water is brought in leaden pipes from a mountain in the neighbourhood, to a cistern on the Castle-hill, from whence it is distributed to public conduits in different parts of the city--From these it is carried in barrels, on the backs of male and female porters, up two, three, four, five, six, seven, and eight pair of stairs, for the use of particular families--Every story is a complete house, occupied by a separate family; and the stair being common to them all, is generally left in a very filthy condition; a man must tread with great circumspection to get safe housed with unpolluted shoes. . . . You [Dr. Richard Lewis, the recipient of Bramble's epistle] are no stranger to their method of discharging all their impurities from the windows, at a certain hour of the night . . . . A practice to which I can by no means be reconciled; for notwithstanding all the care that is taken by their scavengers to remove this nuisance every morning by break of day, enough still remains to offend the eyes, as well as other organs of those whom use has not hardened against all delicacy of sensation.

(Humphry Clinker, p. 196)

On Saturday evening, 14 August 1773, Samuel Johnson and James Boswell--two gentlemen obviously "not hardened against all delicacy of sensation"--strolled arm-in-arm up the High Street, on their way to the latter's house in James Court. "I could not prevent

his being assailed by the evening effluvia of
Edinburgh," recalled Boswell with some embarrassment.
"I heard a late baronet, of some distinction in the
political world in the beginning of the present reign
[of George III], observe that 'walking the streets of
Edinburgh at night was pretty perilous, and a good deal
odoriferous.' The peril is much abated, by the care
which the magistrates have taken to enforce the city
laws against throwing foul water from the windows; but,
from the structure of the houses in the old town, which
consist of many stories, in each of which a different
family lives, and there being no covered sewers, the
odour still continues. A zealous Scotsman would have
wished Mr. Johnson to be without one of his five senses
upon this occasion. As we marched slowly along, he
grumbled in my ear, 'I smell you in the dark!' But he
acknowledged that the breadth of the street, and the
loftiness of the buildings on each side, made a noble
appearance." (Boswell, Tour to the Hebrides, p. 173).
Undoubtedly, the dirt and the aroma remained,
throughout the eighteenth century, as essential
ingredients to the tradition of old Edinburgh.

        Wesley returned to Edinburgh on Monday afternoon,
at 5:00, on 23 April 1753; however, he did not even
remain the night, and thus must have been only passing
through on his way from Glasgow to Tranent. Six years
later--Monday, 28 May 1759--he again rode through the
former capital, possibly not even bothering to stop for
an appreciable length of time as he made his way from
Glasgow to Musselburgh. Not until April 1761 did
Wesley stay in Edinburgh long enough to accomplish
something; we note that we arrived at 4:00 P.M. on
Tuesday, the 28th. First, he met with Christopher
Hopper, who would preach that evening "in a large room

lately an episcopal meeting-house" (Journal, 4:449). The building was located in the north-central section of the city, in the gardens opposite Heriot's (or Orphans') Hospital. Then the next morning (Wednesday, the 29th), Wesley preached in the same room at 7:00; the extreme cold, perhaps, kept him from holding an open-air service. "Some of the reputable hearers cried out in amaze: 'Why, this is sound doctrine! Is this he whom Mr. Wh[itefield] used to talk so?' Talk as he will, I shall not retaliate" (Journal 4:449).

After delivering another sermon in the evening, he stayed the night; the next morning he departed for Dundee, returning again on Saturday, 9 May. No doubt the sixty-six miles from Glamis to Edinburgh had exhausted him; "however, I would not disappoint the congregation, and God gave me strength according to my day" (Journal, 4:452). On Sunday, the 10th, Wesley had planned to preach near the Royal Infirmary Street--but the managers of the institution would not permit it. "So I preached in our room morning and evening, even to the rich and honourable. And I bear them witness they will endure plain dealing, whether they profit by it or not" (Journal, 4:452).

Before John Wesley took his leave of Edinburgh on Monday, 11 May 1761, he found time to set down this impression of the city: "The situation of the city, on a hill shelving down on both sides, as well as to the east, with the stately castle upon a craggy rock on the west, is inexpressibly fine. And the main street, so broad and finely paved, with the lofty houses on either hand (many of them seven or eight stories high), is beyond any in Great Britain. But how can it be suffered that all manner of filth should still be thrown even into this street continually? Where are

the magistracy, the gentry, the nobility of the land?
Have they no concern for the honour of their nation?
How long shall the capital city of Scotland, yea, the
chief street of it, stink worse than a common sewer?
Will no lover of his country, or of decency and common
sense, find a remedy for this?" (Journal, 4:452)
Certainly a remedy was being sought, and Wesley must
have been aware of the plans for the expansion of the
city. However, large schemes meant nothing to him as
long as immediate problems continued to be ignored; he
simply could not recognize that which seemed, to him,
at least, merely a substitute for present, practical
considerations.

In 1763, Wesley spent almost two days in
Edinburgh, arriving there on Saturday, 21 May, and
departing on Monday the 23rd. Part of Sunday he spent
visiting with George Whitefield, who had intended to
leave for America about the middle of April 1763;
however, illness forced him to delay embarkation until
4 June, at which time he sailed form Greenock for his
sixth visit to the American colonies. "Humanly
speaking," observed Wesley, "he is worn out; but we
have to do with Him who hath all power in heaven and
earth" (Journal, 5:13). A week later (Sunday, 29 May),
the leader of the Methodists returned to the city,
preaching this time at 7:00 A.M. in the High School
yard--located off Cowgate Port, northeast of the Royal
Infirmary and directly north of Surgeons' Hall. "It
being the time of the General Assembly [of the Church
of Scotland], which drew together, not the ministers
only, but abundance of the nobility and gentry, many of
both sorts were present; but abundantly more at five in
the afternoon. I spoke as plan as ever I did in my
life; but I never knew any in Scotland offended at

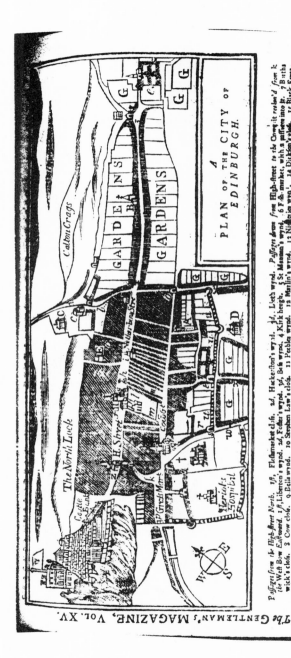

General Assembly of the Church of Scotland, Tron Church, Edinburgh, 1787.

plain dealing. In this respect the North Britons are a pattern to all mankind" (Journal, 5:15). And, speaking of patterns, this would be the first of several occasions upon which Wesley intentionally placed himself in competition with the General Assembly of the Scottish Kirk.

When Wesley came again to Edinburgh on Saturday, 26 May 1764, he preached in the evening on Calton Hill, lying north of the Back of Canongate, bordered on one side by the western road to Leith and on the other by the eastern road to that town; the hill rose some 355 feet beyond sea level. For the residents of the Scottish capital, Calton Hill was considered the country, and maidservants, especially, enjoyed taking the smaller children up there to sit with them or merely to play about. Once more, Wesley had arrived in Edinburgh during the meeting of the General Assembly of the Kirk; thus, on this Saturday evening, "many of the ministry were there. The wind was high and sharp, and blew away a few delicate ones. But most of the congregation did not stir till I had concluded" (Journal, 5:71). The inclement weather continued to be somewhat of a problem during the next day (Sunday, 27 May): at 7:00 A.M. he preached in the High School yard and complained of the extreme cold; in the evening, he addressed a large congregation on Calton Hill in the midst of a storm. "At first the wind was a little troublesome; but I soon forgot it. And so did the people for an hour and a half, in which I fully delivered my own soul" (Journal, 5:71).

Two events of note occurred during this particular visit to Edinburgh. First, on Monday the 28th, Wesley attended a session of the General Assembly, composed, according to his estimate, of over 150 ministers of the

Kirk. "I was surprised to find: (1) that any one was admitted, even lads twelve or fourteen years old; (2) that the chief speakers were lawyers, six or seven on one side only; (3) that a single question took up the whole time, which, when I went away, seemed to be as far from a conclusion as ever, namely, 'Shall Mr. Lindsay be removed to Kilmarnock parish or not?' The argument for it was, 'He has a large family, and this living is twice as good as his own.' The argument against it was, 'The people are resolved not to hear him, and will leave the kirk if he comes.' If, then, the real point in view had been, as their law directs, majus bonum Ecclesiae [the greater benefit of the Church], instead of taking up five hours, the debate might have been determined in five minutes" (Journal, 5:71). Second, Wesley formed an acquaintance with Darcy Brisbane, Lady Maxwell (1743-1810). This young lady had married, in 1760 and at the age of seventeen, Sir Walter Maxwell of Pollock, Bt.; two years later, both her husband and their infant son died. The widow turned immediately to strict piety, then to Methodism, and finally to a life-long friendship and correspondence with John Wesley. In 1770, Lady Maxwell established a school in Edinburgh for the Christian education of poor children; she sustained the institution herself for forty years, and prior to her death set down provisions for the continued existence of the school after her passing.

Wesley was back in Edinburgh by mid June 1764, preaching on the Calton Hill the evening of Saturday, the 16th, to a large gathering. The next day (Sunday, 17 June) he conducted service at 7:00 A.M. for another sizeable congregation in the High School yard. Later in the day he was informed that the Lord's Supper would be administered at the West Kirk, or St. Cuthbert's Parish Church. According to one source, St. Cuthbert's looked "so like a huge stone box, that some wags have described it as resembling a packing-case, out of which the neighbouring beautiful toy-like fabric of St. John's Church has been lifted." Another observer characterized the structure as "completed in the hideous taste and nameless style peculiar to Scottish ecclesiastical architecture during the time of the first three Georges" (Youngson, Classical Edinburgh, pp. 192, 309). Located to the northwest of the Castle, St. Cuthbert's was rebuilt in 1774 and again in 1789; however, its appearance has been considerably altered since the late eighteenth century. At any rate, having been informed of the impending activity there, Wesley found himself in a quandary. ". . .I knew not what to do; but at length I judged it best to embrace the opportunity, though I did not admire the manner of administration. After the usual morning service, the minister enumerated several sorts of sinners, whom he forbade to approach. Two long tables were set on the sides of one aisle, covered with table-cloths. On each side of them a bench was placed for the people. Each table held four or five and thirty. Three ministers sat at the top, behind a cross-table, one of whom made a long exhortation, closed with the words of our Lord; and then, breaking the bread, gave it to him who sat on each side of him. A piece of bread was then given to him who sat first on each of the four benches. He broke off a little piece, and gave the bread to the next; so it went on, the deacons giving more when wanted. A cup was then given to the first person on each bench, and so by one to another. The minister continued his exhortation all the time they were

receiving; then four verses of the twenty-second psalm
were sung, while new persons sat down at the tables. A
second minister then prayed, consecrated, and exhorted.
I was informed the service usually lasted till five in
the evening. How much more simple, as well as more
solemn, is the service of the Church of England!"
(Journal, 5:77-78).

In the evening, Wesley preached again on the
Calton Hill and was uplifted considerably by the
results. "The. . .congregation. . .was far the largest
I have seen in the kingdom, and the most deeply
affected. Many were in tears; more seemed cut to the
heart. Surely this time will not soon be forgotten.
Will it not appear in the annals of eternity?"
(Journal, 5:78)

A bit of a stir preceded Wesley's next visit to
Edinburgh on Tuesday, 23 April 1765. According to his
own account, "My coming was quite seasonable (though
unexpected), as those bad letters, published in the
name of Mr. Hervey, and reprinted here by Mr. John
Erskine, had made a great deal of noise" (Journal,
5:111). The controversy alluded to here actually began
ten years earlier with the publication of Theron and
Aspasio; or, A Series of Dialogues and Letters on the
Most Important Subjects, 3 vols. (London, 1753-1755) by
Reverend James Hervey (1713-1758), vicar of Weston-
Favel and Collingtree. The work strenuously advocates
the doctrine of the imputed righteousness of Christ,
which made it vulnerable to attack from various
quarters. After reading the three volumes, Wesley
wrote an eighteen-page letter to Hervey, dated 15
October 1756, the conclusion of which reads,

Upon the whole, I cannot but wish, that
the plan of these dialogues had been executed

in a different manner. Most of the grand truths of Christianity are herein both explained and proved with great strength and clearness. Why was anything intermixed which could prevent any serious Christian's recommending them to all mankind? Any thing which must necessarily render them exceptionable to so many thousands of the children of God? In practical writings, I studiously abstain from the very shadow of controversy. Nay, even in controversial, I do not willingly write one line, to which any but my opponent would object. For opinions, shall I destroy the work of God? Then am I a bigot indeed? Much more if I would not drop any mode of expression rather than offend either Jew, or Gentile, or the church of God.

(Telford, Letters, 3:388)

The author of the Dialogues and Letters made no reply at the time of receiving this letter; however, when Wesley published his criticisms in Preservative against Unsettled Notions in Religion (1758), Hervey became angry. Almost at once he set to work upon a reply, which he entitled XI. Letters to John Wesley, in Answer to His Remarks on Theron and Aspasio; when he died on 25 December 1758, the response had not been completed. The issue would probably have ended right there had not the manuscript been sent on to one of Wesley's antagonists, the Reverend William Cudworth, who in turn convinced William Hervey, the writer's brother, to publish the tract in 1764. Although the XI. Letters appear free of abuse against Wesley, they contain, nevertheless, highly Calvinistic and misleading evidence upon Wesley's own sentiments--

either Hervey's own comments or the result of Cudworth's revisions and interpolations. John Erskine (1721-1803), the individual who caused Hervey's Letters to be reprinted, had been one of the ministers of the Old Grey-Friars Church, Edinburgh, since 1759. He held membership in the Society for the Propagation of Christian Knowledge (as did Wesley) and was a rather close friend of James Boswell, who on one occasion referred to him as a "primitive saint" (Boswell, The Ominous Years, p. 169).

But perhaps the most significant event of this particular visit to Edinburgh concerns Wesley's initial mention (on Wednesday, 24 April 1765) of the Octagon, in the Low Calton, the first Methodist chapel built in the city. He "preached at four in the afternoon on the ground where we had laid the foundation of our house." On Thursday, the 25th, he devoted most of his time to completing the "Preface" to Notes on the Old Testament; the morning and afternoon of the 26th (Friday) found him in Musselburgh. That evening, "we had another blessed opportunity at Edinburgh, and I took solemn leave of the people" (Journal, 5:112). The entire stay, however, had not been without its share of physical discomfort. While at Newcastle on the 15th, Wesley noticed "a small swelling, less than a pea, but in six days it was as large as a pullet's egg, and exceeding hard. On Thursday [25 April] it broke. I feared riding would not agree with this, especially a hard-trotting horse. However, trusting God, I set out early on Saturday morning [27 April]. Before I reached Glasgow it was much decreased, and in two or three days more it was quite gone. If it was a boil, it was such a one as I never heard of, for it was never sore, first or last, nor ever gave me any pain" (Journal, 5:112).

Indeed, there was a variety of hazards confronting one who flitted back and forth over primitive Scottish roads; this would not be the last of John Wesley's discomforts while in Scotland.

The following year, Wesley returned to Edinburgh, preaching on Saturday evening, 24 May 1766, at the Octagon, which he described on this occasion as "a large and commodious building" (Journal, 5:168). Then, for the fourth successive year, he attended--on Monday, the 26th--some sessions of the General Assembly of the Church of Scotland. "I am very far from being of Mr. Whitefield's mind, who greatly commends the solemnity of this meeting. I have seen few less solemn; I was extremely shocked at the behaviour of many of the members. Had any preacher behaved so at our Conference he would have had no more place among us" (Journal, 5:168). He remained one more day before departing for Leith, Dundee, and Aberdeen, but was back in Scotland's capital on Sunday, 15 June: "Our room [the Octagon] was very warm in the afternoon, through the multitude of people, a great number of whom were people of fashion, with many ministers. I spoke to them with the utmost plainness, and, I believe, not in vain; for we had such a congregation. . .as I never saw in Edinburgh before. It is scarce possible to speak too plain in England; but it is scarce possible to speak plain enough in Scotland. And if you do not, you lose all you labour; you plough upon the sand" (Journal, 5:170).

The next day, Wesley climbed 822 feet to the summit of Arthur's Seat, an extinct volcano rising south of Holyrood Palace and Salisbury Crags, from where he viewed "one of the greatest natural curiosities in the kingdom. . .a small, rocky eminence, six or seven yards across, on the top of an exceeding

high mountain, not far from Edinburgh. The prospect
from the top of the Castle is large, but it is nothing
in comparison of this." He preached in the evening at
the Octagon and again the next day (Tuesday, 17 June),
probably on the Calton Hill. "It rained much," reads
the journal notation, "yet abundance of people came;
and again God made bare His arm. I can now leave
Edinburgh with comfort, for I have fully delivered my
own soul" (Journal, 5:170).

Wesley's visit to Edinburgh in 1767 came somewhat
later than usual--this time in August--probably because
he had spent close to four months in Ireland. Arriving
by stage on Saturday evening, 1 August, he expressed
disappointment at finding "both the society and the
congregations smaller than when I was here last. I
impute this chiefly to the manner of preaching which
has been generally used. The people have been told,
frequently and strongly, of their coldness, deadness,
heaviness, and littleness of faith, but very rarely of
anything that would move thankfulness. Hereby many
were driven away, and those that remained were kept
cold and dead" (Journal, 5:224-225). Actually, the
number of persons listed on the roll of the Edinburgh
Methodist society numbered, in 1767, 150, as compared
with 40 at Dundee, 174 at Aberdeen, and 64 at Glasgow
(Tyerman, Life of Wesley, 2:608). Statistics for the
years preceding can only be speculative, since 1767 was
the initial year in which the Methodist Conference
compiled figures on the membership within the various
circuits.

At 8:00 Sunday morning, 2 August, Wesley preached
at the Octagon; that afternoon, he addressed a
gathering on Castle Hill, another extinct volcano
rising 443 feet above sea level. He spoke on "'There

is joy in heaven over one sinner that repenteth.' The son shone exceeding hot upon my head; but all was well; for God was in the midst of us" (Journal, 5:225). He concluded the Sabbath activities by preaching, in the evening, on Luke 20:34; "many were comforted; especially while I was enlarging on those deep words, 'Neither can they die any more, but are equal to the angels, and are the children of God, being the children of the resurrection'" (Journal, 5:225). During Monday, 3 August, he divided his time between visiting with members of the society, especially the sick among them, and preaching in the evening--first at 7:00 and then from 9:00 until midnight. The current stay came to an end the next morning, when Wesley rode off to Dunbar.

In the following year, Wesley's Edinburgh visit lasted but two days. He arrived on Saturday, 14 May 1768, and spent most of the day walking through Holyrood Palace (see below). At 8:00 A.M., Sunday, the 15th, he preached in the High School yard, "and I believe not a few of the hearers were cut to the heart." From noon until 1:00 P.M., he addressed a large congregation on the Castle Hill, where "my voice commanded them all, while I opened and enforced those awful words, 'I saw the dead, small and great, stand before God.'" Finally, in the evening, he found the Octagon "sufficiently crowded, even with the rich and honourable. 'Who hath warned' these 'to flee from the wrath to come?' Oh may they at length awake and 'arise from the dead!'" (Journal, 5:263)

A period of two years elapsed before John Wesley made another stop at Edinburgh. After spending two days--18 and 19 April 1770--at Glasgow, he determined to ride directly to Perth; "but, being desired to take Edinburgh in my way, I rode thither on Friday [20

April], and endeavoured to confirm those whom many had
strove to turn out of the way. What pity it is that
the children of God should so zealously do the devil's
work! How is it that they are still ignorant of
Satan's devices? Lord, what is man?" (Journal, 5:363)
He departed the next day, returning on Saturday, 12
May. The situation in the city insofar as concerned
Methodism had deteriorated badly. "The congregations,"
observed Wesley, 'were nearly as usual; but the society
which, when I was here before [May 1768], consisted of
above a hundred and sixty members, was now shrunk to
about fifty. Such is the fruit of a single preacher's
staying a whole year in one place! together with the
labours of good Mr. Townsend" (Journal, 5:366). The
Reverend Joseph Townsend, fellow of Clare Hall,
Cambridge, and rector of Pewsey, Wiltshire, had been
sent to Scotland by Selina Shirley, Countess of
Huntingdon; for a time he preached, alternately with
Wesley's itinerants, in Lady Genorchy's St. Mary's
Chapel--located to the southwest of Calton Crags,
between the Orphan Hospital and the College Kirk. A
portion of a lengthy letter from Wesley to Reverend
Townsend--written in Edinburgh and dated 2 August
1767--illustrates the central issue of the controversy:

. . .you did not know the Methodists, unless
one or two honourable ones. You had no
fellowship with them; you neither joined with
them in public, nor strengthened their hands
in private. You stood aloof from them, as
though they would have infected you. Nay,
you preached just by them, at the very hour
of their preaching. You lessened their
congregations; you threw many of the society
into vain reasonings; you opened many mouths

against them; you exceedingly grieved the
spirit of the preachers, and caused their
hands to hang down.

(Telford, Letters, 5:57)

It appears as more than coincidence, then, that at
some point during this visit of May 1770, Wesley met,
for the first time, Willielma, Viscountess Glenorchy
(1741-1786); earlier in the year, she had lost her
husband, which no doubt prompted her to establish St.
Mary's Chapel. Here, she instituted the procedure
whereby Presbyterians, Espiscopalians, and Methodists
conducted services by regular turns. Regarding this
initial contact with Wesley, the Viscountess wrote,
"The Rev. Dr. Webster [Alexander Webster (1707-1784),
minister of the Tolbooth Church, off Parliament Close,
Edinburgh (1737-1784)] and Mr. Wesley met at my house,
and agreed on all doctrines on which they spoke, except
those of God's decrees, predestination, and the saints'
perseverance. I must, according to the light I now
have, agree with Dr. Webster. Nevertheless, I hope Mr.
Wesley is a child of God. He has been an instrument of
saving souls; as such, I honour him, and will
countenance his preachers. I have heard him preach
thrice; and should have been better pleased had he
preached more of Christ, and less of himself" (Jones,
Life of Glenorchy, p. 156). Yet, in spite of this
extremely qualified observation, Lady Glenorchy
appealed to Wesley for assistance in obtaining for her
a schoolmaster, an innkeeper, and a minister. Writing
to him on 29 May 1770, she expressed an obvious degree
of impatience: "When I consider how much you have to
do, and how very precious your time is, I feel
unwilling to give you the trouble of reading a letter
from me; yet I know not how to delay returning you my

best thanks for the pains you have taken to procure me
a Christian innkeeper and a schoolmaster. And, though
you have not as yet been successful, I hope you may
find some before you reach London, who are willing to
leave their native country and friends for the sake of
promoting the interest of Christ's kingdom" (Arminian
Magazine, ed. Wesley and Story, 7 [1784], 279).

Early in June, Wesley had obtained a schoolmaster
for the Viscountess, and in January 1771--almost as a
gesture of his open-mindedness during a period of
intense controversy--sent to her as minister a
pronounced Calvinist, the Reverend Richard DeCourcy (d.
1803). Educated at Trinity College, Dublin, he then
obtained deacon's orders and officiated as curate to
Walter Shirley (1725-1786)--rector of Loughrea, Galway,
and a cousin to the Countess of Huntingdon. Lady
Glenorchy's reaction to the so called "favor" may be
noted here, as set forth in February 1771: "Mr.
DeCourcy is quite the person Mr. Wesley represented
him,--of sweet disposition, and wishes only to preach
Christ to poor sinners wherever he finds an open door"
(Jones, Life of Glenorchy, p. 223). However, the
entire arrangement exploded in Wesley's face--or, more
accurately, behind his back! Although no evidence
exists to support an accusation that Richard DeCourcy
actually and directly undermined Wesley's efforts in
Edinburgh, he certainly must have exercised some
influence upon Lady Glenorchy; for, on 28 June 1771,
she dealt a serious blow to Methodism in the Scottish
capital: "Before I left Edinburgh," announced the
Viscountess, "I dismissed Mr. Wesley's preachers from
my chapel; first, because they deny the doctrines of
imputed righteousness, election, and the saints'
perseverance; secondly, because I find none of our

gospel ministers would preach in the chapel, if they [the Methodists] continued to have the use of the pulpit; thirdly, because I found my own soul had been hurt by hearing them, and I judged that others might be hurt by them also" (Jones, Life of Glenorchy, p. 239). With the expulsion of the Wesleyan Methodist preachers, St. Mary's Chapel stood in possession of DeCourcy and his Calvinistic colleagues. Then, for some strange and unexplained reason, Lady Glenorchy appointed her friend, Lady Maxwell--a close friend to John Wesley, a staunch Methodist, and an avowed Arminian--sole executrix under her will and the principal manager of her chapels in England and Scotland.

Unfortunately, Lady Glenorchy's idiosyncracies, as tempting as they appear within the context of this discussion, must be abandoned to the theologians, historians, and psychologists; for we need to pick up the loose strands of Wesley's visit to Edinburgh in May 1770. On Sunday, the 13th, he preached in the morning at St. Mary's Chapel, and in the afternoon, between noon and 1:00, in the High School yard--"it being too stormy to preach on the Castle Hill." Somewhat before 6:00 P.M., he conducted service at the Octagon, "crowded above and below; but I doubt, with little effect: exceeding few seemed to feel what they heard." He remained in Edinburgh for three more days, and then departed for Musselburgh at 5:00 A.M., Thursday, 17 May (Journal, 5:366-368).

Wesley's next appearance in Edinburgh, coming in the spring of 1772, allows us, first, to observe the hectic pace dictated by his schedule and, second, to realize how Scotland's major city functioned for him as a kind of a base from which to launch his activities in other places. Notice, therefore, this sketch of

Wesley's itinerary between 17 April and 25 May 1772 (a
total of thirty-nine days; less than twelve of them in
Edinburgh):

    Friday, 17 April. Edinburgh

    Saturday, 18. Glasgow (44 miles)

    Sunday, 19. Glasgow

    Monday, 20. Greenock

    Tuesday, 21. Greenock, Port Glasgow, Greenock

    Wednesday, 22. Port Glasgow, Glasgow

    Thursday, 23. Glasgow

    Friday, 24. Glasgow, Edinburgh (44 miles)

    Saturday, 25. Edinburgh, Perth (44 miles)

    Sunday, 26. Perth

    Monday, 27. Perth, Methven, Dunkeld (16 miles)

    Tuesday, 28. Dunkeld, Perth (16 miles)

    Wednesday, 29. Brechin

    Thursday, 30. Brechin

    Friday, 1 May. Aberdeen

    Saturday, 2. Aberdeen

    Sunday, 3. Aberdeen

    Monday, 4. Aberdeen

    Tuesday, 5. Aberdeen, Arbroath (50 miles)

    Wednesday, 6. Arbroath

    Thursday, 7. Arbroath, Dundee (16 miles)

    Friday, 8. Dundee

    Saturday, 9. Edinburgh (53 miles)

    Sunday, 10. Edinburgh

    Monday, 11. Edinburgh

    Tuesday, 12. Ormiston

    Wednesday, 13. Leith

    Thursday, 14. Leith

    Friday, 15. Edinburgh

    Saturday, 16. Edinburgh

    Sunday, 17. Edinburgh

Monday, 18. Edinburgh, Leith
Tuesday, 19. Edinburgh
Wednesday, 20. Edinburgh, Dunbar (11.5 miles)
Thursday, 21. The Bass
Friday, 22. The Bass
Saturday, 23. Alnwick
Sunday, 24. Alnwick
Monday, 25. Morpeth, Newcastle

Returning our attention to the subject at hand, Edinburgh, Wesley arrived at the city late in the evening of 16 April 1772. The following day being Good Friday, he attended service at what he termed "the Episcopal chapel": this being either St. Paul's, at the foot of Carrubber's Close and north of Nether Bow Port, near Bridge Street; or, Dr. Robert Bell's English Chapel (or the Old English Chapel), Blackfriar's Wynd, south of Nether Bow Port. Both were "qualified" English chapels, and a brief pause is in order here to explain the meaning and context of such a term. During the mid and late eighteenth century, two types of Anglican chapels existed in Edinburgh and, indeed, throughout Scotland. The Episcopal Church in Scotland, essentially the direct descendant of the church established under the Stuarts, had been non-juring since the Revolution; thus, it came under severe repressive statutes because of its loyalty to the exiled line. Its priests, even if willing to swear to and pray for King George, were nevertheless forbidden to officiate to congregations of more than four persons at a time (excluding their own families). By the time of Wesley's journeys into Scotland, the statutes against the Episcopal Church in Scotland remained in existence, although magistrates took no efforts to enforce them; thus, the Church's congregations met

quietly and made no attempts to publicize their
services. In the cities of Scotland, the majority of
Scots Anglicans attended what was termed "qualified"
chapels (the second type) served by priests in English
or Irish orders; these clerics read the liturgy of the
Church of England and conducted their congregations as
independents, without obedience to the Scottish
bishops. Although essentially nonconformist,
"qualified" chapels were, apparently, both legal and
public (See Lecky, History of England 2:45-49).

At any rate, no matter what the identification of
the Episcopal chapel, Wesley was agreeably surprised:
not only "the prayers were read well, seriously, and
distinctly, but the sermon, upon the sufferings of
Christ, was sound and unexceptionable. Above all, the
behavior of the whole congregation, rich and poor, was
solemn and serious" (Journal, 5:454). On Friday, the
24th, he left Glasgow at 7:00 A.M. and reached
Edinburgh that evening, having enough energy left after
a ride of forty-four miles to preach on "My son, give
me thy heart" (Journal, 5:455); he preached there the
next morning and then set out for Perth. Back again on
9 May, he attended the Church of England service on the
morning of the 10th and that of the Kirk of Scotland in
the afternoon. "Truly, 'no man having drunk old wine,
straightway desireth new.' How dull and dry did the
latter appear to me, who had been accustomed to the
former!" That evening, most probably at the Octagon,
"I endeavoured to reach the hearts of a large
congregation, by applying part of the Sermon on the
Mount; and I am persuaded God applied it with power to
many consciences" (Journal, 5:459).

The next day, Wesley spoke with members of the
Edinburgh society, now reduced in numbers to

approximately ninety--"so indefatigable have the good
ministers been to root out the seed God had sown in
their hearts" (Journal, 5:459). The reference here, of
course, is to the exclusion of Methodist preachers from
Lady Glenorchy's chapel, as well as to the undermining
of the movement by such ministers as Richard DeCourcy,
Alexander Webster, Joseph Townsend, and John Erskine.
He concluded his activities for this particular visit
by reading prayers and preaching at 'the Episcopal
chapel" on Sunday, 17 May, and conducting a morning
service on Wednesday, the 20th. "I took my leave of
Edinburgh. . .by strongly enforcing the Apostle's
exhortation, 'Be careful for nothing;' but in
everything by prayer and supplication with thanksgiving
let your requests be made known unto God' [Philippians
4:6]" (Journal, 5:461).

By far the most serious concern during the latest
stay in Edinburgh focused not upon the state of the
Methodist society, but on the condition of John
Wesley's health. In May 1772, he was but one month
from being sixty-nine years of age; yet, as evidenced
by the itinerary (see above and also Appendix B) of the
current northern tour, he carried on the affairs of
Methodism with the energy of a man forty years his
junior. Nevertheless, the combination of age and toil
was beginning to exact its toll on John Wesley. "By
all accounts, his valuable health is in a precarious
state," wrote Vincent Perronet to Charles Wesley (from
Shoreham on 18 April 1772); "and unless God provides
(as I doubt not He will), for His people, they will
have abundant reason to mourn" (Arminian Magazine, 8
[1785], 169). The particular problem originated some
eighteen months earlier when the horse upon which
Wesley was riding stumbled and threw him forward on the

pommel of the saddle. "I felt a good deal of pain, but it soon went off, and I thought of it no more. Some months after I observed testiculum alterum altero duplo majorem esse. I consulted a physician; he told me it was a common case, and did not imply any disease at all. In May twelvemonth [1772] it was grown near as large as a hen's egg" (Journal, 6:8). And so, on Monday, 18 May 1772, at Edinburgh, the patriarch of the Methodists was examined by three young physicians-- James Hamilton, Alexander Munro, and James Gregory.

Dr. Hamilton (1740-1827) had been practicing medicine in Dunbar, where earlier he had joined the Methodist society there. Afterward, he moved on to Leeds, then to London, where he served as a physician to the London Dispensary. No doubt Hamilton stood as the chief examiner in this instance, for he surely must have persuaded Wesley to undergo treatment. Alexander Munro, some three years older than Hamilton, had already established a fine reputation as Professor of Anatomy and Surgery at the University of Edinburgh, while James Gregory (1753-1821) was yet to reach his zenith. In two years he would receive the appointment as Professor of the Practice of Medicine at the University of Edinburgh and publish his Dissertatio Medica (Edinburgh, 1774).

The three diagnosed the growth as hydrocele (a tumor with a collection of fluid) and advised their patient to return to London and seek a treatment that would require confinement of more than two weeks. Obviously in no hurry to seek a treatment that would incapacitate him for whatever length of time, Wesley continued on his scheduled rounds and did not reach London until 10 October; however, at York, on Saturday, 27 June 1772, he did consult Joseph Else's Treatise on the Hydrocele (London, 1770): "He supposes the best cure is by a seton [a thread or piece of tape drawn through a fold of skin so as to maintain an opening for discharge] or a caustic; but I am not inclined to try either of them. I know a Physician that has a shorter cure than either one or the other" (Journal, 5:474). Thus, in mid October 1772, Wesley consulted Dr. Samuel Wathen (d. 1787), who "advised me (1) not to think of a radical cure [as suggested by Hamilton, Gregory, and Munro, as well as through Else's Treatise], which could not be hoped for without my lying in one posture fifteen or sixteen days, and he did not know whether this might not give a wound to my constitution which I should never recover; (2) to do nothing while I continued easy; and this advice I was determined to take" (Journal, 6:8). Apparently, his condition caused him no further trouble until early December 1773; the swelling and pain returned and lasted for nearly a month. On 4 January 1774, he again sought out Dr. Wathen; the physician "drew off something more than half a pint of thin, yellow transparent water. With this came out (to his no small surprise) a pearl of the size of a small shot, which he supposed might be one cause of the disorder, by occasioning a conflux of humours to the part" (Journal, 6:8). By the next day the pain was gone, and within one week the seventy year-old Wesley resumed his labors.

It becomes a difficult matter to assess the gravity of the illness described above. For example, on 15 June 1772, Lloyd's Evening Post--a paper with a history of printing its just share of anti-Methodist sentiment--carried the following notice: "By accounts from Scotland, we learn that the Rev. Mr. Wesley has had a dangerous fit of illness, in which he was

attended by three of the most eminent of the faculty
there [Edinburgh], who gave him over; but some younger
gentlemen in practice have been luckily assistant to
him, and they have now hopes that he may continue his
ministry many years longer" (Tyerman, Life of Wesley,
3:123). Yet, on the very evening of the day (18 May
1772) Drs. Hamilton, Munro, and Gregory examined
Wesley, he dedicated a new chapel at Leith; two days
later, he began the journey to Newcastle, with stops at
Dunbar, the Bass, Alnwick, and Morpeth. No doubt,
though, the pain and the swelling were having definite
effect upon his activities. "I am almost a disabled
soldier. I am forbid to ride, and am obliged to travel
mostly in a carriage" (Wesley, Works, 12:369).

In 1774, John Wesley visited Edinburgh on
Wednesday, 11 May, and again on the Wednesday following
(18 May); on both occasions, he remained in the city
only a single day. However, he returned on 1 June for
a longer period, one that--as we shall see--was not
without incident, although it began on a positive note.
Wesley spoke with all members of the Edinburgh society
(Thursday, 2 June), and "was agreeably surprised. They
have fairly profited since I was here last. Such a
number of persons having sound Christian experience I
never found in this society before." That evening he
preached to "a very elegant congregation, and yet with
great enlargement of heart" (Journal, 6:23).

Then, on Saturday, 4 June, occurred the first
trouble Wesley encountered since coming to Edinburgh
twenty-years earlier. As he walked to his lodging
after conducting a service, two men accosted him, one
saying, "Sir, you are my prisoner. I have a warrant
from the sheriff to carry you to the Tolbooth [prison]"
(Journal, 6:23). There was little Wesley could do but

accompany these deputies. The Tolbooth, in the High Street and east of Lawnmarket, proved to be a building "not accommodated with ventilators, with water-pipe, with privy, all parts of it kept in a slovenly condition; but the eastern quarter of it. . . intolerable" (Youngson, Classical Edinburgh, p. 122). Fortunately, Wesley was taken not to the Tolbooth itself, but to a house adjoining the building, where he met his accuser, George Sutherland, once a member of the Edinburgh Methodist society. The deposition stated that "Hugh Saunderson, one of John Wesley's preachers, had taken from his [Sutherland's] wife a hundred pounds in money and upwards of thirty pounds in goods, and had, besides that, terrified her into madness; so that, through the want of her help and the loss of business, he [Sutherland] was damaged five hundred pounds." Further, before the sheriff--Archibald Cockburn, Esq.-- Sutherland deposed "That the said John Wesley and Hugh Saunderson, to evade her pursuit, were preparing to fly the country; and therefore he [Sutherland] desired his warrant to search for, seize, and incarcerate them in the Tolbooth till they should find security for their appearance" (Journal, 6:23-24).

Hugh Saunderson, one of Wesley's Irish preachers, commenced his itinerancy in 1769, in the Armagh circuit. Although certainly a devout Christian and a loyal Wesleyan Methodist, he seemed to attract trouble --certainly not always of his own design. In 1777, Wesley saw fit to expel him from the movement. At any rate, returning to the matter at hand, Sutherland insisted that Mr. Cockburn immediately convey Wesley to the Tolbooth; yet, the sheriff did delay until some friends of the accused arrived to post bond for a hearing, scheduled for 24 June. Before the posting of

the bond could be affected, however, Saunderson arrived
upon the scene, the case was heard at once, and
Sutherland's deposition declared false--for which the
latter had to pay a fine of £1000 Scottish (or £50
British).

Wesley preached the next day (Sunday, 5 June) on
the Castle Hill (at noon) and at the Octagon (in the
evening), where "the house was thoroughly filled, and
many seemed deeply affected. I do not wonder that
Satan, had it been in his power, would have had me
otherwise employed this day" (Journal, 6:24). Thus,
free from the threat of Tolbooth prison, he departed
the city on Wednesday the 8th. It might be remiss,
since it is not altogether removed from the Sutherland
affair, to omit from the account of the 1774 visit to
Edinburgh the following sketch of John Wesley as
written by Joseph Benson (1748-1821), one of
eighteenth-century Methodism's most noted ministers and
scholars. Benson had been with his leader throughout
the week of 1-8 June; therefore,

> I had an opportunity of examining narrowly
> his spirit and conduct; and. . .I am more
> than ever persuaded he is a none such. I
> know not his fellow, first, for abilities,
> natural and acquired; and, secondly, for his
> incomparable diligence in the application of
> those abilities to the best of employments.
> His lively fancy, tenacious memory, clear
> understanding, ready elocution, manly
> courage, indefatigable industry, really amaze
> me. I admire, but wish in vain to imitate,
> his diligent improvement of every moment of
> time; his wonderful exactness even in little
> things; the order and regularity wherewith he

does and treats everything he takes in hand;
together with his quick dispatch of business,
and calm, cheerful serenity of soul. I ought
not to omit to mention, what is very manifest
to all who know him, his resolution, which no
shocks of opposition can shake; his patience,
which no length of trials can weary; his zeal
for the glory of God, and the good of man,
which no waters of persecution or tribulation
have yet been able to quench. Happy man!
Long has thou borne the burden and heat of
the day, amidst the insults of foes, and the
base treachery of seeming friends; but thou
shalt rest from thy labours, and thy works
shall follow thee!

(Wesleyan Methodist Magazine, 3rd ser.,
4 [1825], 356)

Although the preceding passage typifies the ideal (even
the romantic) image of a leader formed by a devoted
follower, it does, at least indicate the personality of
John Wesley; it further captures the sense of the
atmosphere in which he worked.

Two years later, in the spring of 1776, Wesley
journeyed once more to Edinburgh, but stayed only
briefly. He preached in the city on Wednesday evening,
8 May, again on Monday, the 13th, and finally on
Tuesday, 28 May. Obviously, he had intended to stay
longer, but for some reason was delayed in crossing
over from St. Andrews on the 27th. Thus, he had to
wait another three years before he could find the
opportunity to set foot upon the streets of the former
Scottish capital. On Thursday, 27 April 1779, John
Wesley came to Edinburgh from Dunbar. "I was agreeably
surprised," he noted, "at the singing in the evening.

I have not heard such female voices, so strong and clear, anywhere in England" (Journal, 6:235). Returning on Monday, 31 May, he remained only the one day, but was back again on Wednesday, 16 June, making certain that there would be time (on the 17th) to look into the activities of the society. The sight was not at all pleasing! "In five years I found five members had been gained!--ninety-nine being increased to a hundred and four. What, then, have our preachers been doing all this time? (1) They have preached four evenings in the week, and on Sunday morning; the other mornings they have fairly given up. (2) They have taken great care not to speak too plain, lest they should give offense. (3) When Mr. Brackenbury preached the old Methodist doctrine one of them said, 'You must not preach such doctrine here. The doctrine of Perfection is not calculated for the meridian of Edinburgh.' Waiving, then, all other hindrances, is it any wonder that the work of God has not prospered here?" (Journal, 6:239-240).

Robert Carr Brackenbury (b. 1752), mentioned in the passage quoted above, occupied a unique position within the general composition of eighteenth-century Methodist preachers. After becoming one of Wesley's assistants, he was enrolled in the Minutes of Conference and then served as a circuit itinerant preacher, as well as an occasional traveling companion to Methodism's founder and leader. Thus, we find him on this current journey to Scotland. A native of Lincolnshire, specifically Raithby Hall, he attended Cambridge and later served as a county magistrate. Young Brackenbury also owned several country mansions, which made him a landlord over several thousands of broad acres. A Mrs. Richard Smith, biographer of

Hannah More (1844), wrote, in 1854, <u>Raithby Hall, or Memorial Sketches of Robert Carr Brackenbury, Esq., and of Sarah His Wife</u>.

Wesley remained in Edinburgh through practically the entire weekend, 18-20 June 1779, preaching "with all possible plainness; and some appeared to be much stirred up." (<u>Journal</u>, 6:240) But perhaps the most significant event of the visit was his meeting with James Boswell. On Wednesday, 15 April 1778, Boswell, Anna Seward, and Samuel Johnson engaged in a conversation about ghosts, particularly one seen by a young girl at Newcastle-upon-Tyne; Wesley had accepted her testimony, but Johnson would have nothing to do with either the girl's story or Wesley's acceptance of it. The discussion resumed a year later, shortly before Boswell's departure from London for Scotland. "I was. . .desirous to examine the question closely, and at the same time wished to be made acquainted with Mr. John Wesley; for though I differed from him in some points, I admired his various talents, and loved his pious zeal." Boswell therefore requested from Johnson a letter of introduction; the latter complied, and the following note bears the date 3 May 1779: "Sir,--Mr. Boswell, a gentlemen who has been long known to me, is desirous of being known to you, and has asked this recommendation, which I give him with great willingness, because I think it very much to be wished that worthy and religious men should be acquainted with each other" (Boswell, <u>Life of Johnson</u>, p. 1026). And so, the two men met, most probably during this weekend of 18-20 June. According to Boswell, Wesley received him politely and compiled with his request to have Johnson's letter returned to him; however, the leader of the Methodists seems not to have satisfied his

visitor concerning the evidence of the Newcastle ghost.
As for Wesley, he appears not to have considered the
conversation with Boswell of sufficient worth to record
in his journal.

On the evening of Thursday, 18 May 1780, Wesley
"endeavoured to preach to the hearts of a large
congregation at Edinburgh. We have cast much 'bread
upon the waters' here. Shall we not 'find it again,'
at least 'after many days?'" (Journal, 6:278-279) He
left the next day and returned on Saturday, the 20th,
at which time he walked through Holyrood Palace (see
below). The following day, rain cancelled a service
scheduled for the Castle Hill. However, that evening,
the Octagon "was well filled, and I was enabled to
speak strong words. But I am not a preacher for the
people of Edinburgh. Hugh Saunderson and Michael
Fenwick are more to their taste" (Journal, 6:279).
Saunderson, of course, was the Irish itinerant preacher
who had caused, although somewhat indirectly, Wesley's
arrest in Edinburgh sixteen years earlier. As for
Michael Fenwick, he proved to be another of that breed
of Methodist preacher whom Wesley could have done
without. He described Fenwick generally as "an
excellent groom, valet de chambre, nurse, and, on one
occasion, a tolerable preacher" (Wesley, Works,
12:171). However, Wesley probably could never forgive
him for having fallen asleep under a hayrack one day
(25 July 1757) in Clayworth while his mentor delivered
a sermon.

Even after admitting that he was "not a preacher
for the people of Edinburgh," Wesley came back to the
city, on schedule, two years later. On Saturday, 1
June 1782, he spent some time with forty poor children,
housed in a school under the sponsorship of Lady

Maxwell. "They are swiftly brought forward," Wesley
observed, "in reading and writing, and learn the
principles of religion. But I observe in them all the
ambitiosa paupertas [Juvenal, Satires, 3:182-183: "Hic
vivimus ambitiosa paupertate omnes"--Here we all live
in ambitious poverty.]. Be they ever so poor, they
must have a scrap of finery. Many of them have not a
shoe to their foot; but the girl in rags is not without
her ruffles" (Journal, 6:354). Accompanying Wesley on
this particular journey was another of those unusual
personages who seemed to flock around and attach
themselves to the leader of the Methodists. The
Reverend Brian Bury Collins, M.A., of St. John's
College, Cambridge, had been tagging at Wesley's heels
since 1779, preaching to anyone who would offer him an
evangelical pulpit. Although Wesley refused to grant
him a regular appointment or even to recognize him as
being connected with Methodism, Collins' chief aim in
life was to unite the followers of the Wesleys and
those of George Whitefield--the latter's adherants by
now among the flocks administered by Selina Shirley,
Countess of Huntingdon. However, although refused
official recognition by the Wesleyan Methodists,
Collins appears to have been welcomed to the pulpits of
their chapels and open-air services. Thus, on Sunday,
2 June 1782, he was to have preached at noon on the
Castle Hill; "but the dull minister kept us in the kirk
till past one." Later, at 6:00 P.M., Wesley addressed
a full house at the Octagon, where "I did not shun to
declare the whole counsel of God. I almost wonder at
myself. I seldom speak anywhere so roughly as in
Scotland. And yet most of the people hear, and are
just what they were before" (Journal, 6:354).
Undoubtedly, Wesley was fast becoming impatient with

the people of Edinburgh, but he would continue to
include Scotland and its principal city in his regular
itinerary. In fact, ten days later he remarked, "We
had such a congregation both that evening and the next
[12-13 June] as had not been on a week-day for many
years; some fruit of our labours here we have had
already. Perhaps this is a token that we shall have
more" (Journal, 6:357).

However, two years later, on his next visit to
Edinburgh, Wesley had to contend with the climate of
Scotland, as well as with the religious apathy of its
citizens. In the journal for Saturday, 24 April 1784,
he writes, in regard to the journey from Selkirk to the
capital, that "We had frost in the morning, snow before
seven, piercing winds all day long, and in the
afternoon vehement hail, so that I did not wonder we
had a small congregation at Edinburgh in the evening
[7:00]" (Journal, 6: 498-499). The next day, Sunday
the 25th, Wesley attended the 11:00 A.M. service at the
Tolbooth Church, or the western end of St. Giles's
Cathedral, off Parliament Close. He found the "sermon
was very sensible, but having no application, was no
way likely to awaken drowsy hearers" (Journal, 6:499).
At six that evening, he preached at the Octagon. "For
once it was thoroughly filled. I preached on 'God is a
Spirit, and they that worship Him must worship Him in
spirit and in truth.' [John 4:24] I am amazed at this
people. Use the most cutting words, and apply them in
the most pointed manner, still they hear, but feel no
more than the seats they sit upon!" (Journal, 6:499)
The preceding constitutes one of the few occasions in
his journal that Wesley allows himself the luxury of
even mild anger. On Monday, 26 April, he departed for
the Glasgow area, returning to Edinburgh on Thursday,

the 29th. ". . .in the evening [7:00] the house was well filled. So that we must not say 'the people of Edinburgh love the word of God only on the Lord's Day'" (Journal, 6:500).

Wesley was off again early the next morning, remaining from the city until Thursday afternoon, 20 May. On Friday, he "examined the society, and found about sixty members left. Many of these were truly alive to God, so our labour here is not quite in vain" (Journal, 6:509). After spending some time with Lady Maxwell--"who appeared to be clearly saved from sin, although exceedingly depressed by the tottering tenement of clay" (Journal, 6:510)--he visited for an hour (on Saturday, the 22nd) at her school for poor orphans. That evening he preached at the Octagon on Isaiah 57:1-2; however, "A famous actress, just come down from London (which, for the honour of Scotland, is just during the sitting of the Assembly), stole away a great part of our congregation tonight. Now much wiser are these Scots than their forefathers!" (Journal, 6:510) The actress referred to by Wesley, was, no doubt, Sarah Siddons (1755-1831), for she had been engaged by John Jackson, manager of the Theatre Royal, Edinburgh, for part of the 1784 season. In fact, on 1 June she performed at the Theatre Royal in John Home's tragedy, Douglas (Tobin, Plays by Scots, pp. 110-112). This marked the second year in succession that Mrs. Siddons had disrupted the schedule of the General Assembly of the Church of Scotland. As for Wesley, he simply viewed her effect upon his congregation as one more blight upon his labors in Edinburgh.

On Sunday, 23 May, his last day in the city for the current year, Wesley attended morning service at the Tolbooth Church, and in the afternoon went to the

Episcopal chapel on the east side of Carrubber's Close.
Regarding the latter, he remarked that "they have lost
their glorying; they talked the moment service was
done, as if they had been in London." In the evening,
"the Octagon was well filled; and I applied, with all
possible plainness, 'God is a Spirit, and they that
worship Him must worship Him in spirit and truth'"
(Journal, 6:510; see also above, 25 April 1784).

The next visit to Edinburgh came, as usual,
exactly two years later, May 1786. Wesley stopped only
briefly on Wednesday, the 17th, but returned on Sunday,
the 28th. He preached first (at 7:00 A.M.) in the
Octagon on Psalms 50:23, then at noon on the Castle
Hill, basing the sermon text on Revelation 20:12. "I
never saw such a congregation there before. But the
chair was placed just opposite to the sun. But I soon
forgot it while I expounded those words, 'I saw the
dead, small and great, stand before God.' In the
evening [6:00] the whole audience seemed to feel,
'Without holiness no man shall see the Lord'" (Journal
7:165-166). For 1788--a year of personal tragedy for
Wesley because of the death of his brother, Charles--
the Methodist leader made only one stop in the city,
although he remained for three days (19 through 21
May). "I still find a frankness and openness in the
people of Edinburgh," remarked the eighty-five year-old
Wesley, "which I find in few other parts of the
kingdom. I spent two days among them with much
satisfaction; and I was not at all disappointed, in
finding no such increase either in the congregation or
the society, as many expected from their leaving the
Kirk" (Journal, 7:390). Certain of the Edinburgh
Methodists thought that the time was ripe for a general
exodus from the Church of Scotland and into their

society; they were encouraged, no doubt, by the activity of the Associate Presbytery. Yet, no such action of that sort occurred.

Unfortunately, the record of John Wesley's last appearance in Edinburgh--from Thursday, 13 May 1790, through Sunday, 16 May--is incomplete, for the manuscript journal from 10 April through 24 May 1790 was lost. Thus, only the fragmentary notations from the diary allow us to observe his activities there. He arrived in the city at 2:00 P.M. on the 13th, and thus had time for an evening service at 6:30. On Friday and Saturday he preached in the evening, but on Sunday, 16 May, he delivered both a late morning (11:00) and an evening (6:00) sermon.

The question that arises, of course, is how successful was Wesley's effort in the former capital of Scotland. Perhaps the following table may well reflect the erratic nature of those with whom he had to deal, both in the city and even throughout Scotland. These figures (the first two columns extracted from Tyerman, Life of Wesley, 3:534) refer to the Edinburgh circuit, which means the city proper and the surrounding towns of Leith, Musselburgh, Preston Pans, Haddington, and Dalkeith:

Year	Number of Methodists in the circuit	Gain (+)/ Loss (-)
1766	165	---
1770	62	-103
1774	287	+225
1778	161	-126
1785	134	- 27
1788	330	+196
1791	205	-125

Holyrood Palace, Edinburgh

Perhaps the best point at which to begin a discussion of Holyrood Palace is in terms of its physical relationship with the rest of the old town of Edinburgh. According to one late eighteenth-century observer,

> The Palace of Holyroodhouse, the eastmost boundary of the city, stands on a plain within two miles of the river Forth, from which it rises by a gradual assent of ninety-four feet from the high water-mark. From Holyrood-house there begins a narrow point, or, if we may be allowed the expression, the tail of a hill, which gradually, extending itself in breadth, rises in a steep and straight ridge, from which its shelving sides decline; the ridge terminating in an abrupt precipice, the site of the castle, at the distance of a mile in length, and one hundred and eighty feet in heighth from Holyrood-house.
>
> The ridge of this hill forms a continued and very magnificent street. From its sides, lanes, and alleys, which are there called wynds and closes, extend like slanting ribs; so that, upon the whole, it bears a striking resemblance to a turtle, of which the castle is the head, the high street the ridge of the back, the wynds and closes the shelving sides, and the palace of Holyroodhouse the tail.

(Arnot, History of Edinburgh, p. 233)

Daniel Defoe, early in the century, provides us with a fairly detailed account of the palace itself, which he thought "a handsome building, rather convenient than large." Within, he viewed a large, irregular court, where "are very improperly placed the coach-houses and stables, which should much rather have been farther off, either in the park, or without the outgate." Finally, inside the palace, the "great staircase is at the south-west corner of the house, and the guard-chamber and rooms of state take up the south side of the house, as the king's lodgings do the east side, which the Lord Commissioner makes use of in time of parliament; and the west side would be supposed to be the queen's lodgings, if such a thing were to be seen again in Scotland, but at present are out of use. The north side is taken up with one large gallery, reaching the whole length of the house, famous for having the pictures [111 in number; see also below, following the description by Smollett] of all the kings of Scotland" (Defoe, _Tour_, pp. 584-585).

Two of Tobias George Smollett's fictional characters present similar opinions about Holyrood Palace, although slight variations exist. According to Jeremy Melford, Holyrood "is an elegant piece of architecture, but sunk in an obscure, and, as I take it, unwholesome bottom, where one would imagine it had been placed on purpose to be concealed. The apartments are lofty, but [c. 1766] unfurnished; and as for the pictures of the Scottish kings, from Fergus I. to King William, they are all paultry daubings, mostly by the same hand, painted either from the imagination, or porters hired to sit for the purpose" (Smollett, _Humphry Clinker_, p. 201). All one hundred and eleven of these portraits were, indeed, painted by the same hand--one Jacob de Wet; for his efforts, the artist received £120 per year, from which he had to purchase his canvas and paints. Jeremy Melford's uncle, the often irritable Matthew Bramble, saw Holyrood as "a jewel in architecture, thrust into a hollow where it cannot be seen; a situation which was certainly not chosen by the ingenious architect, who must have been confined to the site of the old palace, which was a convent" (Humphry Clinker, p. 123). To understand the last portion of the preceding remark, one needs to know that the Abbey of Holyrood was founded by David I in 1128 for Augustinian Canons regular. When King James IV made Edinburgh the capital of Scotland at the beginning of the sixteenth century, he constructed the palace upon the foundation of the old abbey church and convent. The structure viewed by Defoe and Smollett was the work of a Scottish architect, Sir William Bruce of Kinross (d. 1710); from 1671 to 1679, he worked under a charge from Charles II to complete the project begun by James IV.

John Wesley first saw Holyrood Palace in May 1761--either on Sunday the 10th or on the following day. He claimed it a "noble structure," noting further that "It was rebuilt and furnished by King Charles the Second. One side of it is a picture-gallery, wherein are pictures of all the Scottish kings and an original one of the celebrated Queen Mary. It is scarce possible for any who looks at this to think her such a monster as some have painted her, nor indeed for any who considers the circumstances of her death equal to that of an ancient martyr" (Journal, 4:452, 455). Seven years later, he again walked through Holyrood, "a noble pile of building," but casting his eye with displeasure upon the sorry state of the entire place. "The tapestry is dirty, and quite faded; the fine ceilings dropping down; and many of the pictures in the

gallery torn or cut through. This was the work of good
General Hawley's soldiers (like general, like men!),
who, after running away from the Scots at Falkirk,
revenged themselves on the harmless canvas" (Journal,
5:263). General Henry Hawley--a fairly competent
commander, yet a brutal disciplinarian--commanded a
force of British regulars that set out, on 3 January
1746, to relieve Stirling, then under siege by Prince
Charles Edward's Highlanders. The Scots met Hawley's
army at Falkirk Muir, Stirlingshire, on 17 January. In
what must be termed the final success for the Young
Pretender, his Highlanders dealt a serious blow to the
prestige of George II's army; only the nature of the
ground--a high slope cut by ravines--darkness, and a
severe rainstorm prevented utter disaster for Hawley.
Even so, he left over 500 killed and wounded on the
field, in contrast to approximately forty dead Scots
(see Robertson, England, pp. 102-103).

Wesley's third visit to Holyrood Palace came on
Saturday, 20 May 1780. Again, he was shocked by what
he observed. "The stately rooms are dirty as stables,
the colours of the tapestry are quite faded, several of
the pictures are cut and defaced. The roof of the
royal chapel is fallen in, and the bones of James the
Fifth and the once beautiful Lord Darnley are scattered
about like those of sheep or oxen. Such is human
greatness! Is not 'a living dog better than a dead
lion?'" (Journal, 6:279) The desecration of the
chapel was due in part to Charles II, who closed the
church to the public, and to James II, who shocked the
citizens of Edinburgh by ordering mass to be celebrated
here. Therefore, a mob broke into the building, and
left nothing beyond the bare walls. They even entered
the royal sepulchre and defiled (as Wesley states) the

remains of James V, his wife Magdaline of France, Lord
Darnley, and other nobles and royal children. On
Tuesday, 26 October 1773, while Boswell and Johnson
visited in Inverarny, the former "spoke with peculiar
feeling of the miserable neglect of the chapel
belonging to the palace of Holyrood-house, in which are
deposited the remains of many of the Kings of Scotland,
and of many of our nobility. I [Boswell] said, it was
a disgrace to the country that it was not repaired:
and particularly complained that my friend [Archibald
James Edward] Douglas, the representative of a great
house, and proprietor of a vast estate, should suffer
the sacred spot where his mother lies interred, to be
unfroofed, and exposed to all the inclemencies of the
weather" (Boswell, Tour to the Hebrides, p. 405).

Coates Hall, Edinburgh

In May 1782, Darcy Brisbane, Lady Maxwell, moved
her residence from Gardiner's Hall (off Gardiner's
Crescent) to Coates Hall, which lay approximately one
and one-half miles west of the Octagon in Low Calton.
When, at the end of the nineteenth century, St. Mary's
Episcopal Cathedral was erected between Manor Place and
Palmerston Place, Coates Hall became the Cathedral
song-school. In Wesley's day, of course, the house was
considered a country estate, and Lady Maxwell invited
the founder of Methodism to lodge there on a number of
occasions when he came to Edinburgh. In fact, Wesley
preached a sermon there on Sunday afternoon, 25 April
1784. On Wednesday the 17th and Thursday the 18th of
May 1786, he visited Coates Hall and conversed with
Lady Maxwell; nine days later (Saturday, the 27th), he
walked, at the conclusion of the 6:00 P.M. service at
the Octagon, "to my lovely lodging at Coates, and found

rest was sweet" (Journal, 7:165). Certainly this
residence, surrounded by gardens and lying well outside
the confines of the old city, must have appealed to
Wesley in terms of the eighteenth-century concept of
retirement--at least retirement in the temporary sense.
Finally, he spent some time there during his final
visit to Edinburgh in may 1790. The diary entry for
Tuesday, the 13th, indicates that he might have lodged
at Coates Hall, and he certainly had dinner there the
following afternoon.

Saughton Hall, Edinburgh

Lady Maxwell occupied Saughton Hall until November
1782, when she moved to Gardiner's Hall. Wesley lodged
at Saughton from Thursday, 30 May, through Sunday, 2
June 1782, and described the estate as "a good old
mansion-house, three miles from Edinburgh. . . ." On
Friday, the 31st, Lady Maxwell desired him "to give a
short discourse to a few of her poor neighbours. I did
so, at four in the afternoon, on the story of Dives and
Lazarus" (Journal, 6:354).

Perth

The "Fair City" of Perth has long set forth strong
claim as the first capital of Scotland; in fact, the
city actually was the seat of government until the
middle of the fifteenth century. Scone Palace (see
below) once served as the crowning place for Scottish
kings, and, in 843, King Kenneth Macalpine brought the
Stone of Scone from Dunstaffnage Castle, Argyle, to be
used as the coronation stone. Edward I took the stone
to Westminster Abbey, where it now lies, and in 1651,
Charles II became the last king to be crowned at Scone
Palace.

Visiting Perth at some time after the Jacobite
uprising of 1715, Daniel Defoe recognized that the
"chief business of this town is the linen manufacture;
and it is so considerable here, all the neighbouring
country being employed in it, that it is a wealth to
the whole place." He was amazed that the city could
have profitted highly from the 1715 rebellion,
especially since "the townsmen got so much money by
both parties, that they are evidently enriched by it
and it appears not only by the particular families and
persons in the town, but by their public and private
building which they have raised since that; as
particularly a new Tolbooth or Town-hall." Finally,
Defoe observed that Perth "was well built before
[1715], but now [c. 1725] has almost a new face; (for
as I said) here are abundance of new houses, and more
of old houses new-fitted and repaired, which look like
new. The linen trade too, which is their main
business, has mightily increased since the late Act of
Parliament in England, for the suppressing the use and
wearing of printed calicoes; so that now the
manufacture is greatly increased here, especially of
that kind of cloth which they buy here and send to
England to be printed, and which is so much used in
England in the room of the calicoes, that the worsted
and silk weavers in London seem to have very little
benefit by the bill, but that the linen of Scotland and
Ireland are, as it were, constituted in the room of the
calicoes" (Defoe, Tour, pp. 645-646). By way of
explanation, the Act of 1701 forbade the use and wear
in any form of Indian, as well as Chinese, silks, in
addition to Indian printed or painted calicoes and
striped and checked cottons.

Perth had always been a major textile center, but

it did not really achieve major commercial status until late in the eighteenth century. For instance, of the nineteen cotton mills operating in Scotland in 1788, three were located in Perth, while by 1794, the city could boast of more than 1500 looms. Earlier, in 1727, the Commissioners and Trustees for Improving Fisheries and Manufactures in Scotland embarked upon a program to establish spinning schools; the first of these to be opened were located in Edinburgh, Glasgow, and Perth. The city also became something of a banking center, beginning in 1763 with the establishment, first, of the Perth Banking Company, followed by five other institutions. Two years later, they all merged into the Perth United Company, with a capital of £8000. By 1787, Perth United became the Perth Banking Company, a large joint-stock corporation with a capital of £34,000 and ninety-nine shareholders. Perhaps the ultimate tribute to the city's growth and economic development came on Saturday, 26 May 1770, when the bridge over the River Tay was completed at Perth. Originally estimated, in 1764, to cost £9784, the total expenditures for the structure came to £28,840--some £13,000 of which came from the Forfeited Estates Commissioners in the forms of grants. The remainder was contributed by the city of Perth and by individual subscriptions (Hamilton, _Economic History_, pp. 175, 156, 136-137, 311, 314, 338, 233).

John Wesley first came to Perth on Saturday, 23 April 1768, after having received "magnificent accounts of the work of God in this place; so that I expected to find a numerous and lively society. Instead of this, I found not above two believers, and scarce five awakened persons in it. Finding I had all to begin, I spoke exceeding plain in the evening to about a hundred persons at the room; but knowing this was doing nothing, on Sunday the 24th I preached about eight [A.M.] at the end of Watergate. A multitude of people were soon assembled, to whom I cried aloud, 'Seek ye the Lord while He may be found; call ye upon Him while He is near.' All were deeply attentive, and I had a little hope that some were profitted" (Journal, 5:256). Later that morning he attended service at the Church of St. John, off South Street, afterward preaching on "'God forbid that I should glory, save in the cross of our Lord Jesus Christ.' The congregation was so exceeding large that I doubt many could not hear" (Journal, 5:256).

On this initial visit, Wesley took the opportunity to explain the nature of a Methodist society, "adding that I should not look on any persons at Perth as such [Methodists] unless they spoke to me before I left the city. Four men and four women did speak to me, two of whom I think were believers; and one or two more seemed just awakening, and darkly feeling after God. In truth, the kingdom of God, among these, is as yet but as a grain of mustard-seed" (Journal, 5:256). The next day (Monday, 25 May), he met a Mr. Fraser (see below, Chapter 5, under Monydie), minister of "a neighbouring parish, [who] desired us to breakfast with him. I find him a serious, benevolent, sensible man, not bigoted to any opinions" (Journal, 5:256).

The next visit to Perth occurred on Saturday, 21 April 1770, Wesley arriving there in the afternoon after traveling from Edinburgh through a violent rainstorm. That evening, he preached in the Tolbooth, which "contained the congregation, and at eight in the morning Sunday, [the 22nd]. The stormy wind would not suffer me to preach abroad in the evening; so we

retired into the court-house, as many as could, and had
a solemn and comfortable hour." On Tuesday, the 24th,
he met Dr. James Oswald, another minister and "an
upright, friendly, sensible man. Such, likewise, I
found Mr. Black, the senior minister at Perth, who,
soon after, went to Abraham's bosom" (<u>Journal</u>, 5:363).
So, if Wesley was not making converts at Perth, he
could at least realize some friendships among local
ministers from his efforts.

Two years later, Saturday evening, 25 April 1772,
Wesley came to Perth for what turned out to be a
ceremonious occasion for the effort of Methodism in
Scotland. Upon arriving, he forwarded to the Provost
of the city a request to preach in the Guildhall the
following morning and evening. The request having been
granted and the two services conducted, the leader of
the Methodists "accepted of the Provost's invitation to
lodge at his house, and spent an agreeable evening with
him, and three ministers, concluded with solemn prayer"
(<u>Journal</u>, 5:455). He spend Monday and most of Tuesday
visiting in and around Perth, and on Tuesday evening
(28 April) preached in the city "to a large and serious
congregation. Afterwards they did me an honour I never
though off--presented me with the freedom of the city.
The diploma ran thus:

> Magistratuum illustris ordo et honorandus
> senatorum coetus inclytae civitatis
> Perthensis, in debiti amorus et affectuum
> tessarum erga Johannem Wesley, immutitatibus
> praefatae civitatis, societatis etiam et
> fraternitatis aedilitiae privilegiis
> donarunt.
>
> Aprilis die 28°anno Sal. 1772°

[The illustrious order of Magistrates and

honourable Court of Aldermen of the famous
city of Perth, as a proof of their well-
merited esteem and affection for John Wesley,
have invested him with the immunities of the
above-mentioned city, and with the privileges
of the fellowship and brotherhood of a
burgess. This 28th day of April, in the year
of our salvation 1772.]
I question whether any diploma from the city of London
be more pompous or expressed in better Latin" (Journal,
5:456-457).

The diploma itself was struck off from a copper
plate on parchment, the arms of the city and certain of
the words illuminated, and flowers painted around the
borders. According to Henry Moore, "for the purity of
the Latin it is not perhaps excelled by any diploma,
either from London or any other city in Europe" (Moore,
Life of Wesley, 2:254). The origin of this honor is
associated with a Miss Meston (d. 1804), a native of
Edinburgh and by birth a member of the Church of
Scotland. While still a child, her parents passed
away, and she went to live with an uncle, a minister of
the Kirk. When this gentleman's health failed, the
girl went on to reside with another uncle, a Perth
merchant and thrice elected Provost of the city. A
house servant who had converted to Methodism persuaded
Miss Meston to hear one of Wesley's itinerants, which
resulted in the latter joining the Perth society. She
then aroused her uncle's interest in Methodism, and the
Provost not only became Wesley's host during his visits
to the city, but convinced the council to confer the
honor described above. Miss Meston later married
Charles Kennedy, a devoted London Methodist; upon her
death, she was buried in the graveyard of City Road

Chapel, London (see <u>Methodist Magazine</u>, 29 [1806], 133, 176).

Unfortunately, the honor bestowed upon Wesley did little to advance the results of his labors in Perth. Upon returning to the city on Thursday, 19 May 1774, he found that morning preaching had been abandoned; thus, "the people were few, dead, and cold. These things must be remedied, or we must quit the ground." On Saturday, the 21st, he preached in the evening to a large congregation, but "could not find the way to their hearts. The generality of the people here are so wise that they need no more knowledge, and so good that they need no more religion! Who can warn them that are brimful of wisdom and goodness to flee from the wrath to come?" The following day (Sunday, 22 May), Wesley "endeavoured to stir up this drowsy people by speaking as strongly as I could at five [A.M.] on 'Awake, thou that sleepst'; at seven [A.M.] on 'Where their worm dieth not,' and in the evening on 'I saw the dead, small and great, stand before God.' In the afternoon a young gentleman, in the west kirk, preached such a close, practical sermon on 'Enoch walked with God,' as I have not heard since I came into the kingdom" (<u>Journal</u>, 6:20).

Two years later, Tuesday, 14 May 1776, although the wind was "cold and boisterous," Wesley preached at 6:00 P.M. on the South Inch--one of the two open parks by the banks of the River Tay. "Many are the stumbling-blocks," he lamented, "which have been laid in the way of this poor people. They are removed, but the effects of them still continue" (<u>Journal</u>, 6:106). There followed, then, an absence of eight years before Wesley again found the opportunity to make an appearance in Perth. He came on Friday, 30 April 1784,

observing, strangely, the city to be "now but the
shadow of what it was, though it begins to lift up its
head. It is certainly the sweetest place in all North
Briton, unless perhaps Dundee." Obviously, he had
reference to the spiritual condition of the city, for
even the most disinterested traveler could hardly have
escaped noticing the increased economic activity of
Perth during the late eighteenth century. At any rate,
he preached at 6:00 P.M. in the Tolbooth, on 1
Cornithians 13:1, to a large and well-behaved
congregation. Many of them were present again at five
in the morning, May 1--although the diary for this day
indicates that he preached at 6:00 A.M., on 1
Corinthians 13:13 (see Journal, 6:500-501).

Scone Palace, Perth

Wesley first viewed Scone Palace on Thursday
afternoon, 5 May 1768, and described it as "a large old
house, delightfully situated, but swiftly running to
ruin. Yet there are a few good pictures and some fine
tapestry left in what they call the Queen's and King's
chambers. And what is far more curious, there is a bed
and a set of hangings in the (once) royal apartment,
which was wrought by poor Queen Mary while she was
imprisoned in the castle of Lochleven [see below,
Chapter 5, under Kinross]. It is some of the finest
needlework I ever saw, and plainly shows both her
exquisite skill and unwearied industry" (Journal,
5:258). He toured the grounds again on Monday, 23
April 1770, taking "another view of that palace of
ancient men of renown, long since mouldered into common
dust. The buildings, too, are now decaying apace. So
passes the dream of human greatness!" (Journal, 5:363)
The last sentence calls to mind a similar idea set

forth by Samuel Johnson in <u>The Vanity of Human Wishes</u>
(January 1749):

> Unnumber'd suppliants croud Preferment's gate,
> Athirst for wealth, and burning to be great;
> Delusive Fortune hears th' incessant call,
> They mount, they shine, evaporate, and fall.
>
> (73-76)

The palace at Scone deteriorated to the point
that, in 1808, it was replaced by a fine castellated
mansion. Wesley, of course, did not see the famous
Stone of Scone, which then, as now, lay clamped to the
underside of the Coronation Chair, in the Chapel of St.
Edward the Confessor, Westminster Abbey. It measures
twenty-six inches in length, sixteen inches in width,
and eleven inches thick, and consists of a dull red or
purplish sandstone native to the west coast of
Scotland. Chisel marks indicate that at some time it
was prepared for use in a building.

Dundee

For a considerable period prior to the Union,
Dundee, lying north of the River Tay, had been known
both as a seaport and a center for the manufacturing of
coarse linen. In 1755, its population stood at 12,477;
by the turn of the century, the figure had more than
doubled to 26,084. (Hamilton, <u>Economic History</u>, p.26).
Alexander Webster (1707-1784), the Edinburgh minister
who, in 1755, conducted a population survey of
Scotland--and the same Alexander Webster who met with
Wesley at Lady Glenorchy's house in May 1770 (see
above, under <u>Edinburgh</u>)--observed that Dundee "has
increased so considerably that there have been added
two parish Churches to the Establishment in the course
of last year" (Kyd, <u>Scottish Population</u>, p. 47). The

population increase naturally created a mammoth housing
problem, since most of the dwellings were built of
wood, while only between six and eight stone structures
stood in High Street or in the Market Place. Also, the
streets were terribly narrow, congested, and filthy.
By 1800, however, the number of houses had been
doubled, new streets laid out, and the general
standards of living elevated considerably.

Apparently, the population explosion within
Dundee, accompanied by a general deterioration of
streets and buildings, was a mid-century phenomenon.
Viewing the town prior to 1710, Daniel Defoe thought it
well deserving of the epithet "Bonny Dundee." He noted
a large number of "stately houses, and large handsome
streets; particularly it has four very good streets,
with a large market-place in the middle, the largest
and fairest in Scotland, except only that of Aberdeen"
(Defoe, Tour, p. 651). Taking sight of the religious
climate of the city, Defoe remarked that "The great
church was formerly collegiate, being the cathedral of
the place, and was a very large building; but part of
it was demolished in the Civil War; the remainder is
divided. . .into three churches for the present use of
the citizens. They have also a meeting-house or two
for the episcopal worship; for you are to take it once
for all, that north by Tay, there are far more of the
episcopal persuasion than are to be found in the south;
and the farther north, the more so. . ." (Defoe, Tour,
pp. 651-652).

John Wesley's initial visit to Dundee occurred on
Thursday, 30 April 1761; he remained only the one day,
and made no mention in the journals of his activities
there. Three years later, he came back, stopping there
first on Thursday, 31 May 1764, where at 6:00 P.M. he

"preached on the side of the meadow near the town.
Poor and rich attended. Indeed, there is seldom fear
of wanting a congregation in Scotland. But the
misfortune is, they know everything; so they learn
nothing" (Journal, 5:72). Back again some two weeks
later (Friday, 15 June), he had hoped to catch the boat
for Edinburgh, but the vessel was just departing;
rather than remain in Dundee overnight, he rode on to
Cupar. After an absence of two years, Wesley appeared
once more in Dundee on Monday, 2 June 1766; this would
be his first stay of any significant length. The day
of his arrival proved terribly wet, but "it cleared up
in the evening, so that I preached abroad to a large
congregation, many of whom attended in the morning [3
June]" (Journal, 5:168). The schedule during the next
two days seems to have been the same. On Thursday, 5
June, the weather at last being fair, "we had a more
numerous congregation than ever; to whom, after
preaching, I took occasion to repeat most of the
plausible objections which had been made to use in
Scotland. I then showed our reasons for the things
which had been objected to us, and all seemed to be
thoroughly satisfied." What he said, essentially, was
this:

> I love plain dealing. Do not you? I will
> use it now. Bear with me.
>   I hang out no false colours; but show you
> all I am, all I intend, all I do.
>   I am a member of the Church of England;
> but I love good men of every Church.
>   My ground is the Bible. Yea, I am a
> Bible-bigot. I follow it in all things, both
> great and small.
>   Therefore, 1. I always use a short

private-prayer when I attend the public
service of God. Do not you? Why do you not?
Is not this according to the Bible?

2. I stand whenever I sing the praise of
God in public. Does not the Bible give you
plain precedents for this?

3. I always kneel before the Lord my
Maker when I pray in public.

4. I generally in public use the Lord's
Prayer, because Christ has taught me, when I
pray, to say--[Our Father, etc.]

I advise every preacher connected with me,
whether in England or Scotland, herein to
tread in my steps.

(<u>Journal</u>, 5:168-169)

Essentially, Dundee was never to become one of the
sweetest fruits in Wesley's vineyard. For example, in
June 1766, he noted that "There are about sixty members
there, and scarce more than six scriptural believers"
(<u>Journal</u>, 5:171). Then, on Monday evening, 2 May 1768,
"I preached to a large congregation at Dundee. They
heard attentively, but seemed to feel nothing. The
next evening [3 May] I spoke more strongly, and to
their hearts rather than their understanding; and I
believe a few felt the work of God sharp as a two-edged
sword" (<u>Journal</u>, 5:258). Still, conditions for
Methodism must have improved somewhat during the next
two years. On Wednesday, 9 May 1770, Wesley noted that
"The ministers here, particularly Mr. Small, are bitter
enough; notwithstanding which the society is well
established, and the congregation exceeding large. I
dealt very plainly with them at six [P.M.], and still
more so the next evening; yet none appeared to be
offended" (<u>Journal</u>, 5:366). He took note of another

"huge congregation" at Dundee on the evening of Thursday, 7 May 1772, the fast-day before the sacrament. "Never in my life did I speak more plain or close: let God apply it as pleaseth Him." On the day following, he "laboured to reconcile those who (according to the custom of the place) were vehemently contending with nothing" (<u>Journal</u>, 5:459).

During 1774, Wesley made only two brief visits to Dundee, preaching there on Monday evening, 23 May, and again on the evening of Tuesday, the 31st. Two years later (Sunday, 26 May 1776), he stopped long enough to attend services in one of the new Episcopal churches, a "cheerful, lightsome, and admirably well finished" structure. "A young gentleman preached such a sermon, both for sense and language, as I never heard in North Britain before, and I was informed his life is as his preaching." Then at 5:00 P.M. of the same day, Wesley preached to "an exceeding large congregation; and the people of Dundee, in general, behave better at public worship than any in the kingdom, except the Methodists and those at the Episcopal chapels. In all other kirks the bulk of the people are bustling to and fro before the minister has ended his prayer. In Dundee all are quiet, and none stir at all till he has pronounced the blessing" (<u>Journal</u>, 6:109). However, one had always to distinguish clearly the thin line between decorum and apathy. Preaching in the city on Tuesday evening, 1 June 1779, Wesley observed "The congregation was, as usual, very large and deeply attentive. But that was all. I did not perceive that any one was affected at all. I admire this people; so decent, so serious, and so perfectly unconcerned" (<u>Journal</u>, 6:236).

As late as 1782, Wesley found himself making little or no headway in Dundee. For example, on

Monday, 3 June, he preached before a large and attentive congregation; yet, "I found no increase, either of the society or of the work of God" (Journal, 6:354). Two years later, he did note some improvement, but it was of the type that had nothing whatsoever to do with the development of Methodism. "Handsome houses spring up on every side. Trees are planted in abundance. Wastes and commons are continually turned into meadows and fruitful fields. There wants only a proportionable improvement in religion, and this will be one of the happiest countries in Europe." On the evening of Saturday, 1 May 1784, he preached at an open-air service, and did so again the next afternoon "to one far more numerous, on whom I earnestly enforced, 'How long halt ye between two opinions?' Many of them seemed almost persuaded to halt no longer; but God only knows the heart" (Journal, 6:500-501). His next trip to Dundee occurred in mid-May 1786, but nothing of note transpired during the three days (19, 20, and 26) of his visit. Wesley came once more to the city four years later; his final diary notes only that he arrived at 1:00 P.M. on Tuesday, 18 May 1790, and departed at noon on the next day. Of more than passing interest are the comparative figures from the membership list of 1767--the fist year in which a complete account of the membership within the various Methodist societies was drawn forth. In contrast to 175 members in the Aberdeen society, 150 in Edinburgh, and 64 in Glasgow, the Dundee society numbered but forty persons (Tyerman, Life of Wesley, 2:608). Throughout the next twenty-three years of John Wesley's mission to Dundee, the Methodist society there never increased significantly beyond that figure.

Aberdeen

Early in the eighteenth century, Defoe observed that Aberdeen, in one sense, the capital of northeast Scotland, "is divided into two towns or cities, and stands at the mouth of two rivers; the towns are the new and the old Aberdeen, about a mile distant from one another, one situate on the River Don or Dune, the other on the River Dee, from whence it is supposed to take its name; for Aber, in the old British language, signifies a mouth, or opening of a river. . ." (Defoe, Tour, p. 653). Specifically, he noted the existence of a "great market-place, which, indeed, is very beautiful and spacious; and the streets adjoining are very handsome and well built; the houses lofty and high; but not so as to be inconvenient, as in Edinburgh; or low, to be contemptible as in most other places. But the generality of the citizens' houses are built of stone four stories high, handsome sash-windows, and are very well furnished within, the citizens here being as gay, as genteel, and, perhaps, as rich, as in any city in Scotland" (Defoe, Tour, p. 654). Being a true born son of mercantilism, Defoe could appreciate the activity in salmon and herring fishery, the manufacture of linen and worsted stockings, and the export of pork. "In a word, the people of Aberdeen are universal merchants, so far as trade of the northern part of the world will extend. They drive a very great trade to Holland, to France, to Hambrough, to Norway, to Gottenburgh, and to the Baltick; and it may, in a word, be esteemed as the third city in Scotland, that is to say, next after Edinburgh and Glasgow" (Defoe, Tour, p. 655).

Defoe, of course, wrote of an Aberdeen that had not yet entered into its full potential as an

industrial city. By 1755, its population had reached
to approximately 22,000; this figure would rise to
26,992 in 1801 (Hamilton, Economic History, p. 26).
Thus, the need for expansion became readily apparent.
And, as with Edinburgh, the topography created certain
difficulties: the deep valley of the Den Burn to the
west, a loch to the north, and the sea and the harbor
to the east. In 1768, the planners built Marischal
Street, which provided better access to the harbor; in
1770, they constructed a breakwater to protect the
harbor from the northeasterly gales. Finally, the loch
to the north was drained, and plans drawn for four new
streets: George, Charlotte, St. Andrew, and John
(Hamilton, Economic History, pp. 26-27).

By the time (late August 1773) Samuel Johnson and
James Boswell arrived in Aberdeen, the traveler could
well identify two distinct sections of the city.
Johnson took notice of the differences almost
immediately, remarking that "Old Aberdeen is the
ancient episcopal city, in which are still to be seen
the remains of the cathedral [St. Machar's]. It has
the appearance of a town in decay, having been situated
in times when commerce was yet unstudied, with very
little attention to the commodities of the harbour."
In contrast, he viewed the new city as containing "all
the bustle of prosperous trade, and all the show of
increasing opulence. It is built by the water-side.
The houses are large and lofty, and the streets
spacious and clean. They build almost wholly with the
granite used in the new pavement of the streets of
London, which is well known not to want hardness, yet
they shape it easily. It is beautiful and must be very
lasting" (Johnson, Journey to the Western Islands, pp.
12-13).

Wesley's first visit to Aberdeen, in May 1761, came about through the efforts of Dr. John Memyss, originally of Wrexham, but a resident of Aberdeen since 1747 and a Methodist even before then. Shortly after his removal to the Scottish city, he joined the evangelical congregation of Reverend John Bisset (d. 1756); upon the latter's death, Memyss journeyed to London, where he approached Wesley concerning the immediate need for evangelical preaching in Aberdeen. Wesley therefore dispatched Christopher Hopper, who spent the period 1759-1760 forming a society in the city. The leader of the Methodists was not long in following his preacher there; he arrived on Saturday morning, 2 May 1761, lodging at Dr. Memyss's house, and remained until Thursday morning, the 7th. On the evening preceding his departure (Wednesday, 6 May), he dined at the home of a Mr. Ogilvie, "one of the ministers between whom the city is divided. A more open-hearted, friendly man I know not that I ever saw. And indeed I have scarce seen such a set of ministers in any town of Great Britain or Ireland" (Journal, 4:451).

Late in May 1763, Wesley returned to Aberdeen, inquiring, in his own words, "into the state of things here." In this city, at least, he could find ample reasons for enthusiasm. "Surely never was there a more open door. The four ministers of Aberdeen, the minister of the adjoining town, and the three ministers of Old Aberdeen, hitherto seem to have no dislike, but rather to wish us 'good luck in the name of the Lord.' Most of the townspeople as yet seem to wish us well; so that there is no open opposition of any kind. Oh what spirit ought a preacher to be of, that he may be able to bear all this sunshine!" (Journal, 5;14) At 7:00

P.M., Wednesday, 25 May, "the evening being fair and
mild, I preached to a multitude of people, in the
College Close, on 'Stand in the ways and see, and ask
for the old paths.'" However, the weather changed
abruptly the next day; it "being raw and cold, I
preached in the College Hall. What an amazing
willingness to hear runs through this whole kingdom!
There want only a few zealous, active labourers, who
desire nothing but God; and they might soon carry the
gospel through all this country. . ." (Journal, 5:14).
He departed on Friday, 27 May, for Brechin. By this
time, the Methodist society in Aberdeen contained
nearly ninety members.

Apparently, the Aberdeen society proved
sufficiently successful that Wesley could justify a
return to the city in the following year. Indeed, his
schedule from Saturday, 2 June 1764, through Wednesday,
6 June, allowed little time for rest or leisure. He
preached on the evening of the 2nd in the College Hall,
and again at 7:00 the next morning. At 4:00 that
afternoon, he addressed a crowded audience in the
College kirk at Old Aberdeen, then moved over to the
College Close, New Aberdeen, at 7:00 P.M. "But the
congregation was so exceeding large that many were not
able to hear. However, many did hear, and I think
feel, the application of 'Thou art not far from the
kingdom of God.'" Still, success was not without its
problems. "We want nothing here but a larger house;
and the foundation of one is laid already. It is true
we have little money, and the society is poor; but we
know in whom we have believed" (Journal, 5:74). Since
1759, the first meeting-house of the Aberdeen Methodist
society had been located in Barnett's Close, leading
from the Guest-row to Flourmill Brae; the society moved

from there to a house on the north side of Queen Street, then to another dwelling in Lodge Walk. Although the three houses had been rented by the society, they were located in respectable sections of the city. In the early spring of 1764, the Aberdeen Methodists, finding the dwelling in Lodge Walk too small for their needs, acquired a site on Queen Street; there they erected a chapel, similar in style to the Octagon at Edinburgh. Thus, for Wednesday, and Thursday, 13-14 June 1764, the relevant portions of Wesley's journal read as follows: "We reached Aberdeen about one [P.M., 13 June]. Between six and seven, both this evening and the next, I preached in the shell of the new house, and found it a time of much consolation" (Journal, 5:77).

Two years later, Wesley spent practically an entire week in Aberdeen, arriving on Friday, 6 June 1766, and remaining until Friday morning, 13 June. On his first evening there, he preached to a large congregation; "the number of those who attended in the morning [7 June] showed they were not all curious hearers." The pace quickened on Sunday, the 8th: "Knowing no reason why we should make God's day the shortest of the seven, I desired Joseph Thompson [one of his itinerant preachers, then stationed in Aberdeen] to preach at five [A.M.]. At eight I preached myself. In the afternoon, I heard a strong, close sermon at Old Aberdeen, and afterward preached in the College kirk to a very genteel and yet serious congregation. I then opened and enforced the way of holiness, at New Aberdeen, on a numerous congregation." On Monday, the 9th, he kept a watch-night, "and explained to abundance of genteel people, 'One thing is needful'; a great number of whom would not go away till after the noon of

night" (Journal, 5:169). The watch-night had been
instituted some twenty-five years earlier, among the
colliers at Kingswood. According to Wesley, these men,
prior to their conversions to Methodism, tended to
congregate every Saturday night at the local ale-house;
after having seen the new light, they went, instead, to
Kingswood school, where they spent the greater part of
the evening in prayer, praise, and thanksgiving. Thus,
in John and Charles Wesley's Hymns and Sacred Poems
(Bristol: Felix Farley, 1742), we observe these lines:

> Oft have we passed the guilty night
> In revellings and frantic mirth;
> The creature was our soul delight,
> Our happenings the things of earth;
> But O! suffice the season past,
> We choose the better part at last.

> We will not close our wakeful eyes,
> We will not let our eyelids sleep,
> But humbly lift them to the skies,
> And all a solemn vigil keep:
> So many nights on sin bestow'd,
> Can we not watch one hour for God?

(Poetical Works, 2:193)

After a side trip to Monymusk (see below, Chapter 6),
Wesley came back to Aberdeen on the 11th and found
"many of the people were much alive to God. With these
our labour has not been in vain; and they are worth all
the pains we have taken in Scotland" (Journal, 5:170).

On his next scheduled visit, Tuesday, 26 April
1768, the positivism observed two years earlier was
still evident. Wesley "found a society truly alive,
knit together in peace and love. The congregations
were large both morning and evening, and, as usual,

deeply attentive. . . ." However, there were also the usual distractions: "a company of strolling players, who have at length found place here also, stole away the gay part of the hearers. Poor Scotland! Poor Aberdeen! This only was wanting to make them as completely irreligious as England" (Journal, 5:256). Actually, Wesley could well have counted his blessings, for, other than amateur productions or bands of traveling players, the theatre as such was practically non-existent in Aberdeen during the eighteenth century. In addition to the distractions from the "stage," the problem of direct abuse, so prevalent in England, reared its ugly head during this particular visit. On Sunday, 1 May, he preached at the new house in Queen Street at 7:00 A.M., then at the College kirk in the afternoon. "At six [P.M.], knowing our house could not contain the congregation, I preached in the Castle-gate, on the paved stones. A large number of people were all attention; but there were many rude, stupid creatures round about them, who knew as little of reason as of religion; I never saw such brutes in Scotland before. One of them threw a potato which fell on my arm. I turned to them; and some were ashamed" (Journal, 5:257). Finally, Wesley chose this week to set down (on Wednesday, 27 April) the particulars of his last will and testament (a verbatim copy of which may be seen, most conveniently, in Tyerman's Life of Wesley, 3:15-17). The items within this document were altered considerably in his will of 1789.

Returning to Aberdeen once again in May 1770, Wesley saw fit to spend another six days there--from Tuesday, the 1st, until Sunday morning, the 6th. If nothing else, he provides us with a rather detailed report on the unseasonable weather in the north of

Scotland. "We had storms of snow or rain every day. And it seems the weather was the same as far as London. So general a storm has scarce been in the memory of man" (Journal, 5:365). At the end of this stay, (Saturday, 5 May), he preached in the College kirk "to a very serious (though mostly genteel) congregation," and then to the society at the Methodist meeting-house (Journal, 5:365). Two years later, he spent almost the same amount of time in Aberdeen, arriving on Friday, 1 May 1772, and departing on Tuesday afternoon, the 5th. On Sunday morning, the 3rd, he attended service at St. Andrew's Episcopal Church. "Here likewise I could not but admire the exemplary decency of the congregation. This was the more remarkable because so miserable a reader I never heard before. Listening with all attention, I understood but one single work, 'Balak,' in the First Lesson, and one more 'begat,' was all I could possibly distinguish in the Second. Is there no man of spirit belonging to this congregation? Why is such a burlesque upon public worship suffered? Would it not be far better to pay this gentleman for doing nothing than for doing mischief, for bringing a scandal upon religion?" (Journal, 5:457-458) That afternoon, at 3:00, Wesley preached in the College kirk, and again at 6:00 at the Methodist Meeting-house on the Narrow Way. "I spoke exceeding plain, both this evening and the next [Monday, 4 May]; yet none were offended. What encouragement has every preacher in this country, 'by manifestation of the truth,' to 'commend' himself 'to every man's conscience in the sight of God!'" (Journal, 5:458)

On 25 May 1774, Wesley reached Aberdeen in the evening and remained until Monday morning, the 30th. During his stay he managed to read Sketches in the

History of Man (2 vols., 1774) by Henry Home, Lord
Kames (1696-1782), the Scottish jurist and close friend
of James Boswell. Both Johnson and Boswell thought the
Sketches to be inaccurate and generally inferior, while
Wesley could not understand clearly the purpose or even
the value of the work:

> Undoubtedly the author is a man of strong
> understanding, lively imagination, and
> considerable learning, and his book contains
> some useful truths. Yet some things in it
> give me pain: (1) His affirming things that
> are not true, as that all negro children turn
> black the ninth or tenth day from their
> birth. No: most of them turn partly black
> on the second day, entirely so on the third.
> That all the Americans [Indians] are of a
> copper colour. Not so: some of them are as
> fair as we are. Many more such assertions I
> observed which I impute not to design but to
> credulity. (2) His flatly contradicting
> himself, many times within a page or two.
> (3) His asserting, and labouring to prove,
> that man is a mere piece of clockwork. And,
> lastly, his losing no opportunity of
> vilifying the Bible, to which he appears to
> bear a most cordial hatred. I marvel if any
> but his brother infidels will give two
> guineas for such a work as this!
>
> (Journal, 6:22)

Perhaps the brotherhood of infidels was more
numerous than Wesley thought, for Lord Kames's Sketches
went to an enlarged four volumes in 1778, another two-
volume edition in Dublin the year following, and a
four-volume edition (Edinburgh) in 1788. At any rate,

Wesley managed to break away from his reading on
Sunday, 29 May, preaching at 7:00 A.M. and again in the
evening, at which time "the people were ready to tread
upon each other. I scarce ever saw people so squeezed
together. And they seemed to be all ear while I
exhorted them, with strong and pointed words, not to
receive 'the grace of God in vain'" (Journal, 6:22).

Wesley's visit to Aberdeen in 1776 lasted five
days (17 through 19 May, and 22 through 23 May), part
of which was taken up with reading Samuel Johnson's
Journey to the Western Islands of Scotland and Thomas
Pennant's Tour in Scotland (see Chapter 2). On Sunday,
the 19th, he attended morning service at the
Presbyterian kirk, which he described as "full as
formal as any in England; and no way calculated either
to awaken sinners or to stir up the gift of God in
believers." That afternoon he heard a "useful sermon"
at the Church of England chapel, "and was again
delighted with the exquisite decency both of the
minister and the whole congregation. The Methodist
congregation come the nearest to this; but even these
do not come up to it." Finally, he noted a large crowd
at the Queen Street meeting-house for evening service,
"but some of the hearers did not behave like those at
the [English] chapel" (Journal, 6:106). The English
chapel, located between the Gallowgate and Loch Street,
was founded as a qualified (independent) congregation.
The handsome and spacious building, erected between
1721 and 1722, supposedly held as many as a thousand
persons and contained one of the few church organs in
all of Scotland. In 1866, the chapel was replaced by
Old St. Paul's Episcopal Church.

The next Aberdeen visit occurred three years
later; Wesley arrived on Thursday, 3 June 1779, and

"preached to a people that can feel as well as hear" (Journal, 6:236). He remained only for the one day, but returned on Saturday evening, the 12th. The next day being Sunday, he "spoke as closely as I could, both morning and evening, and made a pointed application to the hearts of all that were present. I am convinced that this is the only way whereby we can do any good in Scotland." In between his own services, Wesley found time to attend the Scottish kirk, where "I heard many excellent truths. . .; but, as there was no application, it was likely to do as much good as the singing of a lark. I wonder the pious ministers in Scotland are not sensible of this. They cannot but see that no sinners are convinced of sin, none converted to God, by this way of preaching. How strange it is, then, that neither reason nor experience teaches them to take a better way!" (Journal, 6:239) However, he must have felt that all was going well with the Methodist society in Aberdeen, for he waited another three years before he came again. And, he remained only for two days, remarking--on Wednesday, 5 June 1782--that the "congregations were large both morning and evening, and many of them much alive to God" (Journal, 6:354,357). In regard to the Aberdeen Methodist preachers, it is interesting to note the specific conditions under which they worked. For instance, each was provided a house and, in addition to a quarterly stipend of £3, received an allowance of eleven shillings per week. Thus, the total came to £40 12s. a year. From this sum, the preacher provided his own meat, drink, washing, attendance, coals, candles, and letters. As added benefits, the stewards of the society donated to the preachers their lodging and all necessary furniture (see Journal, 12:164, note 1).

The first sign of any slight deterioration among
the Aberdeen Methodists was noticed by John Wesley in
May 1784. Specifically, he discovered that "the
morning preaching had been long discontinued, yet the
bands and the select society were kept up. But many
were faint and weak for want of morning preaching and
prayer-meetings, of which I scarce found any traces in
Scotland," So, despite the success of the Aberdeen
society in terms of its numbers, it could not escape
the same problems common to the societies in Glasgow,
Edinburgh, and Dundee. On Wednesday evening, 5 May,
Wesley spoke with his preachers, showing "them the hurt
it did both to them and the people for any one preacher
to stay six or eight weeks together in one place.
Neither can he find matter for preaching every morning
and evening, nor will the people come to hear him:
Hence he grows cold by lying in bed, and so do the
people. Whereas, if he never stays more than
a fortnight together in one place, he may find matter
enough, and the people will gladly hear him. They
immediately drew up such a plan for this circuit, which
they determined to pursue" (Journal, 6:502). The next
morning (Thursday, 6 May), at 5:00, he preached before
"the largest congregation. . .which I have seen since I
came into the kingdom" (Journal, 6:502). He departed
immediately, returning on the 15th for a single service
in the evening. At 2:00 the following afternoon, he
preached in Trinity Chapel, a English Episcopal church
in Shiprow. "It was crowded with people of all
denominations. I preached from 1 Cor. xii, 1, 2, 3, in
utter defiance of their common saying, 'He is a good
man, though he has bad tempers.' Nay, if he has bad
tempers, he is no more a good man than the devil as a
good angel." At 5:00 that evening, Wesley preached "in

our own chapel, exceeding crowded, on the form and power of godliness. I am now clear of these people, and can cheerfully commend them to God" (Journal, 6:508). The next morning, at 4:30, he left for Arbroath.

After 1784, there would be two further visits to Aberdeen. Wesley arrived in the city at 4:00 P.M. on Monday, 22 May 1786, and remained there until Thursday morning (3:30 A.M.), the 25th. On the evening of the 24th, "We had an exceeding solemn parting, as I reminded them [the members of the society] that we could hardly expect to see each other's face any more till we met in Abraham's bosom" (Journal, 7:164). However, he came again, four years later, on Thursday, 20 May 1790, and took his leave for the final time at 6:00 P.M., Wednesday, 26 May. ". . .I took a solemn farewell of a crowded audience. If I should be permitted to see them again, well; if not, I delivered my own soul" (Journal, 8:66).

King's College, Aberdeen

Founded in 1500 by William Elphinstone (1431-1514), Bishop of Aberdeen (1488-1514), and located in the old city of Aberdeen, King's College received its charter from James IV in 1598. Defoe informs us that Bishop Elphinstone "lies buried in the chapel or college church, under a very magnificent and curious monument. The steeple of this church was the most artificial that I have seen in Scotland, and very beautiful, according to the draught of the building. But it is much more so now [c. 1710], having been injured, if not quite broken down by a furious tempest anno 1361; but rebuilt after the first model" (Defoe, Tour, p. 654).

John Wesley walked about King's College at noon on
Monday, 4 May 1761--two days after he first arrived in
Aberdeen. "It has three sides of a square, handsomely
built, not unlike Queen's College in Oxford. Going up
to see the hall, we found a large company of ladies,
with several gentlemen. They looked and spoke to one
another, after which one of the gentlemen took courage
and came to me. He said: 'We came last night to the
College Close, but could not hear, and should be
extremely obliged if you would give us a short
discourse here.' I knew not what God might have to do,
and so began without delay on 'God was in Christ,
reconciling the world unto Himself.' I believe the
word was not lost; it fell as dew on the tender grass"
(Journal, 4:450).

Marischal College, Aberdeen

Although located in the new city of Aberdeen, on
the north side of the Dee, Marischal College (the
Marshallian or Marshal's College) dates from 1593. The
old buildings, essentially those of the former
Greyfriar's monastery, were torn down to make way for
the present quandrangle, built between 1836 and 1844;
however, one stone from the original was preserved and
inserted over the vestibule under the Mitchell Tower.
It bears the College motto, "They haif said; what say
thay; lat theme say." Samuel Johnson described the
main hall as "large and well-lighted. One of its
ornaments is the picture of Arthur Johnston, who was
principal of the college, and who holds among the Latin
poets of Scotland the next place to the elegant
Buchanan" (Johnson, Journey to the Western Islands, p.
14). Johnston (1587-1641), a physician as well as a
writer of Latin verse, served as rector of King's

College before moving over to Marischal, while George Buchanan (1506-1582), a Latin poet and scholar, studied at St. Andrews and later became tutor to James VI. By far the noblest asset of Marischal was its library, "well stocked with books, as well by the citizens as by the benefactions of gentlemen, and lovers of learning; as also with the finest and best mathematical instruments" (Defoe, Tour, p. 654).

On the very afternoon of his arrival in Aberdeen (Saturday, 2 May 1761), Wesley approached Marischal's principal, George Campbell, for permission to preach in the College Close. Dr. Campbell (1719-1796), a native of Aberdeen, studied at Marischal in preparation for the law. However, he re-directed his interests toward divinity, and in 1746 received his license from the Presbytery of Aberdeen as a probationer. Before assuming the principalship at Marischal, he held pastorates at Banchory-Ternan (1750) and Aberdeen (1756). Among his writings we may take note of A Dissertation on Miracles (Edinburgh, 1762), Philosophy of Rhetoric (London, 1776), The Four Gospels Translated from the Greek (London, 1790), Lectures on Systematic Theology and Pulpit Eloquence (London, 1807), Lectures on Ecclesiastical History (London, 1800), and Lectures on the Pastoral Character (London, 1811). The principal readily granted Wesley's petition, "but as it began to rain, I was desired to go into the hall. I suppose this is full a hundred feet long, and seated all round. The congregation was large, notwithstanding the rain, and full as large as five in the morning" (Journal, 4:450).

On Monday afternoon, 4 May 1761, Wesley toured the College library, where he met George Campbell and the Professor of Divinity at Marischal, Alexander Gerard

(1728-1795). Prior to his appointment to the Divinity
professorship in 1760, Gerard held the chair in
Philosophy at Marischal from 1758 to 1760. In 1771, he
moved to King's College as Professor of Divinity. His
published works include An Essay on Taste (London,
1759), Sermons (1759-1761), Dissertations (1766), An
Essay on Genius (1767), Sermons (1776-1778), Nineteen
Sermons (London, 1780-1782), Pastoral Care (1799), and
Evidences of Natural and Revealed Religion (1828). On
23 August 1773, in Aberdeen, James Boswell "talked of
the differences of genius, to try if I could engage
Gerard in a disquisition with Dr. Johnson; but I did
not succeed" (Boswell, Journal of a Tour, p. 218).
Wesley fared somewhat better, for he had read Dr.
Gerard's Essay on Taste on Wednesday, 24 March 1779,
and again on Thursday, 1 November 1787. He was hardly
impressed: "It is lively and pretty; but neither deep
nor strong. Scarce any of the terms are accurately
defined; indeed, defining is not this author's talent.
he has not by any means a clear apprehension; and it is
through this capital defect that he jumbles together
true and false propositions, in every chapter and in
every page" (Journal, 6:225).

Another invitation came the next day, Tuesday, 5
May, from Principal Campbell; thus, he and Wesley spent
an hour together at the former's house. "I observed no
stiffness at all, but the easy good-breeding of a man
of sense and learning. I suppose both he and all the
professors, with some of the magistrates, attended
[service] in the evening. I set all the windows open,
but the [College] hall, notwithstanding, was as hot as
a bagnio. But this did not hinder either the attention
of the people or the blessing of God." Finally, on
Wednesday, evening, 6 May, at 6:30, Wesley "stood in

the College Close and proclaimed Christ crucified. My voice was so strengthened that all could hear, and all were earnestly attentive. I have now 'cast' my 'bread upon the waters'; may I 'find it again after many days!'" (Journal, 4:451) If the question should arise as to why, both at King's and Marischal, Wesley had no contact with the students, the answer lies in the simple fact that none were on the premises. At both colleges during the mid and late eighteenth century, the term began on 1 November and ended on 1 April.

Gordon's Hospital, Aberdeen

On Wednesday noon, 25 May 1763, Wesley visited Gordon's Hospital, a charitable institution for poor children located on the outskirts of Old Aberdeen. He described the place as "an exceeding handsome building, and (what is not common) kept exceeding clean. The gardens are pleasant, well laid out, and in extremely good order; but the old bachelor who founded it has expressly provided that no woman should ever be there" (Journal, 5:14). Possibly, the old bachelor was Robert Gordon (1665-1732), who early in the century founded a school for boys at Aberdeen. Or, perhaps, the reference is to the same Dr. Gordon who, in 1781, opened a dispensary in Aberdeen, which served also to allow medical students the opportunity for observation and acquisition of practical knowledge in medicine (see Hamilton, Economic History, p. 387).

Chapter Four

SOUTH

Flow gently, sweet Afton, among the green
   braes,
Flow gently, I'll sing thee a song in thy
   praise;
My Mary's asleep by thy murmuring stream,
Flow gently, sweet Afton, disturb not her dream.

Thou stock-dove whose echo resounds through the
   glen,
Ye wild whistling blackbirds in yon thorny den,
Thou green-crested lapwing, thy screaming
   forbear,
I charge you disturb not my slumbering fair.

How lofty, sweet Afton, they neighboring hills,
Far marked with the courses of clear winding
   rills;
There daily I wander as noon rises high,
My flocks and my Mary's sweet cot in my eye.
   (Robert Burns, "Afton Water," ll. 1-12)

Port Patrick

Defoe identified Port Patrick as "the ordinary place for the ferry or passage to Belfast or other ports in Ireland. It has a tolerable good harbour, and a safe road; but there is very little use for it, for the packet boat, and a few fishing vessels are the sum of the navigation. . . ." However, since the Union,

Port Patrick had been important for the shipment of Irish cattle to Newton Stewart and Dumfries. Also, since 1737, the only military road built in the Lowlands, constructed to facilitate movements of troops between Scotland and Ireland, stretched from near Carlisle to Port Patrick. Of course, these improvements came after Defoe's visit; he found nothing about the town "to invite our stay, 'tis a mean dirty homely place; and as we had no business here, but to see the coast, we came away very ill satisfied with out accommodations" (Defoe, Tour, pp. 598-599).

John Wesley first came to Port Patrick at 3:00 P.M., Tuesday, 30 April 1765. He and James Kershaw, one of the Methodist itinerant preachers, "were immediately surrounded with men, offering to carry us over the water [to Ireland]. But the wind was full in our teeth. I determined to wait till morning, and then go forward or backward, as God should please" (Journal, 5:113). Two years later, Saturday, 28 March 1767, he came again for the same purpose--transportation to Ireland. The packet-boat was ready the next morning (Sunday, 29 March), "but waited for the mail, hour after hour, till past three in the afternoon. Hereby we avoided a violent storm, and had only what they called a fresh breeze. . ." (Journal, 5:201-202). There exists no evidence that Wesley attempted anything in behalf of Methodism during the two occasions upon which he set foot in Port Patrick.

Stranraer

Located a short distance northeast of Port Patrick. Stranraer, also, existed as a stop-over for travelers awaiting passage to Northern Ireland. However, the town was not unattractive, containing a

sixteenth-century castle and North West Castle house
(now a hotel), once the home of the Arctic explorer,
Sir John Ross (1777-1856).

Wesley paused at Stranraer on at least two
occasions, first on Tuesday, 30 April 1765, as he and
James Kershaw traveled from Girvan (see immediately
below) to Port Patrick. He indicated that the two "met
with as good entertainment of every kind as if we had
been in the heart of England" (Journal, 5:112). The
second instance proved equally brief. He landed at
Stranraer on Wednesday night, 30 August 1767, after a
five-hour passage from Donaghadee. On the following
morning, he departed early for Ayr, Glasgow, and,
ultimately, Edinburgh.

Girvan

Thirty miles north of Stranraer, along the
Ayrshire coast, the town of Girvan functioned, during
the eighteenth century, in much the same manner as the
present, depending largely upon its fishing and boat
building activities. On Monday, 29 April 1765, Wesley
and James Kershaw spent the night at Girvan, on their
way from Ayr to Port Patrick. The founder of the
Methodists saw only enough of the place to describe it
as "a little town on the sea-shore" (Journal, 5:112).
The two men left the next morning, riding over the
mountains between Ballantrae and Stranraer.

Maybole

To the northeast of Girvan lies the town of
Maybole, where Wesley spent the afternoon of Wednesday,
29 April 1765. Interestingly enough, he relies upon
the colloquial to describe his stay there: "After a
short bait at Maybole in the afternoon, we went on to

Girvan. . ." (Journal, 5:112). A Scotch bait referred
(between c. 1780 and c. 1850) to a halt and a rest on
one's staff, especially on the part of traveling
pedlars.

Although Wesley did not note it in his journal, he
must have seen Maybole Collegiate Church, the roofless
ruin of a fifteenth-century church built for a small
college established in the town in 1373 by the
Kennedies of Dunure. The remains include a rich door
in a revived First Pointed style, and an Easter
Sepulchre, also an imitation of early work. In the
provost's house (no longer standing), John Knox had his
famous disputation with Quentin Kennedy in 1561.

Ayr

Aside from having, in the eighteenth century, a
fair reputation as a port town, Ayr, of course, has
long been known for its association with Robert Burns.
The Scottish poet was, in 1759, baptised in the Auld
Kirk, a structure that dates from 1655. Other
noteworthy sites that were certainly available for the
eighteenth-century traveler include the late-medieval
Auld Brig, spanning the River Ayr, and the sixteenth-
century Loudon hall, formerly the residence of the
sheriffs of Ayrshire.

Daniel Defoe saw Ayr as a contrast between its
seventeenth-century greatness and early eighteenth-
century decline to mediocrity:

. . .it has certainly been a good town, and
much bigger than it is now. At present like
an old beauty, it shows the ruins of a good
face; but is also apparently not only decayed
and declined, but decaying and declining
every day, and from being the fifth town in

Scotland, as the townsmen say, is now like a
town forsaken; the reason of its decay, is,
the decay of its trade. . . . There is a
good river here, and a handsome stone bridge
of four arches.

The town is well situated, has a very
large ancient church, and has still a very
good market for all sorts of provision. But
nothing will save it from death, if trade
does not revive, which the townsmen say it
begins to do since the Union.

(Defoe, <u>Tour</u>, p. 601)

John Wesley and James Kershaw were in Ayr on
Monday morning, 29 April 1765, as they began their
journey from Glasgow to Port Patrick. However, they
must not have lingered there long--if, indeed, they
stopped at all--for the same day they rode on to
Maybole, and then to Girvan.

Kilmarnock

An inland industrial town, Kilmarnock served as a
market for sheep and lambs; toward the end of the
eighteenth century, facilities were established there
for the manufacture of carpets and bonnets. Its
single-most claim to fame, however, stems from the
publication, on 31 July 1786, of the Kilmarnock edition
of Robert Burns' poems: <u>Poems, chiefly in the Scottish
dialect</u> (Kilmarnock: Printed by John Wilson, 1786),
8vo. Born in Kilmarnock in 1750, Wilson was the town's
major printer and publisher from 1770 until his death
in 1821. He founded, in 1803, the first Ayrshire
newspaper, the <u>Ayr Advertiser</u>.

On Monday morning, 29 April 1765, John Wesley and
James Kershaw rode through Kilmarnock, perhaps stopping

for no more than an hour or so before they resumed
their journey to Maybole, Girvan, Stranraer, and,
finally, Port Patrick. Obviously, these small towns in
Ayrshire were to play an insignificant role in Wesley's
attempts to establish Methodism in Scotland. Instead,
he chose to concentrate his efforts upon the larger
towns and cities.

Solway Firth

Depending upon the weather or the season, Wesley
(and certainly other travelers of the period) would
enter Scotland from or leave it for Cumberland; such
places as Carlisle, Wigton, and Cockermouth contained
active Methodist societies that he visited regularly
during his tours of northern England and Scotland.
Thus, on at least seven occasions between 1753 and
1768, he crossed Solway Firth, the forty mile-long
inlet of the Irish Sea, at the Esk River estuary, that
separates northwestern England from southwestern
Scotland. Initially, he crossed from Bowness, some
thirty miles from Cockermouth, early on Monday morning,
16 April 1753. "Our landlord [at Bowness], as he was
guiding us over the Firth, very innocently asked how
much a year we got by preaching thus. This gave me an
opportunity of explaining to him that kind of gain
which he seemed utterly a stranger to. He appeared to
be quite amazed; and spoke not one word, good or bad,
till he took his leave" (Journal, 4:61).

The second crossing occurred on Monday, 30 May
1757, between 4:00 and 5:00 in the afternoon. Wesley
had left Wigton at about 1:00 P.M., crossed the Firth,
and "before seven reached an ill-looking house called
the Brow, which he came to by mistake, having passed
the house we were directed to. I believe God directed

us better than man. Two young women, we found, kept the house, who had lost both their parents, their mother very lately. I had great liberty in praying with them and for them. Who knows but God will fasten something upon them which they will not easily shake off?" (Journal, 4:216) Two years later, Monday 12 May 1759, he came the same way (through Wigton) and arrived at Solway Firth "just as the water was fordable. At some times it is so three hours in twelve; at other times, barely one" (Journal, 4:315). Again, on Monday, 27 April 1761, he found himself departing Wigton in the morning and reaching the Firth shortly before noon. "The guide told us it was not possible, but I resolved to try, and got over well" (Journal, 4:449).

Five years later, on Tuesday evening, 24 June 1766, Wesley crossed from the Scottish side; he had arrived in Dumfries before 8:00 A.M., and after a short pause there, "pushed on in hopes of reaching Solway Firth before the sea was come in. Designing to call at an inn by the Firth side, we inquired the way, and were directed to leave the main road and go straight to the house which we saw before us. In ten minutes Duncan Wright [one of Wesley's itinerant preachers from Limerick, in Ireland] was embogged. However, the horse plunged on and got through. I was inclined to turn back; but Duncan telling me I needed only to go a little to the left, I did so, and sunk at once to my horse's shoulders. He sprung up twice, and twice sunk again, each time deeper than before. At the third plunge he threw me on one side, and we both made shift to scramble out. I was covered with fine soft mud from my feet to the crown of my head; yet, blessed be to God, not hurt at all. But we could not cross till between seven and eight o'clock [P.M.]. An honest man

crossed with us, who went two miles out of his way to
guide us over the sands to Skinburness, where we found
a little clean house, and passed a comfortable night"
(Journal, 5:172).

During the last ten days of March 1767, central
and northern England were struck by severe rainstorms
and high winds, Wesley rode through all of this from
Liverpool to Whitehaven, and on Thursday, 26 March,
traversed "miserable roads [from Whitehaven] to Solway
Firth; but the guides were so deeply engaged in a cock-
fight that none could be procured to show us over. We
procured one, however, between three and four [P.M.].
But there was more sea than we expected, so that,
nothwithstanding all I could do, my legs and the skirts
of my coat were in the water. The motion of the waves
made me a little giddy; but it had a stranger effect on
Mr. [John] Atlay--he lost his sight, and was just
dropping off his horse when one of our fellow
travellers caught hold of him" (Journal, 5:201). The
final journey across the Firth, unlike the preceding
two, passed without incident. Wesley left Caldbeck, in
Cumberland, at 4:00 A.M., Monday, 18 April 1768. He
reached Solway Firth "before eight [A.M.], and, finding
a guide ready, crossed without delay. . ." (Journal,
5:255).

Ruthwell

The village of Ruthwell lies some eight and
one-half miles east-southeast of Dumfries, and therein
stands the famous Ruthwell Cross, one of the most
notable of early Christian monuments in all of western
Europe. Preserved in an annex to the parish church of
Ruthwell, the Cross dates from the end of the seventh
century and ranks, along with the Bowcastle Cross in

Cumberland, as one of the two foremost examples of Anglican sculpture, as well as one of the major monuments of Europe from the so-called Dark Ages. The main faces have figure-sculpture, mostly scenes from Scripture, associated with Latin inscriptions; on the sides are rich vine scrolls with birds and beasts. On the margins are inscribed, in runes, portions of the Old English poem <u>The Dream of the Rood</u>, generally ascribed to Caedmon.

John Wesley visited Ruthwell twice during the years he traveled in Scotland; on both occasions he stopped there after having just crossed the Solway Firth. Thus, we find him in the village first on Monday, 21 May 1759; he remained but a short while before riding on to Dumfires. Eight years later, on Thursday, 26 March 1767, he and John Atlay crossed the Firth, "rode on nine or ten miles, and lodged at a village called Ruthwell" (<u>Journal</u>, 5:201). The next morning, they proceeded toward Dumfries and then on to Port Patrick.

Dumfries

Daniel Defoe, ever ready to impress upon his readers (and his patron) the benefits obtained by Scotland as a result of the Union with England, thought Dumfries, lying at the mouth of the River Nith, as "always a good town, and full of merchants. By merchants, here I mean. . .not mercers and drapers, shopkeepers, &c. but merchant-adventurers, who trade to foreign parts, and employ a considerable number of ships. But if this was so before, it is much more so now [c. 1706-1710]; and as they have (with success) embarked in trade, as well to England as to the English plantations, they apparently increase both in shipping

and people. . ." (Defoe, Tour, p. 590). Certainly a
major reason for the expansion of Dumfries after the
Union, specifically during the middle of the century,
was that the town lay on the drove roads from the north
and the west to Carlisle and the English markets;
therefore, the nearby landed proprietors took a natural
interest in the growing cattle trade.

Defoe also described the town as possessed of a
"very fine stone bridge. . .over the River Nid [Nith];
as also a castle, though of old work, yet still good
and strong enough; also an exchange for the merchants,
and a Tolbooth, or town-hall for the use of the
magistrates. They had formerly a woollen manufacture
here. But as the Union has, in some manner, suppressed
those things in Scotland, the English supplying them
fully, both better and cheaper; so they have more than
an equivalent by an open trade to all the English
plantations, and to England itself" (Defoe, Tour, pp.
590-591). However, the results of the Union turned out
not always to be positive, as witnessed by severe
rioting in Dumfries in the early 1770's because of crop
failures and a general food shortage. Mobs attacked
ships in the harbor, whose crews were unloading a
consignment of meal for Irvine (on the Ayrshire coast,
north of Kilmarnock). Troops had to be called out, the
rioters suffered casualties, and prisoners taken and
brought before the High Court at Edinburgh--some
sentenced to transportation for from three to seven
years, others sent directly to prison. Interestingly
enough, the prisoners included tailors, smiths, and
shoemakers, as well as fleshers, masons, and weavers
(Hamilton, Economic History, pp. 375-376).

Dumfries became a regular rest stop for John
Wesley during his mission to Scotland. On Monday

evening, 16 April 1753, after crossing Solway Firth, he dined there and took note of "a clean, well-built town, having two of the most elegant churches (one at each end of the town) that I have seen" (Journal, 4:61). In the churchyard of one, St. Michael's, lie the bodies of Robert Burns, his wife Jean Armour, and their sons; the poet died at Dumfries on 21 July 1796. Four years later, again after coming across the Firth the previous afternoon, Wesley "breakfasted at Dumfries [Tuesday, 31 May 1757], and spent an hour with a poor backslider of London, who had been for some years settled there" (Journal, 4:216). At around 6:00 P.M., Monday, 21 May 1759, he returned to the town. "Having time to spare, we took a walk in the churchyard, one of the pleasantest places I ever saw. A single tomb I observed there, which was about a hundred and thirty years old; but the inscription was very hardly legible:

> Quandoquidem remanent [or data sunt] ipsis quoque fata sepulchris! [For sepulchres themselves must crumbling fall/In time's abyss, the common grave of all. (Juvenal, Satire X, trans. John Dryden, 146)]

So soon do even our sepulchres die! Strange that men should be so careful about them! But are not many self-condemned therein? They see the folly while they run into it. So poor Mr. [Matthew] Prior, speaking of his own tomb, has those melancholy words, 'For this last piece of human vanity, I bequeath five hundred pounds.'" (Journal, 4:315)

From 1766 to 1770, Wesley made at least four brief visits to Dumfries. On Tuesday, 24 June 1766, he paused there before moving on to cross Solway Firth, while in the next year (Friday, 27 March 1767), he rode through on his way to Port Patrick. He dined in the

town on Monday evening, 18 April 1768, and on Easter
Sunday, 15 April 1770, spent the night at "an admirable
inn at Dumfries" (Journal, 5:362).

Until 1787, there exists no evidence of any
serious Methodist activity at Dumfries. However, at
the Manchester Conference of August 1787, Wesley
ordered Robert Dall, one of his itinerant preachers, to
establish a society in the Lowland town. Apparently,
the latter's efforts bore quick results, for on 1
December 1787, Wesley wrote to him from London: "You
have reason to praise God, who has prospered you, and
given you to see the fruit of your labours. Our all
dispensing God has called us to preach the plain
gospel. I am glad your hands are strengthened in
corresponding with the brethren. I will desire any to
change with you when you see it best, and, if I live
till spring, please God, I will visit you at Dumfries"
(Tyerman, Life of Wesley, 3:532). Encouraged by his
leader's remarks, Dall requested permission to begin
construction of a chapel to replace the rented rooms
presently occupied by the society. Wesley replied on
11 February 1788: "I allow you to build at Dumfries,
providing any one will lend a hundred guineas on
interest. I hope to see you, God willing, in May"
(Tyerman, Life of Wesley, 3:532).

True to his word, Wesley arrived in Dumfries on
Tuesday, 13 May 1788; obviously, his spirits were high
regarding the potentials for Methodism in the town.
"Dumfries is beautifully situated; but as to wood and
water, and generally rising hills, &c., is, I think,
the neatest, as well as the most civilised town that I
have seen in the kingdom. Robert Dall soon found me
out. He has behaved exceeding well, and done much good
here; but he is a bold man. He has begun building a

preaching-house, larger than any in Scotland, except those in Glasgow and Edinburgh. In the evening, I preached abroad in a convenient street on one side of the town. Rich and poor attended from every quarter, of whatever denomination; and everyone seemed to hear for life. Surely the Scots are the best hearers in Europe!" (Journal, 7:387)

The visit of 1788 was to be more than one of the usual stop-overs of preceding years. The next day, Wednesday, 14 May, Wesley preached at 5:00 A.M. in the house occupied by the Dumfries society pending the completion of Robert Dall's chapel. ". . .such a one I never saw before," exclaimed the founder of the Methodists regarding the condition of this interim meeting house. "It had no windows at all, so that, although the sun shown bright, we could see nothing without candles. But I believe our Lord shone on many hearts while I was applying those words [Matthew 8:2-3], 'I will, be thou clean.' I breakfasted [at 8:00 A.M.] with poor Mr. Ashton, many years ago a member of our society in London; but far happier now in his little cottage than ever he was in his prosperity" (Journal, 7:387). He also found time to comment upon the increase in the diets of the citizens. "When I was in Scotland first [1751], even at a nobleman's table we had only flesh meats of one kind, but no vegetables of any kind; but now they are as plentiful here as in England. Near Dumfries there are five very large public gardens, which furnish the town with greens and fruit in abundance" (Journal, 7:387-388). That evening, he preached again in the Methodist meeting-house, finding the congregation "nearly double to that we had the last, and, if it was possible, more attentive. Indeed, one or two gentlemen, so called,

laughed at first; but they quickly disappeared, and all
were still while I explained the worship of God in
spirit and in truth. Two of the clergy followed me to
my lodging, and gave me a pressing invitation to their
houses. Several others intended, it seems, to do the
same. . ." (Journal, 7:388). However, he could remain
no longer; arising at 3:30 the next morning (Thursday,
15 May), he was on the road by 4:00, bound for Moffat
and then Glasgow.

The reaction to this first extended stay of Wesley
in Dumfries is worthy of attention at this point. One
resident of the town, a Mrs. Gordon Playdell, wrote to
Robert Dall, stating that "such was the general
prejudice against Mr. Wesley, that I really feared his
coming would end your hopeful prosperity; but God has
disappointed all my fears, and outdone all my hopes.
The popularity, which met him here, was marvellous.
The turn in his favour was such as none but God could
have brought about. You have been all along respected,
and the esteem for you grows more and more. Your
pious, unwearied attentions to the poor criminals have
increased the general regard for you, and your sermons
in the jail been much approved" (Tyerman, Life of
Wesley, 3:532-533). Charles Atmore, another of John
Wesley's itinerant preachers, also wrote to Dall,
declaring that "Mr. Wesley was much pleased with
Dumfries and you. He has given you a place in his
journal [see 8:387], and what you have done at Dumfries
will be a memorial of you to all generations" (Tyerman,
Life of Wesley, 3:533).

Wesley's final visit to Dumfries occurred on
Monday, 31 May 1790. Arriving at 6:30 P.M., he found
the congregation waiting, and "after a few minutes, I
preached on Mark iii.35: 'Whatsoever shall do the will

of God, the same is my brother, and sister, and
mother.'" Alexander Mather, whom Wesley had converted
in London on 14 April 1754, preached to the Dumfries
society at 5:00 the following morning, while Wesley
spent the day conversing with the townsfolk, "a candid,
humane, well-behaved people, unlike most that I have
found in Scotland. In the evening the house was
filled; and truly God preached to their hearts. Surely
God will have a considerable people here" (Journal,
8:68). By 1790, Dumfries had become a part of the
Glasgow circuit, and, as a result, merited its own
resident preacher, Zechariah Yewdall, who had served in
Bradford, Glamorganshire, and Edinburgh. In the last
city, he supervised the erection of a chapel in 1788,
described by one observer as "a dirty, damp, dark,
dangerous hole, seating six hundred people; twenty-
seven years later, the commissioners of Edinburgh
purchased the structure for £1900 to make way for a
bridge from Shakespeare Square to Calton Hill (Tyerman,
Life of Wesley, 2:471). At any rate, Mr. Yewdall
supplies us with a rather pathetic picture of Wesley on
his last visit to Dumfries: "He came from Glasgow that
day [by way of Moffat], (about seventy miles [actually,
seventy-four]) but his strength was almost exhausted,
and, when he attempted to preach, very few could hear
him. His sight was likewise much decayed, so that he
could neither read the hymn or text. The wheels of
life were ready to stand still; but his conversation
was agreeably edifying, being mixed with the wisdom and
gravity of a parent, and the artless simplicity of a
child" (The Arminian Magazine, 18 [1795], 423). At
that moment John Wesley was in his eighty-seventh year
and had but nine months of life remaining.

Thornhill

Thornhill lies on the River Nith, in Dumfries-
shire, northwest of Dumfries and southwest of Moffat.
It was, essentially, a stop for Wesley on his route
from Dumfries to Glasgow and Edinburgh. Thus, we
observe him lodging there on Monday, evening, 16 April
1753, and commenting on the general state of Scottish
accommodations: "What miserable accounts pass current
in England of the inns in Scotland! Yet here, as well
as wherever we called in our whole journey, we had not
only everything we wanted, but everything readily and
in good order, and as clean as I ever desire" (Journal,
4:61). Wesley passed through Thornhill on Tuesday, 31
May 1757; on Tuesday, 22 May 1759; and, finally, on
Monday, 23 June 1766. Upon this last visit, he rested
in the town long enough to begin his reading of John
Knox's History of the Reformation of Religion within
the Realm of Scotland (see above, Chapter 2).

Drumlanrig

Twelve miles from Dumfries and two or three miles
from Thornhill lies Drumlanrig, outside of which stood
the palace of the Dukes of Queensberry: William
Douglas (1637-1695), James Douglas (1622-1711), William
Douglas (1724-1810). Defoe described the town as "like
a fine picture in a dirty grotto, or like an equestrian
statue set up in a barn; 'tis environed with mountains,
and that of the wildest and most hideous aspect in all
the south of Scotland. . ." (Defoe, Tour, p. 591).
Thus, he was surprised to see "a palace so glorious,
gardens so fine, and every thing so truly magnificent,
and all in a wild, mountainous country. . . ." Upon
closer inspection, the palace itself "stands on the top
of a rising ground, which, at its first building, lay

with steep and uncouth descent to the river [Nith], and which made the lookers-on wonder what the duke meant to build in such a disproportional place. But he best understood his own design; for the house once laid out, all that unequal descent is so beautifully levelled and laid out in slopes and terraces, that nothing can be better designed, or, indeed, better performed than the gardens are, which take up the whole south and west sides of the house; and, when the whole design will be done, the rest will be more easy, the ground being a plain the other way, and the park and avenues completely planted with trees" (Defoe, Tour, pp. 591-592).

John Wesley passed by Drumlanrig castle on Tuesday, 31 May 1757, taking full notice of "an ancient and noble pile of building, delightfully situated on the side of a pleasant and fruitful hill. But it gives no pleasure to its owner, for he does not even behold it with his eyes. Surely this is a sore evil under the sun: a man has all things and enjoys nothing" (Journal, 4:216). Apparently, some two years later, the scene had become altered radically. Riding by on Tuesday 22 May 1759, Wesley sadly observed, "How little did the late Duke [of Queensberry] imagine that his son would plough up his park and let his house run to ruin! But let it go! In a little time the earth itself, and all the work of it, shall be burned up" (Journal, 4:316). Finally, on Monday evening, 18 April 1768, the leader of the Methodists lodged at Drumlanrig, coming from Dumfries on his way to Glasgow.

Enterkin Mountains

Daniel Defoe termed the Enterkin Mountains "the frightfullest pass, and most dangerous that I met with,

between that [southern Scotland] and Penmenmuir in
North Wales. . ." (Defoe, Tour, p. 591). Coming from
Drumlanrig, he ascended "through a winding bottom for
near half a mile," seeing "vast high mountains on
either hand, though all green, and with sheep feeding
on them to the very top; when, on a sudden, turning
short to the left, and crossing a rill of water in the
bottom, you mount the side of one of those hills,
while, as you go on, the bottom in which that water
runs down from between the hills, keeping its level on
your right, begins to look very deep, till at length it
is a precipice horrible and terrifying; on the left the
hill rises almost perpindicular, like a wall; till
being come about half way, you have a steep, unpassable
height on the left, and of a monstrous calm or ditch on
your right; deep, almost as the monument is high, and
the path, or way, just broad enough for you to lead
your horse on it, and, if his foot slips, you have
nothing to do but let go the bridle. . ." (Defoe, Tour,
pp. 594-595).

    After pausing at Thornhill and Drumlanrig castle
on Tuesday, 31 May 1757, John Wesley rode "partly over
and partly between some of the finest mountains, I
believe, in Europe--higher than most, if not than any,
in England, and clothed with grass to the very top"
(Journal, 4:216). Thirteen years later, on Monday
morning, 16 April 1770, as he made his way from
Dumfries to Glasgow, he wrote of the morning being fair
"till we began to climb up Enterkin, one of the highest
mountains in the west of Scotland. We then got into a
Scotch mist, and were drooping wet. . ." (Journal,
5:362).

Leadhills

Leadhills, at the foot of the Enterkin Mountains in Lanarkshire, rises approximately 1300 feet above sea level, which makes it the highest village in all of Scotland. Here, in 1685, the Scottish poet Allan Ramsay (d. 1758) was born; his father managed the mines owned by Sir Charles Hope, Earl of Hopetoun, while his mother, Alice Bower, was the daughter of a Derbyshire mining expert.

When he first came to Leadhills on Tuesday, 17 April 1753, John Wesley observed "a village of miners, resembling Plessey, near Newcastle" (Journal, 4:62). This observation he repeated ("wholly inhabited by miners") when he came again on Tuesday, 31 May 1757; in all probability, he remained there overnight. When he came through Leadhills two years later, Wesley undoubtedly had been given more specific information, for he described the place as "a village containing five hundred families, who have had no minister for these four years. So, in Scotland, the poor have not the gospel preached! Who shall answer for the blood of these men?" (Journal, 4:316) Here, certainly, was a choice opportunity for Methodism, but Wesley never remained long enough even to preach a single word here. He had determined, early in his mission to Scotland, to concentrate upon the larger towns and the cities. Therefore, each time that he came to Leadhills (as well as other villages of similar size), he was usually in a hurry to press on to Glasgow. On Monday, 16 April 1770, he passed through the village for what appears to have been the final time.

Lesmahawgo

Although Wesley described Lesmahawgo as a village

smaller than neighboring Leadhills, he found some
consolation in knowing that the former place had two
ministers, while the latter could not accommodate even
one. Further, he took note of the "churchyard, by the
side of which a little clear river runs, near the foot
of a high mountain. The wood which covers this makes
the walks that run on its sides pleasant beyond
imagination. But what taste have the good people of
the town for this? As much as the animals that graze
on the river bank" (Journal, 4:316). Wesley dined at
Lesmahawgo on Tuesday, 17 April 1753; remained there
overnight on Tuesday, 22 May 1759; and again lodged in
the village on Monday, 16 April 1770.

Moffat

Situated northeast of Dumfries, Moffat proved a
convenient stopover for the traveler who, in the
eighteenth century, entered Scotland across the Solway
Firth and who wished to proceed either to Glasgow or
Edinburgh. Thus, Wesley spent the night of Monday, 27
April 1761, there; by 4:00 the next afternoon he was in
Edinburgh. On Friday, 12 May 1786, he left Carlisle at
9:00 A.M. and arrived at Moffat by seven that evening;
he was on the road by 4:00 A.M. the following morning,
reaching Glasgow by 6:15 P.M. Finally, in what can
only be termed an incredible display of energy for a
man of eighty-seven, Wesley left Glasgow at 2:00 A.M.
on Monday, 31 May 1790, came to Moffat shortly after
3:00 P.M., and arrived in Dumfries at 6:30 P.M. Of
course, by this time in his life, he was traveling by
chaise rather than upon horseback, which might have
allowed him some brief periods of rest while enroute.

Selkirk

Selkirk, the county seat of Selkirkshire and a royal burgh, lay south of Galashiels, ten miles from Melrose. The craft of shoemaking had always flourished there, and during the rebellions of 1715 and 1745, the inhabitants were forced to supply shoes to the Jacobite armies. Although, by the end of the eighteenth century, the industry was almost non-existent, the citizens continued to be termed "the souters of Selkirk."

John Wesley first arrived at Selkirk on Wednesday afternoon, 15 April 1772, coming through a hard storm of rain and snow. In the town he "observed a little piece of stateliness which was quite new to me: the maid came in and said, 'Sir, the lord of the stable wants to know if he should feed your horses.' We call him ostler in England" (Journal, 5:453). No doubt there was a momentary lapse in communication here; either Wesley thought he heard lord when the maid really said laad or lahd,, or the woman was simply being sarcastic. Two years later, on Tuesday, 10 May 1774, he returned to Selkirk, where he spent the night before moving on to Edinburgh. On his next visit, Tuesday, 7 May 1776, he performed a service for the family with which he lodged. Following evening prayers, the mistress of the house said to him, "'Sir, my daughter Jenny would be very fond of having a little talk with you. She is a strange lass; she will not come down on the Lord's day but to public worship, and spends all the rest of the day in her own chamber.' I desired she would come up; and found one that earnestly longed to be altogether a Christian. I satisfied her mother that she was not mad; and spent a little time in advice, exhortation, and prayer" (Journal, 6:105).

Finally, he lodged again at Selkirk on Friday night, 23
April 1784, arriving from Carlisle at 7:00 P.M., and
departing the next morning at 5:00 for Edinburgh.

Floors Castle, Roxburgh

Within walking distance (south, approximately
one-half mile) of Kelso lay the seat of John Ker, first
Duke of Roxburghe (1680-1741). The ancient Roxburgh
Castle, which played no small part in the early history
of Scotland, once stood in this area; by the end of the
eighteenth century, little remained but a pile of
stones. In 1718, Sir John Vanbrugh, the playwright and
architect, built Floors Castle for the Duke for
Roxburghe, and William Henry Playfair remodeled and
enlarged the structure in 1839. Daniel Defoe came upon
Floors at the outset of its construction, and observed
that "those who viewed it fifteen or sixteen years ago
[c. 1698, when he, himself, was there last], will
scarce know it again, if they should come a few years
hence, when the present Duke may have finished the
additions and embellishments, which he is now making,
and has been a considerable time upon. Nor will the
very face of the country appear the same, except it be
that the River Tweed may, perhaps, run in the same
channel. But the land before, lying open and wild, he
will find enclosed, cultivated and improved, rows, and
even woods of trees covering the champaign country, and
the houses surrounded with large green vistas, and well
planted avenues, such as were never seen there before"
(Defoe, Tour, pp. 619-620).

Wesley walked from Kelso to Floors Castle shortly
after 7:00 P.M., Thursday, 27 May 1784. From a
distance, he could see that it was "finely situated on
a rising ground, near the ruins of Roxburgh Castle. It

has a noble castle; the front and office round make it look like a little town. Most of the apartments within are furnished in an elegant but not in a costly manner. I doubt whether two of Mr. [Edwin] Lascelles's rooms at Harewood House [near Leeds, and designed by Robert Adam] did not cost more in furnishing than twenty of these. But the Duke's house is far larger, containing no less than forty bedchambers" (Journal, 6:511-512).

Kelso

In the early eighteenth century, Kelso, situated on the bank of the River Tweed, was a clean and neat market town. Its most popular attraction for the traveler, Kelso Abbey, dates from the reign of David I (1124-1153), who established the four Border monasteries--the others being at Melrose, Jedburgh, and Dryburgh. Founded for the monks of the Tironensian Order, the building, almost entirely of Norman and transitional work, is unique in Scotland because the plan has had western as well as eastern transepts, with a tower over both of the crossings.

Defoe saw Kelso as a "considerable thorough-fare to England, one of the great roads from Edinburgh to Newcastle lying through this town, and a nearer way by far than the road through Berwick. They only want a good bridge over the Tweed: at present they have a ferry just at the town, and a good ford through the river, a little below it; but, though I call it a good ford, and so it is when the water is low, yet that is too uncertain; and the Tweed is so dangerous a river and rises sometimes so suddenly, that a man scarce knows when he goes into the water, how it shall be ere he gets out at the other side; and it is not very strange to them at Kelso, to hear of frequent

disasters, in the passage, both to men and cattle"
(Defoe, Tour, p. 620).

Wesley came to Kelso from Berwick-upon-Tweed late
Friday afternoon, 10 June 1757. At 6:00 P.M. he and
William Coward (d. 1770; Wesley preached his funeral
sermon) went to the market-house, where they remained
for some time; however, "neither man, woman, nor child
came near us. At length, I began singing a Scotch
psalm, and fifteen or twenty people came within
hearing, but with great circumspection, keeping their
distance as though they knew not what might follow.
But while I prayed their number increased, so that in a
few minutes there was a pretty large congregation. I
suppose the chief men of the town were there, and I
spared neither rich nor poor. I almost wondered at
myself, it not being usual with me to use so keen and
cutting expressions, and I believe many felt that, for
all their form, they were but heathens still." The
next morning (Saturday, 11 June) he spoke to another
crowd at 5:00: "Many looked as if they would look us
through; but the shyness peculiar to this nation
prevented their saying anything to me, good or bad,
while I walked through them to our inn" (Journal,
4:219).

Wesley next visited Kelso on Friday, 14 June 1782,
where he lodged at the home of Dr. Robert Douglas,
minister of the parish church of Kelso. Mrs. Planche,
the minister's sister, writes that "Wesley spent a
night with us, and the morning at five he preached from
1 Cor. xiii" (The Arminian Magazine, 14 [1791], 420).
Wesley, himself, reports that "I spoke strong words in
the evening [14 June], concerning judgement to come;
and some seemed to awake out of sleep. But how shall
they keep awake, unless they 'that fear the Lord speak

often one to another?'" (Journal, 6:357). The next morning, as he came down the outside steps of the Douglas house, "the carpet slipped from under my feet, which, I know not how, turned me round, and pitched me back, with my head foremost, for six or seven stairs. It was impossible to recover myself till I came to the bottom. My head rebounded once or twice from the edge of the stone stairs. But it felt to me exactly as if I had fallen on a cushion or a pillow. Dr. Douglas ran out, sufficiently affrighted. But he needed not. For I arose as well as ever; having received no damage, but the loss of a little skin from one or two of my fingers. Doth not God give His angels charge of us, to keep us in all our ways?" (Journal, 6:357) One needs to be reminded, that when he took this spill, Wesley was seventy-nine years of age! At any rate, that afternoon, he departed from Kelso for Alnwick; Mrs. Planche followed, then proceeded to Newcastle, where she heard one of Wesley's ministers, Reverend William Hunter. She then wrote to Wesley, requesting Hunter's presence in Kelso; a month later, the leader of the Methodists dispatched Hunter to form a Methodist society in the town.

The final visit of John Wesley to Kelso occurred on Thursday, 27 May 1784; departing Berwick at 10:45 A.M., he arrived two hours later. He found that "the two seceding [Associate Presbytery of the Church of Scotland; see Chapter 1] ministers have taken true pains to frighten the people from hearing us, by retailing all the ribaldry of Mr. [William] Cudworth, [Augustus Montague] Toplady, and Rowland Hill [three of the most outspoken critics of Methodism]. But God has called one of them [Toplady] to his account already, and in a fearful manner. As no house could contain the

congregation, I preached in the churchyard, and a more
decent behaviour I have scarce ever seen" (Journal,
6:511). It must have been on this day that young
Walter Scott--a student at the University of Edinburgh,
but sent to Kelso, because of illness, to live with his
aunt, Jane Scott--heard John Wesley preach:

> When I was about twelve years old I heard
> Wesley preach more than once, standing on a
> chair in Kelso churchyard. He was a most
> venerable figure, but his sermons were vastly
> too colloquial . . . . He told many
> excellent stories. One I remember which he
> said had happened to him at Edinburgh. "A
> drunken dragoon," said Wesley, "was
> commencing an assertion in military fashion,
> 'G-d eternally d--n me,' just as I was
> passing. I touched the poor man on the
> shoulder, and when he turned round fiercely,
> said calmly, "You mean, 'God bless you.'" In
> the mode of telling the story he failed not
> to make us sensible how much his patriarchal
> appearance, and mild, yet bold, rebuke, over-
> awed the soldier, who touched his hat,
> thanked him, and, I think, came to chapel
> that evening.

                    (Lockhart, Memoirs, 6:45-46)

There can be no doubting the possibility of young Scott
having heard Wesley preach at Kelso. However, one must
assess carefully the ability of a twelve or thirteen
year-old boy to pass serious judgment upon the language
level of the sermons he heard. Also, the story of the
drunken dragoon may be more anecdotal than factual;
Wesley noted no such incident in the journal accounts
relative to his numerous visits to Edinburgh. Finally,

Walter Scott's most recent biographer, Professor Edgar Johnson (see the entry in Appendix D), makes no mention of his subject having been present upon any occasion when Wesley spoke at Kelso.

Chapter Five

CENTRAL

When chapman billies leave the street,
And drouthy neebors, neebors meet,
As market days are wearing late,
An' folk begin to tak the gate,
While we sit bousing at the nappy,
An' getting fou and unco happy,
We think na on the long Scots miles,
The mosses, waters, slaps, and styles,
That lie between us and our hame,
Whare sits our sulky, sullen dame,
Gathering her brows like gathering storm,
Nursing her wrath to keep it warm.
　　(Robert Burns, Tam o' Shanter, ll. 1-12)

Old Cambus

　　John Wesley and Christopher Hopper left
Berwick-upon-Tweed (Northumberland) at 4:00 A.M.,
Wednesday, 24 April 1751, crossed the River Tweed, and
by 7:00 A.M. had arrived in the small village of Old
Cambus, about a mile south of Cockburnspath. Wesley
remarked, in his journal, that "Scotch towns are none
which I ever saw, either in England, Wales, or Ireland.
There is such an air of antiquity in them all, and such
a peculiar oddness in their manner of building"
(Journal, 3:522). He came here again fifteen years
later, on Friday, 23 May 1766, where he "found notice
had been given of my preaching about a mile off"
(Journal, 5:167). So, he immediately rode off for
Cockburnspath.

Cockburnspath

Cockburnspath lies on the east coast of Scotland,
roughly north of Coldingham and south of Dunbar. Defoe
tells us of descending the Lammermuir Hills and coming
directly upon "a village called Cockburnspeth, vulgarly
Cobberspeth, where nature forms a very steep and
difficult pass, and where, indeed, a thousand men well
furnished, and boldly doing their duty, would keep out
an army, if there was occasion" (Defoe, Tour, p. 565).

Wesley preached in this village on Friday
afternoon, 23 May 1766, where the congregation had
gathered prior to his arrival (see above, under Old
Cambus). "I spoke as plain as I possibly could, but
very few appeared to be at all affected. It seems to
be with them as with most in the north--they know
everything and feel nothing" (Journal, 5:167).

Dunbar

One of the chief port towns for the east coast
Scottish herring trade, Dunbar underwent considerable
expansion toward the end of the eighteenth century
when, in 1792, the construction of a cotton works
factory was begun there. At the beginning of the
century, Daniel Defoe saw it as "a handsome well-built
town, upon the sea-shore where they have a kind of a
natural harbour, though in the middle of dangerous
rocks. They have here a great herring-fishery, and
particularly they hang herrings here, as they do at
Yarmouth in Norfolk, for the smoking them; or, to speak
the ordinary dialect, they make red herrings here. I
cannot say they are cured so well as at Yarmouth, that
is to say, not for keeping and sending on long voyages,
as to Venice and Leghorn, though with a quick passage,
they might hold it thither too. However, they do it

very well" (Defoe, Tour, p. 566). Obviously, the curing process became improved, for during the winter of 1786-1787, several sloops of unpacked herring were loaded at Avoch, in Ross-shire, and shipped off to Dunbar (Hamilton, Economic History, p. 122).

Dunbar was one Scottish town where Methodism had gained some slight foothold prior to the arrival of John Wesley. In 1752, a company of British dragoons-- or, at least the more pious among them--held a prayer- meeting in the town, and one of the inhabitants, Andrew Affleck, became converted. He then joined the first Methodist society established there, remaining until his death in 1811 (The Methodist Magazine, 36 [1813], 73-74). Thus, when Wesley made his entrance on Wednesday, 8 June 1757, he "found a little society, most of them rejoicing in God their Saviour. At eleven [A.M.] I went out into the main street, and began speaking to a congregation of two men and two women. These were soon joined by above twenty little children, and not long after by a large number of young and old. On a sudden the sun broke out and shone full in my face, but in a few moments I felt it not" (Journal, 4:218). Two years later, he came to Dunbar on Wednesday afternoon, 30 May 1759. That evening, as well as the one following, he preached at 6:00 "in a large, open place. . . .Both poor and rich quietly attended, though most of them shivering with cold; for the weather was so changed within a few days that it seemed more like December than May." For the two nights that Wesley remained in Dunbar, he lodged "with a sensible man" (Andrew Affleck?) of whom he "inquired particularly into the present discipline of Scotch parishes. In one parish it seems there are twelve ruling elders; in another there are fourteen. And what

are these? Men of great sense and deep experience?
Neither one nor the other. But they are the <u>richest</u>
men in the parish. And are the <u>richest</u>, of course, the
<u>best</u> and <u>wisest</u> men? Does the Bible teach this? I
fear not. What manner of governors, then, will these
be? Why, they are generally just as capable of
governing a parish as of commanding an army" (<u>Journal</u>,
4:317).

Wesley's next visit to Dunbar occurred on Tuesday,
12 May 1761; at 7:00 P.M., because of a steady rain, he
preached at the Methodist meeting-house. As usual, the
weather underwent an ubrupt change, and on the 13th, "a
fair, mild evening, I preached near the quay to most of
the inhabitants of the town, and spoke full as plain as
the evening before. Everyone seemed to receive it in
love; probably, if there was regular preaching here
much good might be done" (<u>Journal</u>, 4:455). It must be
noted that Wesley's estimates of the congregations at
open-air meetings always tended to be inflated, and not
too much faith can be placed in the phrase, "most of
the inhabitants of the town." When he came once more
on Monday, 30 June 1763, he again faced the problem of
the weather, the evening being "very cold, and the wind
was exceeding high; nevertheless I would not pen myself
up in the room, but resolved to preach in the open air.
We saw the fruit; many attended; notwithstanding the
cold, who never set foot in the room; and I am still
persuaded much good will be done here, if we have zeal
and patience" (<u>Journal</u>, 5:15). Thus, he returned to
Dunbar on Thursday, 24 May 1764; Tuesday, 23 April
1765; and Friday, 23 May 1766. On the last-mentioned
date, he "designed to preach abroad. . .in the evening,
but the rain drove us into the house. It was for good.
I now had a full stroke at their hearts, and I think

some <u>felt</u> themselves sinners" (<u>Journal</u>, 5:167-168). In
the next year, Wesley came to Dunbar later in the
season than usual, riding over from Edinburgh on his
way to Newcastle and reaching the coastal town on
Tuesday, 4 August 1767. here he "endeavoured, if
possible, to rouse some of the sleepers, by strongly,
yea, roughly, enforcing those words, 'Lord, are there
few that be saved?' And this I must say for the Scots
in general, I know no men like them for hearing plain
dealing" (<u>Journal</u>, 5:225).

For the sixth year in succession, Wesley visited
Dunbar, where he preached--on Monday evening, 16 May
1768--"near the shore, to an unusually large
congregation" (<u>Journal</u>, 5:264). Remaining there
overnight and part of the next day, he took some time
to read Thomas Shaw's <u>Travels and Observations relating</u>
<u>to Several Parts of Barbary and the Levant, with</u>
<u>Supplement</u> (2nd. ed., London, 1757), a work which he
found dull and unentertaining. In 1769, Wesley's
northern travels took him to Wales and Ireland, which
meant that he did not get back to Dunbar until 1770,
arriving late on Thursday afternoon, 17 May. During
his absence, a new chapel had been built in the town,
"the cheerfullest in the kingdom." He preached there
that evening, and again on the one following, hoping
that "God broke some of the stony hearts of Dunbar. A
little increase here is in the society likewise; and
all the members walk unblameably" (<u>Journal</u>, 5:368). He
preached in the town on Wednesday, 20 May 1772;
Wednesday, 8 June 1774; Thursday, 30 May 1776; and
Wednesday, 26 May 1779. On the last-mentioned date, he
made note in his journal (see 6:235) of "such a
congregation at Dunbar as I have not seen there for
many years." Returning from Edinburgh some three weeks

later (Sunday, 20 June), he planned to preach in the
open air; however, a rainstorm canceled the service,
and Wesley simply stayed the night. When he returned
the following year (Wednesday, 17 May 1780), he was
momentarily taken aback by the manner of the
congregation. "Indeed, some of them seemed at first
disposed to mirth, but they were soon as serious as
death. And truly the power of the Lord was present to
heal those that were willing to come to the throne of
grace" (Journal, 6:278). Six days later (Tuesday, the
23rd), he was back again and found time, the following
afternoon, for some touring. ". . .I went through the
lovely garden of a gentleman in the town, who had laid
out walks hanging over the sea and winding among the
rocks. One of them leads to the castle wherein that
poor injured woman Mary, Queen of Scots, was confined.
But time has wellnigh devoured it; only a few ruinous
walls are now standing" (Journal, 6:280).
Unfortunately, Wesley somewhat confused the facts.
Dunbar fortress, dating from the ninth century, served
the Queen as a retreat and a rallying place, rather
than as a prison. In fact, on 15 June 1567, she and
Borthwick marched from the fortress at the head of 2000
men, bound for Carberry.

On Monday, 27 May 1782, Wesley came north from
Alnwick to Dunbar, arriving in the town on Wednesday,
the 29th. "The weather was exceeding rough and stormy,
yet we had a large and serious congregation" (Journal,
6:353). In fact, the rain proved so severe that the
next day he found the road to Edinburgh flooded and
required a guide to take him on to the capital. He
preached in the town two years later, on Monday, 24 May
1784. During his next visit, Tuesday, 30 May 1786, "I
had the happiness of conversing with the Earl of

Haddington and his Lady, at Dunbar. I could not but observe both the easiness of his behaviour (such as we find in all the Scotch nobility), and the fineness of his appearance, greatly set off by a milk-white head of hair" (Journal, 7:166). The reference here is to Thomas Hamilton, seventh Earl of Haddington, who had succeeded to the title only the previous year. The following morning Wesley set out for Berwick and had the opportunity to view "the stupendous bridge, about ten miles form Dunbar, which is thrown over the deep glen that runs between the two mountains, commonly called the Pease. I doubt whether Louis the Fourteenth ever raised such a bridge as this" (Journal, 7:166). The Pease Bridge, standing three hundred feet in length and one hundred twenty-seven feet in height, formed part of the old road from Edinburgh to Berwick-upon-Tweed. Wesley saw it again on Friday, 23 May 1788, after departing from Dunbar for the last time. He termed it "one of the noblest works in Great Britain, unless you would except the bridge at Edinburgh, which lies directly across the Cowgate" (Journal, 7:391). During this final visit to Dunbar--extending from 1:00 P.M., Thursday, the 22nd, to about 6:00 the next morning--he preached first in the Methodist meeting-house, "tolerably well filled, on Job xxii. 21, I believe with--'The spirit of convincing speech' [line 1, verse 8, from the hymn "When Christ had left His flock below," in Hymns and Sacred Poems. Published by John Wesley and Charles Wesley (London: William Strahan, 1739)]: But much more at five in the morning, Friday the 23rd. And will God manifest His power among these dry bones also?" (Journal, 7:391)

Dun (Doon) Hill, Dunbar

Some two miles southeast of Dunbar stands Dun Hill where was fought, on 2-3 September 1650, the Battle of Dunbar--one of the last engagements of the Civil War. In late August, the loyalist Scottish army, commanded by David Leslie (d. 1682), had completely outmaneuvered Cromwell's troops; the English tried to fall back from Edinburgh toward Berwick. However Leslie blocked the only passage between the hills and the sea by which Cromwell could move southward. Believing that the English army was already embarking guns and troops for passage out of Scotland, Leslie was in no mood for an engagement. In fact, he would have avoided one altogether had not the ministers of the Kirk threatened him with censures if he allowed Cromwell to escape. Thus, on the evening of 2 September, the Scot commander moved his forces from their impregnable position on Dun Hill. Cromwell, whose army numbered but half of Leslie's, turned from the sea, attacked through a gap in the Scottish lines, and completely carried the field.

The statistics surrounding the Battle of Dunbar differ slightly, depending upon the source one consults. One historian states that in July, Cromwell stood at Berwick with 16,000 men; at Dun Hill, his force was half the size of Leslie's (32,000?). After the engagement, the English losses amounted to a scant twenty, while 3000 Scots lay dead and another 10,000 were captured (Fletcher, History of England, pp. 448-449). Another agrees on the number of Scots slain by the English, but reduces the captured to 9,000 (Churchill, History of the English People, 2:297). Finally, Daniel Defoe, ever willing to be specific, calculates Cromwell's army at 8,000 and the Scottish casualties at 6000 killed and 10,000 captured (Defoe, Tour, pp. 566-567).

John Wesley, when he toured the area around Dun Hill on Friday, 22 May 1772, was too caught up with the scene and its broad historical significance to bother much with particulars. "We took a view of the famous Roman camp, lying on a mountain [Dun Hill] two or three miles from the town [Dunbar]. It is encompassed with two broad and deep ditches, and is not easy of approach on any side. Here lay General Leslie with his army, while Cromwell was starving below. He had no way to escape; but the enthusiastic fury of the Scots delivered him. When they marched into the valley to swallow him up, he mowed them down like grass" (Journal, 5:462).

North Berwick

North Berwick is situated on the east coast, some twelve and one-half miles from Dunbar. Preaching there at 1:00 P.M. on Tuesday, 12 May 1761, Wesley described it as "a pretty large town close to the sea-shore. . ." (Journal, 4:455). He may well have been there on a market day or when the fishing boats had just returned, for the label of large could only have been applied in relative terms to the area and population of eighteenth-century North Berwick. For, two hundred years later, the town numbered but 4161 inhabitants.

Tantallon Castle, North Berwick

Tantallon Castle, on the rocky coast of the Firth of Forth, opposite the Bass Rock (see below) and three miles east of North Berwick, once stood as the stronghold of the Earls of Douglas. And, of course, considerable of its fame rests with its role within the

cantos of Walter Scott's poem <u>Marmion, a Tale of
Flodden Field</u> (1808). The great frontal curtain wall
of the Castle, flanked by round towers and having an
imposing central gatehouse, dates from the fourteenth
century, and may be considered one of the grandest of
its kind in all Scotland. Outside the structure are
extensive earthworks, some of which represent the
defences thrown up against the cannons of James V, in
1526; other earthworks, still farther out, date from
the Civil War when, in 1651, the guns of General George
Monk dealt considerable damage to the structure. The
legendary impregnability of the Castle is certainly
suggested by the lines from the old rhyme--"Ding down
Tantallon--/Mak' a brig to the Bass!"

On Thursday, 21 May 1772, Wesley "walked over the
ruins of Tantallon Castle, once the seat of the great
Earls of Douglas. The front walls (it was four-square)
are still standing, and by their vast height and huge
thickness give us a little idea of what it once was.
Such is human greatness!" (<u>Journal</u>, 5:462).

The Bass (Bass Rock)

The Bass is one of the rocky islands in the Firth
of Forth, lying just northeast of North Berwick.
During the first uprising in the Glenkens at the
Conventicle of 1666, a band of insurgents occupied
Dumfries; their number grew to 2000 before they reached
Lanark, but the force was routed at Rullion Green by
General Thomas Dalyell. As a result, thirty-five
persons were marched off to be executed, while an even
larger number found themselves imprisoned on the Bass
Rock. The place has always been noted as the home of
hundreds of screeching gannets--those large seabirds
which the Scots term <u>Solands</u>.

John Wesley toured the Bass on Thursday, 21 May
1772, and in his journal recorded a rather detailed
description of the island:

> I went to the Bass, seven miles from it
> [Dunbar], which, in the horrid reign of
> Charles the Second, was the prison of those
> venerable men who suffered the loss of all
> things for a good conscience. It is a high
> rock surrounded by the sea, two or three
> miles in circumference, and about two miles
> from the shore. The strong east wind made
> the water so rough that the boat could hardly
> live: and when we came to the only landing-
> place (the other side being quite
> perpendicular), it was with much difficulty
> that we got up, climbing on our hands and
> knees. The castle, as one may judge by what
> remains, was utterly inaccessible. The walls
> of the chapel, and of the governor's house,
> are tolerably entire. The garden walls are
> still seen near the top of the rock, with the
> well in the midst of it. And round the walls
> there are spots of grass that feed eighteen
> or twenty sheep. But the proper natives of
> the island are Solund [Soland] geese, a bird
> about the size of a Muscovy duck, which breed
> by thousands, from generation to generation,
> on the sides of the rock. It is peculiar to
> these that they lay but one egg, which they
> do not sit upon at all, but keep it under one
> foot (as we saw with our eyes) till it is
> hatched. How many prayers did the holy men
> confined here offer up in that evil day! And
> how many thanksgivings should we return for

all the liberty, civil and religious, which
we enjoy!
(Journal, 5:461-462)
Obviously, Wesley felt strongly against the treatment
meted out to the rebels of 1666 by Dalyell's troops.
In 1663, the Edinburgh Parliament, in reality an arm of
Charles' government, passed an act forbidding
Covenanter ministers to hold Conventicles--assemblies
for public worship in some place other than a parish
church. Thus, those who gathered at the Glenkens
consisted of perhaps several hundred armed peasants,
with their wives, from as many as thirty or forty
parishes. And, of course, all violently opposed
Charles II and his Council, as well as those Scots who
did not rise in rebellion against them.

St. Andrews

The ancient Royal Burgh of St. Andrews, on the
North Sea coast, received its charter form King David
in 1140. Because the town contains so much of
historical and architectural value, one can sympathize
with James Boswell's complaint that "there should be a
short printed directory for strangers, such as we find
in all the towns of Italy, and in some of the towns in
England" (Tour to the Hebrides, p. 198). Foremost
among the landmarks of the town stands the University
of St. Andrews, founded in 1412 and at one time
consisting of three colleges: St. Salvatore's (1450),
St. Leonard's (1512), and St. Mary's (1537, remodeled
during 1765-1767). In 1747, St. Salvatore's and St.
Leonard's incorporated into one institution, the
property of the latter--exclusive of the church--being
sold in 1772 to Robert Watson (1730-1781), Professor of
Logic, Rhetoric, and Belles-Lettres, and (1777)

Principal of the United College of St. Leonard and St.
Salvatore. The area also claimed St. Andrew's Castle,
the archiepiscopal castle of the primate of Scotland.
There, on 29 May 1546, Archbishop David Beaton fell at
the hands of assassins, and the initial round of the
Reformation struggle occurred in the great siege that
followed. The oldest parts of the extensive ruin date
from the thirteenth century, but considerable of the
work pre-dates the destruction of 1547. The grim
"Bottle-dungeon" and the mine and counter-mine tunneled
in the living rock during the siege comprise the most
notable features. St. Andrew's Castle itself stood on
a promontory thrust out into the North Sea, isolated by
a deep and wide ditch.

Naturally, St. Andrews contained a number of
churches, the most inspiring being its twelfth-century
Cathedral. Once the largest church in Scotland, with a
length of 391 feet, little remains except parts of the
east and west gables, the south wall of the nave, and
portions of the choir and south transept. The
Cathedral served also as the church of a Priory of
Augustinian Canons Regular. Fortunately, the structure
did not suffer significantly during the reformation;
however, it was allowed to fall into bad condition and
functioned principally during the seventeenth and
eighteenth centuries as a quarry. Nearby stood the
Church of St. Rule's, or St. Regulus' Church, built by
Bishop Robert (1126-1159) for the Augustinian Canons.
The remains consist of a choir and a western tower,
which rises to a height of 108 feet. On the edge of
the cliff behind St. Andrew's Cathedral one can still
see the scanty foundations of a small cruciform church,
once known as St. Mary's. Supposedly the church of the
Culdee fraternity, the structure was pulled down by the

Reformers in 1559. Finally, St. Andrews housed Blackfriars' Chapel, situated on South Street; an apsidal, groin-vaulted aisle, built in 1525, is all that remains of the structure.

Daniel Defoe, coming upon St. Andrews in the first decade of the eighteenth century, spent considerable time touring the antiquities of the town and noting, with the satisfaction of a true Dissenter, the decay of the Castle and the churches. "The city is not large," he observed, "nor is it contemptibly small; there are some very good buildings in it, and the remains of many more. The college are handsome buildings, and well supplied with men of learning in all sciences [i.e. academic disciplines], and who govern the youth they instruct with reputation; the students wear gowns here of a scarlet-like colour, but not in grain [not _dyed_], and are very numerous" (Defoe, _Tour_, pp. 640-641). Despite the destruction of the Castle, the Cathedral, and several smaller churches and buildings, Defoe was undoubtedly impressed by what he saw: ". . .it is still a handsome city, and well-built, the streets straight and large, being three streets parallel to one another, all opening to the sea" (Defoe, _Tour_, p. 643).

To the eye and mind of Samuel Johnson, walking about St. Andrews in mid August 1773, the sights were not at all pleasant. Of course, the town had changed since the days of Defoe, and Johnson interpreted past events from the viewpoint of a loyal Tory and a staunch Anglican. Thus, when the place "had lost its Archiepiscopal preeminence, [it] gradually decayed: One of its streets is now lost; and in those that remain, there is the silence and solitude of inactive indigence and gloomy depopulation." In spite of the decline of the University, at least in terms of numbers

of students, he found the institution a "place
eminently adapted to study and education, being
situated in a populous, yet a cheap country, and
exposing the minds and manners of young men neither to
the levity and dissoluteness of a capital city, nor to
the gross luxury of a town of commerce, places
naturally unpropitious to learning; in one the desire
of knowledge easily gives way to the love of pleasure,
and in the other, is in danger of yielding to the love
of money" (Johnson, Journey to the Western Islands, pp.
6-8). When Johnson and Boswell made ready to depart
St. Andrews, the former reflected carefully upon the
town and the meaning of its past greatness and present
decline:

> But whoever surveys the world must see many
> things that give him pain. The kindness of
> the professors did not contribute to abate
> the uneasay remembrance of an university
> declining, a college alienated, and a church
> profaned and hastening to the ground.
>
> St. Andrews indeed has formerly suffered
> more atrocious ravages and more extensive
> destruction, but recent evils affect with
> greater force. We were reconciled to the
> sight of archiepiscopal ruins. The distance
> of a calamity from the present time seems to
> preclude the mind from contact or sympathy.
> Events long passed are barely known; they are
> not considered. We read with as little
> emotion the violence of Knox and his
> followers, as the irruptions of Alaric and
> the Goths. Had the university been destroyed
> two centuries ago, we should not have
> regretted it; but to see it pining in decay

and struggling for life, fills the mind with
mournful images and ineffectual wishes.
        (Johnson, Journey to the Western Islands,
        p. 8)

One cause for certain of the deterioration in and
around St. Andrews resulted, simply, from Nature. The
North Sea, rushing in upon the coast from a
northeasterly direction, gradually destroyed not only
the harbor, but the potential of the town as a center
for trade. Thus, what in the thirteenth and fourteenth
centuries were once streets became, by the second
decade of the eighteenth century, meadows and gardens.

John Wesley visited St. Andrews on Monday, 27 May
1776. He described "Three broad, straight, handsome
streets. . .all pointing at the old cathedral, which,
by the ruins, appears to have been above three hundred
feet long, and proportionably broad and high; so that
it seems to have exceeded York Minster, and to have a
least equalled any cathedral in England. Another
church, afterwards used in its stead, bears the date
1124. A steeple standing near the cathedral is thought
to have stood thirteen hundred years" (Journal, 6:110).
The University of St. Andrews did not at all impress
Wesley, and he appeared totally negative to the conduct
within the colleges, as well as to the buildings:

        What is left of St. Leonard's College is
        only a heap of ruins. Two colleges remain.
        One of them [St. Salvatore's] has a tolerable
        square, but all the windows are broke, like
        those of a brothel. We were informed the
        students do this before they leave the
        college. Where are their blessed Governors
        in the meantime? Are they all fast asleep?
        The other college [St. Mary's] is a mean

building, but has a handsome library newly
erected. In the two colleges, we learned,
were about seventy students; near the same
number as at Old Aberdeen. Those at New
Aberdeen are not more numerous; neither those
at Glasgow. In Edinburgh I suppose there are
a hundred. So four universities contain
three hundred and ten students! These all
come to their several colleges in November,
and return home in May! So they may study
five months in the year, and lounge all the
rest! Oh where was the common sense of those
who instituted such colleges? In the English
colleges everyone may reside all year, as all
my pupils [at Lincoln College, Oxford] did;
and I should have thought myself little
better than a highwayman if I had not
lectured them every day in the year but
Sundays.

(<u>Journal</u>, 6:110)

Arbroath (Aberbrothock)

Formerly known as <u>Aberbrothock</u>, "the mouth of the
Brothock," Arbroath proved to be one of those fishing
villages that made almost no contribution to the growth
of the Scottish fishing industry during the mid and
late eighteenth century. Instead, the town developed a
small grain industry to help supply the demands of
Glasgow. Its main attraction consists of the remains
of Arbroath Abbey, a Tironensian monastery founded in
1176 by William the Lyon (1143-1214), King of Scotland
(1165-1214), and dedicated to St. Thomas of Canterbury.
William was eventually buried here. In 1320, a great
assembly of Scotland issued the famous Declaration of

Arbroath, in which the delegates asserted Scottish independence against the encroachments of Plantagenet England. Considerable portions of the cruciform abbey church still remain, including an aisle-less presbytery, transeptal chapels, and two western towers. The best preserved portion is the south transept, with its rose window.

For the eighteenth-century traveler, the inn of the town was the White Hart, located on the corner of the High Street and Kirk Wynd; in 1821, the inn was removed and White Hart Hotel built on the same site. Sir Walter Scott lodged more than once at the White Hart; in fact, he represented the town of Arbroath in The Antiquary, (1816) as "Fairport." Also, in Robert Southey's ballad, Inchcape Rock, the poet focuses upon a warning bell fixed on a float by the abbot of Arbroath. Sir Ralph the Rover, to plague the abbot, cuts the bell from the float; later, however, on his way home, his boat smashes upon the Inchcape Rock.

According to Mr. Ernest F. Cobb, the town chamberlain in 1913, there exists evidence of at least thirty-two different spellings of Arbroath and Aberbrothock. The seal of the burgh bears the legend Sigillum Aberbrothici; however, as late as the first decade of the twentieth century, Aberbrothwick was deemed the appropriate designation in regard to official matters pertaining to the harbor (see Wesley, Journal, 5:458, note 3).

James Boswell and Samuel Johnson came to Arbroath on Friday, 20 August 1773, and spent most of their time touring the ruins of the Abbey. "The arch of one of the gates is entire," wrote Johnson, "and of another only so far dilapidated as to diversify the appearance. A square apartment of great loftiness is still standing [the regality tower?]; its use I could not conjecture, as its elevation was very disproportionate to its area. Two corner towers, particularly attracted our attention" (Journey to the Western Islands, p. 10). At this point, Boswell climbed through a high window of one of the towers; however, he found the stairs broken and thus could not achieve his goal of reaching the top. At the departure, Johnson claimed that "I should scarcely have regretted my journey, had it afforded nothing more than the sight of Aberbrothick [still another variant spelling]" (Journey to the Western Islands, p. 10).

When John Wesley first came to Arbroath on Monday evening, 7 May 1770, a Methodist society had been in existence for about nine months. Thus, he observed that the entire town "seems moved. The congregation [on 7 May] was the largest I have seen since we left Inverness [on 29 April]; and the society. . .is the largest in the kingdom, next that of Aberdeen" (Journal, 5:365). Although Wesley did not reveal the number of members belonging to the Arbroath society, we may calculate that it was somewhere between 174, the total of the Aberdeen society, and 150, the number of the society at Edinburgh. The next day, he toured the remains of Arbroath Abbey, exclaiming, "I know nothing like it in all North Britain. I paced it, and found it a hundred yards long. The breadth is proportionable." Remember, however, that Wesley, at little more than five feet two or three inches in height, may have paced off less than an actual distance of one hundred yards. At any rate, to continue with his description: "Part of the west end, which is still standing, shows it was full as high as Westminster Abbey. The south end of the cross aisle likewise is standing, near the

top of which is a large circular window. The zealous
Reformers, they told us, burnt this down. God deliver
us from reforming mobs" (Journal, 5:366). The circular
windows to which Wesley referred came to be known as
the "O of Arbroath," and functioned, when illuminated
at night, as a mark for ships. As to the town proper,
he reported having seen none other in Scotland "which
increases so fast, or which is built with so much
common sense, as this. Two entire new streets, and
part of a third, have been built within these two
years. They run parallel with each other, and have a
row of gardens between them. So that every house has a
garden; and thus both health and convenience are
consulted" (Journal, 5:365).

Between the visit recounted above and the next one
in May 1772, the society at Arbroath acquired a new
meeting-house. Wesley preached there on Tuesday,
evening, the 6th, noting that in the town "there is a
change indeed! It was wicked to a proverb; remarkable
for Sabbath-breaking, cursing, swearing, drunkenness,
and a general contempt of religion. But it is not so
now. Open wickedness disappear; no oaths are heard, no
drunkenness seen in the streets. And many have not
only ceased from evil, and learned to do well, but are
witnesses of the inward kingdom of God, 'righteousness,
peace, and joy in the Holy Ghost.'" (Journal, 5:458).
The next day, the town magistrates made him an honorary
citizen of the burgh, as had been done at Perth one
week earlier (see Chapter 3, under Perth). "I value it
as a token of their respect, though I shall hardly make
any further use of it" (Journal, 5:458-459). Two years
later, Wesley returned, intending to hold an open-air
service on Tuesday, 24 May 1774. "The high and
piercing wind made it impracticable to preach abroad in

the evening; but the house contained the people tolerably well. . ." (Journal, 6:21). He left the following morning for Aberdeen, and then came back to Arbroath on Monday evening, the 30th. "I know no people in England who are more loving and more simple of heart than these" (Journal, 6:22). On Thursday, 16 May 1776, enroute to Aberdeen, he attended an ordination at the kirk in Arbroath. "The service lasted about four hours; but it did not strike me. It was doubtless very grave; but I thought it was very dull" (Journal, 6:106). Eight days later he came back that way, lodging at the home of a Mr. Grey, the chief magistrate (provost) of the town. "So," he mused, "for a time we are in honour! I have hardly seen such another place in the three kingdoms as this is at present. Hitherto there is no opposer at all, but every one seems to bid us God-speed!" (Journal, 6:109)

However, three years later appeared what could be termed as opposition to the cause of Methodism in Arbroath. Wesley preached in the town on Wednesday, 2 June 1779, to nearly "as large a congregation as at Dundee [on 1 June], but nothing so serious. The poor Glassites here, pleading for a merely notional faith, greatly hinder either the beginning or the progress of any real work of God" (Journal, 6:236). John Glass (or Glas)--1695-1773, and from 1719 until his death minister of Tealing, near Dundee--published, in 1729, a tract entitled The Testimony of the King of Martyrs, in which he attempted to prove that the civil establishment of religion is inconsistent with the Gospel, for the kingdom of Christ is not of this world. As a result, the Church of Scotland expelled him, and those who rallied to his cause were termed Glassites. Glass's son-in-law Robert Sandeman (1718-1771), carried

on the founder's work in London and in America, where
the group became known as Sandemanians. Wesley became
involved with Glass and Sandeman in 1757, as a result
of a publication, Theron and Aspasio; or, A Series of
Dialogues and Letters on the Most Important Subjects, 3
vols. (London, 1753-1755), by James Hervey (1713-1758).
This work essentially advocates, very strenuously, the
doctrine of the imputed righteousness of Christ, while
denying the notion of Glass and Sandeman that faith is
a mere asset to the truthfulness of the Gospel history.
The Glassites responded through Sandeman, who replied
in a two-volume work, Letters to the Author of Theron
and Aspasio (Edinburgh, 1757). Then, Wesley threw his
pen into the skirmish with a twelve-page essay entitled
A Sufficient Answer to "Letters to the Author of Theron
and Aspasio" (Bristol: E. Farley, 1757), wherein he
defended his friend from Lincoln College on the subject
of saving faith (for more on Wesley's relations with
Hervey and problems arising from Theron and Aspasio,
see Chapter 3, under Edinburgh). Yet, the effect of
the Glassites in Arbroath was at best an inconvenience,
for returning to the town twelve days later, on Monday,
14 June, Wesley noted only that he preached there
before leaving the next morning for Dundee and then
Edinburgh.

Two more visits were carried out in late spring
1782. On Tuesday, 4 June, the "house at Arbroath was
well filled with serious and attentive hearers. Only
one or two pretty flutterers seemed inclined to laugh,
if any would have encouraged them" (Journal, 6:354).
The next morning, Wesley was on his way to Aberdeen,
but returned to Arbroath on Monday, the 10th. During
the next scheduled visit, Monday, 3 May 1784, he
noticed the preaching-house to be completely filled,

and thus "spoke exceeding plain on the difference of building upon the sand an building upon the rock [Matthew 7:24]. Truly, these 'approve the things that are excellent,' whether they practice them or no" (Journal, 6:501). Prior to delivering this sermon (at 6:00 P.M.), Wesley was the afternoon dinner guest of David Patterson, a merchant of Arbroath, whose father, Alexander Patterson, died on 12 June 1761. According to one John Rhind, the merchant's nephew, Wesley wrote the following lines at the dinner-table, and they were later inscribed upon the elder Patterson's tombstone:

Reader, awake, in time repent;
Thine house or mine are only lent;
The day is hastening when, like me,
Thou too shalt dust and ashes be;
Forsake thy sins, in Christ believe,
And thou shalt with Him ever live.
(Journal, 6:501, note 2)

On Monday, 17 May 1784, Wesley preached at 6:00 P.M. on 1 Corinthians 1:24, and inquired into an aspect of local history, "an odd event which occurred there in the latter end of the last war. The famous Captain Fall came one afternoon to the side of the town, and sent three men on shore, threatening to lay the town in ashes unless they sent him thirty thousand pounds. That not being done, he began firing on the town the next day, and continued it till night. But perceiving the country was alarmed, he sailed away the next day, having left some hundred cannon-balls behind him; but not having hurt man, woman, or child, or anything else, save one old barn-door" (Journal, 6:508). Wesley spent the afternoon and evening with a Mr. Watson, and presumably heard this story from him. One interesting item that may be related to the visit of Methodism's

founder to Arbroath in 1784 occurs within the pages of
the Arminian Magazine for that year. Wesley informed
his readers that he wished to be buried in the ground
adjoining City Road Chapel, London, and expressed
further the determination that his epitaph--as well as
all epitaphs--ought to be prepared with attention to
grammatical and topographical accuracy. To prove his
point, he cited an example from a tombstone in Arbroath
churchyard:

> Here   lyis   Alexand   Peter,   present   Town
> Treasurer of Arbroath, who died _____ day
> January 1630.
>
> > Such a Treasurer was not since, nor yet
> > before,
> > For common works, calsais, brigs, and
> > schoir--
> > Of all other he did excel;
> > He deviced our skoel, and he hung our
> > bell.
>
> (Tyerman, Life of Wesley, 3:457)

In 1786, Wesley arrived in Arbroath at 5:00 P.M.,
Saturday, 20 May. Here he preached one sermon at 7:00
in the evening (on Hebrews 12:14) and three more on the
following day--the texts being 2 Kings 5:12, Matthew
5:24, and Luke 16:31. Returning on Thursday, the 25th,
he preached at 7:00 P.M., at which time "a large
congregation was deeply attentive while I applied 'To
him that hath shall be given; but from him that hath
not shall be taken away even what he assuredly hath
[Luke 8:18]" (Journal, 7:164). The final diaries
indicate that Wesley's last visit to the town came
about on Wednesday noon, 19 May 1790; he preached at
6:00 P.M. on 2 Corinthians 8:9 and spent an hour with
the members of the society. He arose at 3:00 the next

morning, and by 3:30 was in his chaise, bound for the ferry to Montrose. Undoubtedly, Arbroath was one of the few towns in Scotland where Wesley could envision some positive results from his work. In fact, on Monday, 3 May 1784, he noted in his journal, "I found this to be a genuine Methodist society. They are all thoroughly united to each other; they love and keep our Rules; they long and expect to be perfected in love; if they continue so to do, they will and must increase in number as well as in grace" (Journal, 6:501-502).

Dalkeith

"The town of Dalkeith," wrote Daniel Defoe, "is just without the park [of Dalkeith Palace], and is a pretty large market-town, and the better market for being so near Edinburgh; for there comes great quantities of provisions hither from the southern countries, which are brought up here to be carried to Edinburgh market again, and sold there. The town is spacious, and well built, and is the better, no doubt, for the neighbourhood of so many noblemen's and gentlemen's houses of such eminence in its neighbourhood" (Defoe, Tour, p. 626). Defoe had in mind, specifically, Dalkeith Palace, the property of the Dukes of Buccleuch. During the first decade of the eighteenth century, Anne Scott (1651-1732), Countess of Buccleuch in her own right, had just completed the structure on what might well have been the foundations of the old castle of Dalkeith; for, when Defoe saw the palace--probably between 1706 and 1710--the formal gardens had not yet been completed.

In his journal and diary, John Wesley records but a single visit to Dalkeith, from 5:00 A.M. to perhaps 10:00 or 10:30 A.M., Thursday, 22 May 1788. Here was

another example of a Scottish town wherein Methodism
had made some small headway prior to the arrival of its
leader and founder, as well as without regular visits
from him. For, even though the militant Calvinists of
Dalkeith provided strong opposition to the Wesleyan
Methodists, the foundation for a new chapel had been
laid some three weeks earlier, on 1 May, to replace the
existing meeting-house. "The house at Dalkeith," noted
Wesley, "being far too small, even at eight in the
morning, to contain the congregation, I preached in a
garden on 'Seek ye the Lord while he may be found
[Isaiah 55:6]'; and, from the eager attention of the
people, I could not but hope that some of them would
receive the truth in love" (Journal, 7:390).

Ormiston

Ormiston, some ten miles southeast of Edinburgh,
had, by 1740, established itself as an important
contributor to the Scottish linen industry. Any
success achieved in this town came, principally,
through the efforts of one John Cockburn--a member of
the Edinburgh Parliament even before the Union, a
holder of a seat in the Parliament at Westminster until
1741, and the owner of a large estate in Ormiston.
Cockburn devoted considerable energy to improving the
agricultural productivity of his land and of the
surrounding area. He even sent a number of his
tenants' sons to England so they might study the latest
farming methods; in turn, skilled farmers from the
south were brought to Ormiston as advisors. Further
contributions on the part of this reformer included
rebuilding the village of Ormiston; establishing, in
1736, the Ormiston Club, one of the earliest
agricultural societies in Scotland; and instituting the

involvement in the linen industry by laying down a bleach-field and encouraging his tenants to grow flax. By 1735, a Dutch press for folding cloth was purchased and set up at Ormiston; not long afterward, the Commissioners and Trustees for Improving Fisheries and Manufactures in Scotland (established in 1727) granted a subsidy for the extension of the Ormiston bleach-field, specifically to carry forth on experiments in the bleaching of medium-priced cloths (Hamilton, Economic History, pp. 60, 61, 134, 138, 140).

Wesley preached at Ormiston on Tuesday, 12 May 1772, "to a large and deeply serious congregation. I dined at the minister's, a sensible man, who heartily bid us God-speed. But he soon changed his mind: Lord H. informed him that he had received a letter from Lady Huntingdon, assuring him that we were 'dreadful heretics, to whom no countenance should be given.' It is pity! Should not the children of God leave the devil to do his own work?" (Journal, 5:460) The incident serves well to demonstrate the ongoing divisions within the ranks of the Methodists. By 1770, a small body of aristocrats that comprised Lady Huntingdon's inner circle began to press for a clear separation between the Countess's Connexion and the Wesleyan Methodists. The opportunity for alienation from Wesley, Lady Huntingdon's friend of over thirty years' duration, came in the form of the Conference Minutes of 1770. The Countess maintained that the document contained serious and dangerous errors, and therefore charged her cousin, Walter Shirley, with the task of composing and circulating a letter that, essentially, accused the followers of John and Charles Wesley of heresy. Lady Hopetoun, whose husband's seat was Ormiston Hall, belonged to Lady Huntingdon's inner

circle--or, more accurately, to her select hand called
together for prayer and the reading of Scriptures.
Obviously, Lord Hopetoun and his Lady had received
Shirley's letter in advance of Wesley's arrival in
Ormiston (see also below, this chapter, under
Haddington). However, when the Methodist patriarch
returned to the town two years later, Sunday, 5 June
1774, the effect of the circular letter had run its
course. He preached at 8:00 A.M. and, because the
meeting-house proved too small, "stood in the street
and proclaimed 'the grace of our Lord Jesus Christ.'
The congregation behaved with the utmost decency," and
Wesley departed almost immediately after the sermon for
Edinburgh (Journal, 6:24).

Tranent

Tranent lies but three miles north-northwest of
Ormiston, and simply served Wesley as a stopping-off
point, depending upon how late he left or planned to
arrive in nearby Edinburgh. Thus, he lodged in the
village on Monday night, 23 April 1753. There is no
further mention of Tranent in Wesley's journal,
although the diary entry for Thursday, 13 May 1790,
strongly suggests that he rested in the village for an
hour or so in the morning, as he made his way by chaise
from Berwick-upon-Tweed to Edinburgh.

Joppa

Even before the Union, and certainly throughout
the eighteenth century, the growth and development of
the Scottish cities created a heavy domestic demand for
coal. This was especially true in Edinburgh, since the
former capital could lay claim to the largest
concentration of people in all of Scotland. Thus, coal

from East Lothian, especially, was shipped to nearby Leith, while increasing amounts poured into Edinburgh from scores of small pits within a close radius of the city. (see Hamilton, Economic History, pp. 185-189).

And so, on Friday, 19 May 1780, we find John Wesley preaching at Joppa, which he described as "a settlement of colliers, three miles from Edinburgh. Some months ago, as some of them were cursing and swearing, one of our local preachers, going by, reproved them. One of them followed after him and begged he would give them a sermon. He did so several times. Afterwards, the travelling preachers went, and a few quickly agreed to meet together. Some of them now know in whom they have believed, and walk worthy of their profession" (Journal, 6:279). This single sermon appears to have marked the only occasion upon which Wesley visited the Joppa coal miners.

Roslin Castle, Roslin

Seven and one-half miles due south of Edinburgh lie Rosslyn (or Roslin) Chapel and Castle. Now in total ruin, the Castle once stood on a pinnacle of rock overlooking the River North Esk, and it dates from the early fourteenth century. The Chapel, only a short distance away, was founded in 1446 by William St. Clair, Earl of Orkney and Roslin. In essence, this chapel stands as the choir of a much larger church never completed, built in a highly ornate Gothic. Every stone in the place appears to have been decorated, while the vaulting is a mass of stone flowers and stars; carved lintels stretch from carved corbels on the walls. The Earls of Roslin lie buried in the Chapel and also in the graveyard; James Boswell and Samuel Johnson surveyed the Castle and Chapel in

mid November 1773, the former describing the area in
terms of a "romantick scene." They toured the
"beautiful Gothick chapel, and dined and drank tea at
the inn. . ." (Boswell, Journal to the Hebrides, p.
432).

On Tuesday, 23 May 1780, a "gentleman" from
Edinburgh escorted John Wesley to Roslin Castle. "It
is now all in ruins; only a small dwelling-house is
built on one part of it. The situation of it is
exceeding fine, on the side of a steep mountain,
hanging over a river, from which another mountain
rises, equally steep, and clothed with wood. At a
little distance is the chapel, which is in perfect
preservation, both within and without. I should never
have thought it belonged to any one less than a
sovereign prince! the inside being far more elegantly
wrought with variety of Scripture histories in
stonework than I believe can be found again in
Scotland; perhaps not in all England" (Journal, 6:279).

Queensferry

For almost forty years after the Union,
Queensferry existed as a small and even insignificant
port on the Firth of Forth. This royal burgh had taken
its name from Queen Margaret (1045-1093), who married
the rude Scottish king, Malcolm Canmore and whom
Innocent IV canonized in 1251. Apparently, Margaret
made frequent use of the ferry here while on her
numerous excursions between Dunfermline and Edinburgh.
Shortly after the Union, Defoe took a quick notice of
Queensferry as "not a passage over the water only, but
a very good town also, and a corporation" (Defoe, Tour,
p. 587). Conditions improved beginning in 1754, at
which time the Convention of Royal Burghs determined to

extend the lesser ports on the Firth of Forth--
specifically, Bo'ness, Alloa, Prestonpans, and
Queensferry. The last mentioned town drew, for this
purpose, upon local funds and grants from the
Convention and also from the Commissioners of Forfeited
Estates (Hamilton, Economic History, pp. 220-221).

Wesley crossed over the Firth of Forth from
Queensferry, on his way from Edinburgh to Perth, at
6:30 A.M., Friday, 3 April 1784. Later the next month,
at 11:30 A.M., Thursday, 20 May, he came again, this
time from Kinross to Edinburgh. In his own words, "It
blew a storm; nevertheless, with some difficulty, we
crossed the Queen's Ferry" (Journal, 6:509). He
reversed this route on Monday, 17 May 1790; according
to the diary, he left Edinburgh at 5:00 A.M., reached
Queensferry at 6:00, and was in Kinross by 10:45 A.M.

Kirk of Shotts

Kirk of Shotts, in Lanarkshire, lay on the route
from Hamilton (south of Glasgow) to Edinburgh. After
leaving Hamilton, the traveler would pass through
Newarthill, Newhouse, Kirk of Shotts, Whitburn,
Blackburn, Livingston, Mid Calder, Long Hermiston, and
Gorgie Mills before coming to Edinburgh--in all a
distance of thirty-seven miles (see Boswell's Journal
of a Tour, ed. Pottle, p. 486). Presumably, one would
also pass through Kirk of Shotts on his way between
Glasgow and Edinburgh. Thus, on Monday, 23 April 1753,
Wesley informs us that upon leaving Glasgow, he "rode
on, straight by the Kirk o' Shotts" and reached
Edinburgh by five in the afternoon (Journal, 4:64).
Four years later, on Monday, 6 June 1757, he "took
horse early [from Glasgow], and in three hours reached
the Kirk o' Shotts, where the landlord seemed to be

unusually affected by a few minutes' conversation, as
did also the women of the house where we dined"
(Journal, 4:217).

Leith

Because of its function as the seaport of
Edinburgh, the growth and development of Leith during
the mid and late eighteenth century naturally
paralleled the economic rise of the former Scottish
capital. In 1753 came the initial Act for the
improvement of Edinburgh; a year later, Parliament
granted approval for improving and enlarging the harbor
at Leith. Throughout the remainder of the century, the
Edinburgh council periodically raised funds for further
extensions of the harbor, yet that body quickly
discovered that the trade activity was increasing at a
rate faster than it could provide for expanded
facilities. In the last decade of the century, the
Council authorized plans for additions to the harbor,
and even borrowed £20,000 from the Bank of Scotland and
the Royal Bank for the specific purpose of constructing
a wet dock. The advantages to Leith, Edinburgh, and to
the entire area of Scotland from these additions and
improvements were to become obvious. For instance, by
about 1790, Leith could boast of five master
shipbuilders, who in turn employed no less than 152
carpenters, and in 1793, the ships launched from this
port ranged from small fishing craft to trading vessels
of between 200 and 300 tons. Also, as the city of
Edinburgh expanded toward its harbor town, the trade of
the latter rose sharply; by 1784, the estimated worth
of the trade at Leith rose to £500,000. Finally, in
the same year, 1,774 ships cleared the Leith customs
house--782 of these being coasters, of which 361 were

engaged in the coal trade (see Hamilton, Economic
History, pp. 220, 290, 214).

Shortly after the Union, Daniel Defoe saw Leith as
"a large and populous town, or rather two towns, for
the river or harbour parts them, and they are joined by
a good stone bridge, about half a mile, or more, from
the mouth of the river." He noticed, also, the harbor,
and surmised--quite correctly, as it turned out--that
expansion would have to come about. "Here is a very
fine quay well wharfed up with stone, and fenced with
piles, able to discharge much more business than the
place can supply, though the trade is far from being
inconsiderable too. At the mouth of the harbour is a
very long and well built pier, or head, which runs out
beyond the land a great way, and which defends the
entrance into the harbour from filling up with sand, as
upon hard gales of wind at north east, would be very
likely. There are also ranges of piles, or break-
waters, as the seamen call them, on the other side of
the harbour, all which are kept in good repair; and by
this means the harbour is preserved, and kept open in
spite of a flat shore, and a large swell of the sea."
Finally, Defoe observed, on the other side of the
bridge, "the remains of a strong castle, built by
Oliver Cromwell to command the port, but demolished;
yet not so much, but that a little expense and a few
hands would soon restore it" (Defoe, Tour, pp.
586-587).

The first account of John Wesley's visits to Leith
appears in his journal for Saturday, 28 May 1763. On
the preceding day he had left Aberdeen, on his way to
Edinburgh, and obviously lodged in the seaport town
before proceeding to the capital. Not until Wednesday,
28 May 1766, can we find concrete evidence of him

preaching a sermon at Leith. The brief journal entry
reads, "I. . .spoke exceeding plain. A few received
the truth in the love thereof" (Journal, 5:168).
Wesley preached in the town again on Wednesday, 13 May
1772, in what he termed "the most horrid, dreary room I
have seen in the kingdom. But the next day I found
another kind of room--airy, cheerful, and lightsome;
which Mr. Parker undertook to fit up for the purpose,
without any delay" (Journal, 5:460). He had been
scheduled to preach again on Sunday, the 17th, at noon
in the Lady's Walk; however, when he found the
Episcopal Chapel in Edinburgh to be available, his
schedule was quickly changed. On Monday evening, 18
May, in spite of a sever storm and his own poor health
(see above, Chapter 3, under Edinburgh), Wesley
"preached in the new house at Leith to a lovely
audience on 'Narrow is the way that leadeth unto life.'
Many were present again at five in the morning
[Tuesday, 19 May]. How long have we toiled here almost
in vain! Yet I cannot but hope God will at length have
a people even in this place" (Journal, 5:461).

Only two further visits by Wesley to Leith are
mentioned. On Friday, 19 May 1786, he spent perhaps
more than an hour there before boarding the ferry at
5:45 A.M. Eight days later, on his way from Arbroath
to Edinburgh, he arrived in Leith at 12:45 P.M.
(Saturday, 27 May); after spending two hours at work on
the Arminian Magazine, he preached at 6:00 P.M. on
Galatians 6:14. Considering the proximity of Leith to
Edinburgh, we may assume that Wesley spent more time
there than he noted anywhere in his writings.

Musselburgh
Situated some five miles east of Edinburgh,

Musselburgh's contribution to the economy of eighteenth-century Scotland was its woolen industry, particularly shalloons, hats, carpets, and blankets. Apparently, in the early decades of the century, the relationship between the town and its subdivisions was, for the traveler, somewhat complex; Defoe described it as "a large borough-town and populous, and may, indeed, be said to be a cluster of towns, all built together into one, namely, Muscleboro, Innerask, or Inneresk, and Fisheraw; all which amount to no more than this. Muscleboro, or the main or chief town of Muscleboro; Inneresk, or that part of Muscleboro which stands within, or on the inner side of the River Esk, and Fisheraw, or the row of houses where the fishermen usually dwell; for here is still many fishermen, and was formerly many more, when the mussel fishing was counted a valuable thing. . . ." He noticed a considerable number of people "busy on the woolen manufacture; and as the goods they made here were an ordinary kind of stuff for poor people's wearing, we do not find they are out-done at all from England, so that the manufacture is carried on here still with success" (Defoe, Tour, p. 573).

Finally, Defoe observed that although the inhabitants referred to Musselburgh as a seaport town, "their river, though sometimes full enough of water, is not navigable; for at low water, people ride over the mouth of it upon the sands, and even walk over it; so they do not meddle much with trading by sea. At that part of the town, called Inner-Esk are some handsome country houses with gardens, and the citizens of Edinburgh come out in the summer and take lodgings here for the air, as they do from London at Kensington Gravel-Pits, or at Hampstead and Highgate" (Defoe,

Tour, pp. 573-574).

John Wesley had come to Scotland in the spring of 1751 at the invitation of his friends, Colonel and Mrs. Gallatin; the officer had been transferred some months earlier from Manchester to Musselburgh. Thus, the town holds a significant place in the history of Scottish Methodism, for (according to the record set forth in the journals) Wesley preached his first sermon on Scottish soil here. He and Christopher Hopper arrived in Musselburgh around 4:30 P.M., Wednesday, 24 April 1751. "I had no intention to preach in Scotland," wrote Wesley of that initial journey, "nor did I imagine there were any that desired I should. But I was mistaken. Curiosity (if nothing else) brought abundance of people together in the evening. And whereas in the kirk (Mrs. G[alatin] informed me) there used to be laughing and talking, and all the marks of the grossest inattention; but it was far otherwise here--they remained as statues from the beginning of the sermon to the end" (Journal, 3:523).

While Colonel Gallatin remains fresh in the mind, it may not be altogether digressive to point out that Wesley saw him last more than twenty-seven years later, on Friday, 18 December 1778. "But what a change is here! The fine gentleman, the old soldier, is clean gone, sunk into a feeble, decrepit old man; not able to rise off his seat, and hardly able to speak" (Journal, 6:221). One verse (stanza 3) from Charles Wesley's funeral hymn, "On the Death of Colonel Gallatin," illustrates the extent to which the brothers respected the man whom, among other contributions toward the advancement of their mission, opened the door to the Methodist effort in Scotland:

By our old companion left,

> Of our bosom-friend bereft,
> Gentle, generous, and sincere,
> Galatin demands the tear.

(Poetical Works, 6:363)

After several hours in Edinburgh, on Thursday, 25 April, Wesley and Hopper returned to Musselburgh for dinner, "whither we were followed in the afternoon by a little party of gentlemen from Edinburgh. I know not why any should complain of the shyness of the Scots toward strangers. All I spoke with were as free and open with me as the people of Newcastle or Bristol; nor did any person move any dispute of any kind, or ask me any question concerning my opinion." At 6:00 P.M. he preached on "'Seek ye the Lord', while He may be found.' I used great plainness of speech toward them, and they all received it in love; so that the prejudice which the devil had been several years planting was torn up by the roots in one hour. After preaching, one of the bailies [magistrates] of the town, with one of the elders of the kirk, came to me, and begged I would stay with them a while, if it were but two or three days, and they would fit up a far larger place than the school, and prepare seats for the congregation. Had not my time been fixed, I should gladly have complied. All I could now do was to give them a promise that Mr. Hopper would come back the next week and spend a few days with them" (Journal, 3: 523-524). Indeed, Wesley's time was not his own, for the ninth Methodist Conference would take place at Leeds on 15 May. In the interim, he had engagements at Berwick-upon-Tweed, Alnwick, Almouth, Widdrington, Plessey, Newcastle, Sheep Hill, Sunderland, Painshaw, Durham, Stockton, Acomb, Epworth, Hainton, Conigsby, Ludborough, Grimsby, Misterton, Upperthorpe, and York--which meant that he was to visit at least twenty towns and cities within nineteen days (26 April through 14 May). Small wonder, then, that throughout his seasonal trips to Scotland, Wesley could concentrate only upon the five larger cities and certain key towns.

Wesley again came to Musselburgh on Monday, 6 June 1757, at 5:00 P.M. "I went to an inn, and sent for Mr. Bailiff Lindsey, whom I had seen several years ago [25 April 1751?]. He came immediately, and desired me to make his house my home. At seven I preached in the Poorhouse to a large and deeply attentive congregation; but, the number of people making the room extremely hot, I preached in the morning, [Tuesday, 7 June] before the door. Speaking afterwards to the members of the society, I was agreeably surprised to find more than two-thirds knew whom they had believed. And the tree was known by its fruits. The national shyness and stubornness were gone, and they were as open and teachable as little children. At seven [P.M.] five or six and forty of the fifty Dragoons, and multitudes of the town's-people, attended. Is the time come that even these wise Scots shall become fools for Christ's sake?" (Journal, 4:217-218) Two years later, on Monday, 28 May 1759, after leaving Edinburgh and on his way to Dunbar, he stopped at Musselburgh, preaching "in the evening to a deeply attentive congregation" (Journal, 4:317). He held another evening service there on Monday, 11 May 1761, stopping over enroute from Edinburgh to Haddington.

Three more visits to the town followed, although Wesley's remarks appear far from enthusiastic regarding present and future prospects for Methodism there. He delivered a sermon on Friday evening, 25 May 1764, and again at noon on Friday, 26 April 1765. On the latter occasion, he noted that the town contained "a few living souls still" (Journal, 5:112). Finally, after leaving Edinburgh at 5:00 A.M., Thursday, 17 May 1770, Wesley came to Musselburgh; at 8:00 A.M. he preached "and found some hope there will be a blessing in the remnant" (Journal, 5:368). Apparently, however, the hope did not linger for any considerable length of time, for he never again provides mention of the town in his journal. No doubt he must have returned to Mussleburgh at some time after 1770--the close proximity of the town to Edinburgh (as with Leith: see immediately above) would at least suggest that. In all likelihood, the enthusiasm that had been generated in 1751 abated steadily, and there was little about or within the place worthy of note.

Prestonpans

Some eleven miles east of Edinburgh, on the Firth of Forth, the port town of Prestonpans rates mention in both the historical and economic annals of eighteenth-century Scotland. Regarding the former, Prestonpans was the scene of Prince Charles Edward's first significant victory of the 1745 uprising. On the morning of 21 September, Lord George Murray's 2500 Highlanders attacked Sir John Cope's 2300 British regulars and volunteers; according to one historian, whose account may be more dramatic than accurate, the Scots "gave one volley and fell on with the claymore. Cope's six guns were fired once and killed one man; then the Gunners fled, then the Dragoons; the Infantry had little time left them to fly. As for the Volunteers, 'they were na worth a louse, man,' says Mr. Alick Skirving, who saw the field covered with loose heads and hands (the sword wounds inflicted by the claymore made an unusual and unpleasing impression on troops accustomed to be killed by decent bullets). It was all over in ten minutes, with 400 killed and 1000 prisoners, and Cope led the shameful race to Berwick" (Fletcher, <u>History of England from the Restoration</u>, p. 268). The victory of the Young Pretender at Prestonpans--or, perhaps Cope's defeat and retreat--is celebrated in the Jacobite song, "Hey Johnny Cope, are ye waukin' yet?"

Prior to mid century, Prestonpans made only an insignificant contribution to Scottish trade and to its growing fishing industry. However, in 1749, Dr. John Roebuck (1718-1794) founded in the town the first works in Scotland for the production of sulphuric acid--which was to improve the bleaching process for linen. Prior to that time, the acid had to be imported by the bleaching firms from either Holland or England, and this proved to be an expensive as well as dangerous endeavor. Almost immediately, the Prestonpans works established itself as an important center for the manufacture of chemicals, and the products were demanded both within and outside of Scotland. Also, the Vitriol works caused a sudden increase in trade activity for Prestonpans. By 1790, its merchants were trading with London in fish and a variety of manufactured goods, while return cargoes included raw materials for the sulphuric acid (vitriol) and pottery works in the area, as well as English barley destined for local distilleries (Hamilton, <u>Economic History</u>, pp. 140-141, 214).

As for John Roebuck--born in Sheffield, educated for a time at Edinburgh, and graduated M.D. from the University of Leyden--Prestonpans became only one of his ports of call. In 1759, he founded the Carron Iron

Works in Sterlingshire, principally for the production
of cannon and cannonballs to be directed against the
French armies; by 1768, 1200 men were employed at this
task. Afterward, the former physician became a lessee
of the Duke of Hamilton's coal and salt works at
Barrowstounness, and still later a friend and patron of
James Watt. Primarily because of his involvement with
the manufacture of weaponry for the Royal Army, Roebuck
wrote a pamphlet entitled An Enquiry Whether the Guilt
of the Present Civil War in America ought to be Imputed
to Great Britain or America (London, 1776).
Essentially, he placed the entire blame for the war on
the American colonists, charging them with folly,
wickedness, and downright ingratitude.

Shortly after his initial arrival on Scottish
soil--on the afternoon of Wednesday, 24 April 1751--
Wesley rode by Prestonpans "and saw the place of battle
and Colonel Gardiner's house. The Scotch here affirm
that he fought on foot after he was dismounted, and
refused to take quarter. Be it as it may, he is now
'where the wicked cease from troubling, and where the
weary are at rest'" (Journal, 3:523). James Gardiner
(1688-1745), born at Carriden in Linlithgowshire,
obtained, at the age of fourteen, a commission in a
Scottish regiment in the Dutch service. The same year
(1702), he passed into the British army; in 1706 he
suffered serious wounds during the Battle of Ramillies.
However, that did not prevent him from participating in
the remainder of Marlborough's campaign. Nine years
later, during the Jacobite rebellion, Gardiner, now and
captain of dragoons, and eleven others (eight of whom
were killed) fired the barricades of the Highlanders at
Preston. Noted for his licentiousness, he supposedly
received, in 1719, a vision which immediately brought

about his conversion to religious enthusiasm. Two
years prior to the 1745 uprising, Gardiner received
promotion to colonel, the rank he held at the Battle of
Prestonpans. Deserted by his own troops at the head of
an infantry platoon, but was cut down by the stroke of
a Highland scythe. As a child of six, Walter Scott,
taken by his Aunt Jenny on a visit to Prestonpans,
explored the battlefield in company with a half-pay
retired ensign named Dalgetty. The old man and the
youngster viewed the thorn tree marking the center of
the battle, and stood upon the very spot where James
Gardiner fell (Johnson, Scott, 1:25). Thirty-seven
years later, the memory of that visit returned within
the pages of Waverley (1814); for, prior to joining the
Jacobites forces at Prestonpans, Edward Waverley served
as an officer in Colonel Gardiner's regiment of
dragoons.

In 1746, Reverend Dr. Philip Doddridge (1702-1751)
published A Sermon on the Heroic Death of Colonel James
Gardiner, followed the next year by Some Remarkable
Passages in the Life of Col. James Gardiner, from His
Birth, January 10, 1687, to His Death, in the Battle of
Prestonpans, September 21, 1745; with an Appendix
Relating to the Ancient Family of the Munroes of Fowlis
(Edinburgh, 1747). Wesley read the latter account on
Tuesday, 20 October 1747, in London, questioning, "what
matters it whether his [Gardiner's] soul was set at
liberty by a fever or a Lochaber axe, seeing he had
gone to God?" (Journal, 3:321) The name of the hero of
Prestonpans entered Wesley's mind some twenty-two years
later, on Wednesday, 16 August 1769, while at
Havorfordwest in Wales. He had been reading John
Newton's Narrative of His Life, in a Series of Letters
to Mr. Hawes (1764), and determined that the author's,

"as well as Colonel Gardiner's, conversion was an answer to his mother's prayers" (Journal, 5:332-333). In May 1763, James Gardiner's widow heard Wesley preach in Edinburgh. The next week she wrote to the Methodist leader, congratulating him upon his and his itinerants' efforts in the Scottish capital. I have never, I own, been at the preaching house in a morning yet, as they preach so early; but I ventured to the High School yard the morning you left Edinburgh [7:00 A.M., Sunday, 29 May 1763]; and it pleased God, even after I got home, to follow part of your sermon with a blessing to me" (The Arminian Magazine, 5 [1782], 443).

Wesley's one recorded experience of preaching at Prestonpans did not turn out well at all, although some care had been taken in arranging the event. On Saturday afternoon, 24 May 1766, "notice having been given a week before, I went to the room at Preston Pans; and I had it all to myself, neither man, woman, nor child offered to look me in the face. So I ordered a chair to be placed in the street. Then forty or fifty crept together; but they were mere stocks and stones--no more concerned than if I had talked Greek" (Journal, 5:168).

Haddington

Due east of Prestonpans and thirteen miles south of North Berwick, the River Tyne runs by Haddington, which Defoe regarded as "an old half ruined, yet remaining town; which shows the remarks of decayed beauty, for it was formerly a large, handsome, and well built town, or city rather; for besides the walls of stone, which were in those times esteemed strong, the English fortified it with lines and bastions, four of which bastions were very large, as may be seen by the

remains of them, to this day [c. 1710]; also they had
a large ditch; as for counterscarps, they were scarce
known in those times." Despite the decline in its size
and reputation, and of its architecture, Defoe thought
Haddington "still a good town, has some handsome
streets, and well built; and they have a good stone
bridge over the Tyne, though the river is but small.
The church was large, has suffered in the ruin of the
rest, and is but in part repaired, though 'tis still
large enough for the number of inhabitants; for, though
the town is still what may be called populous, 'tis
easy to see that it is not like what it has been.
There are some monuments of the Maitlands, ancient
lords of this part of the country, remaining; but as
the choir of the church is open and defaced, the
monuments of the dead have suffered with the rest"
(Defoe, Tour, p. 569).

Haddington at one time could boast of two fine
churches, St. Mary's and St. Martin's, and the remains
of both would have been obvious attractions for any
eighteenth-century traveler. The former, known once as
"the Lamp of Lothian," served as the parish church of
the town. In fact, to the present day, the nave still
serves the town as a place of worship, although the
remainder of the building is but a ruin. Dating from
the fifteenth century, St. Mary's represents one of the
largest and noblest examples of Scottish ecclesiastical
architecture of the period. For instance, the east
walls of the transepts and the end walls of the choir
aisles proved windowless, while the flamboyant tracery
of the large windows and the triple windows of the
lofty tower predominated. During the great siege of
Haddington in 1548, the church sustained considerable
damage and narrowly escaped total destruction. The

other structure, St. Martin's, is essentially the ruined nave of a Romanesque church, altered in the thirteenth century, at which time the building was vaulted and buttresses added.

Throughout the eighteenth century, Haddington served as a center for the manufacture of woolen goods, particularly blankets and broadcloth. Defoe observed "English workmen employed," who "really made very good cloth, well mixed and good colours. But I cannot say they made it as cheap, or could bring it so cheap to market as the English; and this was the reason, that, though before the late Union, the English cloth being prohibited upon severe penalties, their own cloth supplied them very well; yet, as soon as the Union was made, and by that means the English trade opened, the clothiers from Worcester, and the counties adjoining such as Gloucester and Wilts, brought in their goods, and under selling the Scots, those manufactories were not able to hold it: (Defoe, _Tour_, pp. 569-570). The general condition of the woolen industry in Haddington, as well as throughout Scotland, improved later in the century with a fuller development of the sheep industry and the establishment of factories for manufacturing woolen cloth.

John Wesley preached at Haddington at 9:00 A.M., Tuesday, 12 May 1761, after having ridden from Musselburgh through a heavy rainstorm. There he conducted the service in the parlor of one Mr. Dickson, the chief magistrate (or _provost_) of the town and the man who would serve as host during the Methodist leader's early visits to Haddington. Three years later, on Friday, 25 May 1764, Wesley preached at 10:00 A.M. in Provost Dickson's yard "to a very elegant congregation. But I expect little good will be done here, for we begin at the wrong end. Religion must not go from the greatest to the least, or the power would appear to be of men" (Journal, 5:70-71). Obviously, his efforts were having little or no effect upon the working classes of the town.

On his next visit, occurring on Friday, 18 May 1770, he rode by the estate of Thomas Hamilton, sixth Earl of Haddington (d. 1785), a place "finely situated between two woods. The house is exceeding large and pleasant, commanding a wide prospect both ways; and the Earl is cutting walks through the woods, smoothing the ground, and much enlarging and beautifying his garden. Yet he is to die!" (Journal, 5:368). In 1766, the Earl had published his Treatise on Forest Trees, in which he conveyed his "pleasure in planting and in inclosing; but, because I did not like the husbandry practised in this country, I got some farmers from Dorsetshire. This made me divide my ground; but as I knew the coldness of the climate, and the bad effects of the high winds had, I made strips of planting betwixt every inclosure, some forty, fifty, or sixty feet broad, as I thought best. . . .From these Englishmen we came to the knowledge of sowing and management of the grass seeds" (quoted from Hamilton, Economic History, p. 60). This planting took place shortly after the Union (1707), and the results produced the famous Tyninghame Woods of East Lothian.

In May 1772, Wesley left Edinburgh on Wednesday morning, the 20th, intending "to preach (as usual) at Provost Dickson's, in Haddington, in the way to Dunbar. But the Provost, too, had received light from the 'Circular Letter [of the Countess of Huntingdon],' and durst not receive those heretics" (Journal, 5:461; see also above, this chapter, under Ormiston). Thus, the

desertion of Mr. Dickson marked the real termination of
Wesley's personal effort in Haddington, although he did
make at least two more brief stops in the town: first,
on Monday, 24 May 1784 (from 10:00 A.M. to 11:30 A.M.),
and again on Tuesday, 30 May 1786, from about 10:00
A.M. until shortly before noon. On neither occasion
did he preach, but merely paused there to partake of
his customary diversion, tea and conversation.

Marquis of Tweeddale's Seat, Yester

On Wednesday, 20 May 1772, when Wesley determined
that he would not receive further welcome at Haddington
(see immediately above and also, in this chapter, under
Ormiston), he went "round by the Marquis of Tweeddale's
seat, completely finished within and without. But he
that took so much delight in it is gone to his long
home, and has left it to one that has not taste or
regard for it. So rolls the world away!" (Journal,
5:461). George Hay, sixth Marquis of Tweeddale (d.
1782) had succeeded in 1770; however, the development
of the seat resulted from the efforts of John Hay, Earl
and first Marquis of Tweeddale (1625-1697), who took
Greenwich Palace as his architectural model and St.
James's Park, London, as the plan for his landscape
design.

When Daniel Defoe toured the area, the seat was
occupied by young John Hay, fourth Marquis of Tweeddale
(1695-1762). At that time (c. 1710), the traveler
generally focused his attention upon the park and the
woods, "because, though there the design of a noble
house of palace, and great part of it built; yet, as it
is not yet, and perhaps, will not soon be finished,
there is no giving a complete description of it."
Further, according to Defoe, the first Marquis "was a

great favourite of King Charles II though not much
concerned in politic affairs at least, not in England,
yet took in from the king the love of managing what we
call forest trees, and making fine vistas and avenues"
(Defoe, Tour, p. 567). Perhaps one reason John Hay
demonstrated a disinterest in politics stems from the
simple fact that few among those who knew him placed
any real trust or interest in his ability. For
example, when, in 1689, George Savile, Marquis of
Halifax, suggested Tweeddale's name as a possible
Secretary for Scotland, King William responded with,
"Pish, he cannot be!" (Hamilton, William's Mary, p.
222) His heirs, however, fared somewhat better. In
March 1704, after Anne and Godolphin dismissed James
Douglas, Duke of Queensbury, as the chief minister in
Scotland, the burden of government fell to the
Presbyterian Country Party, led by the second Marquis
of Tweeddale, described by the Jacobites as "a well
meaning but simple man," and by the British Whigs as "a
very good man, but not perfectly qualified for Court
intrigues" (Trevelyan, Ramillies, p. 260). The son of
the second Marquis, Lord John Hay, was a colonel of the
Scots Grays, had fought with Marlborough in Flanders
for three years (1705-1708), and died of fever at
Courtrai on 25 August 1708 (see Trevelyan, Ramillies,
p. 147).

Kinghorn Ferry

In 1710, Defoe noted that the "ferry, from Leith
to the shore of Fife, is fixed in this town [Kinghorn],
though sometimes the boats in distress, and by force of
wind and weather, are driven to run into Borunt Island
[Burntisland]. This constant going and coming of the
ferry-boat, and passengers, is also a considerable

benefit to the town of Kinghorn, and is a very great
article in its commerce" (Defoe, Tour, p. 632).
Indeed, the crossing by this busy ferry often proved a
crowded and rough passage; as late as 1794, there were
nine passage boats of about fifty or sixty tons, as
well as a few pinnaces, engaged on this ferry. Thus,
the town of Kinghorn tended to be filled to capacity
with passengers waiting for fairer weather to make the
crossing (see Walker, Correspondence of Boswell and
Johnston, pp. 48-49, note 3).

In his journal and diary, John Wesley recorded
four occasions upon which he made use of the Kinghorn
ferry. On Saturday, 28 May 1763, enroute from Aberdeen
to Edinburgh, he "rode on to Kinghorn Ferry, and had a
pleasant passage to Leith" (Journal, 5:15). He came
that way again the following year, on Saturday, 16 June
1764, and the passage proved uneventful; not until his
third crossing--Saturday, 14 June 1766--did he
encounter any inconvenience. "It rained from the
moment we set out [from Dundee] till (about one [P.M.])
we came to Kinghorn. Finding the boat was not to move
till four o'clock, I proposed to hire a pinnace; but
the wind springing up fair, I went into the large boat.
Quickly it fell calm again, so that we did not get over
till past seven" (Journal, 5:170). The final crossing
recorded by Wesley took place on still another
Saturday--this one 27 May 1786. He arrived at Kinghorn
at 9:30 A.M., read for two hours, and then boarded the
ferryboat at 11:30; by 12:45 P.M., after a "pleasant
passage" (Journal, 7:165), he landed in Leith. Thus,
we may determine that in decent weather, the crossing
consumed about one hour and fifteen minutes.

New Inn, King's Kettle

The New Inn was an old coaching-house near King's Kettle, approximately nineteen miles southwest of Newport. On Friday, 26 May 1786, at 11:00 P.M., Wesley boarded a boat at Dundee and crossed the Firth of Tay for Newport, which he reached at 2:00 A.M. After an hour's ride in his chaise, he arrived at the New Inn, where he slept until 6:30 A.M. (Saturday, the 27th). By 7:15 A.M., he was back in his chaise, bound for Kinghorn Ferry, Leith, and then on to Edinburgh (see Journal, 7:164-165). Thus, Wesley had enjoyed but little more than three hours' sleep from the time he left Aberdeen--3:00 A.M., Thursday, 25 May--until he retired at 9:30 P.M., Saturday, the 27th. This seems all the more amazing when one pauses to realize that the Methodist patriarch had entered the eighty-third year of his life.

Melville House, Leslie

Built sometime before 1681 by John Leslie, Duke of Rothes (1630-1681), Melville House was, at the time of Wesley's journeys through Scotland, the seat of David Leslie, sixth Earl of Leven and an active supporter of Methodism north of the River Tweed. In fact, George Whitefield had been a guest at Melville House during one of his forays into Scotland in 1751. In the gardens stood a square tower, one of the retreats of Archbishop David Beaton (1494-1546).

Wesley reports that on Wednesday, 19 May 1784, "I crossed over the pleasant and fertile country of Fife [he had come from Dundee] to Melville House, the grand and beautiful seat of Lord Leven. He was not at home, being gone to Edinburgh as the King's Commissioner; but the Countess was, with two of her daughters, and both her sons-in-law. At their desire, I preached [at 7:30] in the evening on 'It is appointed unto man once to die' [Hebrews 9:27]; and I believe God made the application" (Journal, 6:509). He remained the night, and the next morning, at 5:45, took chaise for Kinross. It is interesting to note that Wesley dated his Thought on Nervous Disorders with the citation, "Melville House, 20 May 1784." According to the diaries, he enjoyed another stay at Lord Leven's estate, that occasion being Monday, 17 May 1790. After arriving from Kinross at 3:15 P.M., he preached in the evening on 1 Peter 1:24; the next morning at 5:00, he was off for Dundee.

Cupar

Cupar, in the early eighteenth century the shire town (or county seat) of Fife, had been, before the Union, a significant commercial center. Between 1775 and 1796, more than one-third of the town was rebuilt, and the traveler could view considerable expansion. Samuel Johnson, who passed through the town in August 1773, just two years before construction began, simply identified Cupar (along with Kinghorn and Kirkaldy) as "not unlike the small or straggling market-towns in those parts of England where commerce and manufactures have not yet produced opulence" (Johnson, Journey to the Western Islands, p. 4).

On Friday, 15 June 1764, Wesley left Aberdeen early in the morning "and came to Dundee just as the boat was going off. We designed to lodge at the house on the other side; but could not get either meat, drink, or good words, so we were constrained to ride on to Cupar. After traveling near ninety miles, I found no weariness at all [meaning, of course, ninety miles

from Aberdeen to Cupar]; neither were our horses hurt.
Thou, O Lord, doth save both man and beast!" (Journal,
5:77). Possibly, he stopped at the Tontine Inn, owned
by a Mr. McNabb, situated on St. Catherine's Street,
next door to the County Hall (see Boswell's Journal of
a Tour to the Hebrides, ed. Pottle, p. 455). Some
years later, on Thursday, 27 May 1790, Wesley again
passed through Cupar, on his way from Forfar to
Auchterader. However, it is unlikely that he even
stopped.

Carse of Gowrie, Perthshire

Wesley noted, in his journal for Thursday, 5 May
1768, that he "rode through the pleasant and fruitful
Carse of Gowrie, a plain, fifteen or sixteen miles long
between the River Tay and the mountains, very thick and
inhabited. . ." (Journal, 5:258). Actually the Carse
is some fourteen miles long, four miles wide, and
consists of approximately 18,000 acres of extremely
rich and fertile soil. In fact, it may be considered
as the finest alluvial or delta land in Scotland,
similar to those fertile tracts adjacent to the mouths
of the Nile, the Ganges, the Indus, or the Mississippi.
Wesley certainly must have passed through this area on
several occasions during his journeys into Scotland,
especially as he came to and departed from Dundee and
Perth.   Matthew   Bramble,   Tobias   George   Smollett's
irritable Welsh squire, praised the Carse as being
"equal in fertility to any part in England. . ."
(Humphry Clinker, p. 224).

Rait

According to Wesley's own description, Rait was "a
little town in the middle of that lovely valley called

the Carse of Gowrie." Here he preached at 10:00 A.M.,
Monday, 23 May 1774, "to a considerable number of plain
serious country people. . ." (Journal, 6:21).

Broughty Castle, Broughty Ferry

Situated in Broughty Ferry, a small town on the
Firth of Tay, some four miles east of Dundee, Broughty
Castle--a large oblong structure with a battlemented
top--was erected about the beginning of the sixteenth
century.

On Friday, 27 May 1763, Wesley left Edinburgh,
preached at Brechin, and rode on to Broughty Castle,
which he determined to be "two or three miles below
Dundee. We were in hopes of passing the river here,
though we could not at the town; but we found our
horses could not pass till eleven or twelve at night."
Therefore, he and the members of his party determined
to cross by boat and leave the horses behind. For this
purpose they "procured a kind of a boat, about half as
long as a London wherry, and three or four feet broad."
As soon as they had cast off, Wesley discovered that
the craft leaked in a number of places, and there was
nothing on board with which to bail. "When we came
toward the middle of the river, which was three miles
over, the wind being high and the water rough, our
boatmen seemed a little surprised; but we encouraged
them to pull away, and in less than half an hour we
landed safe [probably at Tayport]" (Journal, 5:14-15).
The horses, by the way, were transported over in
another vessel.

West Haven

Wesley described West Haven simply as "a town of
fisherman" (Journal, 6:109). He preached there at noon

on Saturday, 25 May 1776, and afterward departed for Dundee.

East Haven

On Monday, 30 May 1774, Wesley left Arberdeen early in the morning, preached and spent the night at Arbroath, and the next day (the 31st) preached at East Haven, another of those small Scottish fishing villages. "I suppose," he remarked in reference to the service, that "all the inhabitants were present, and all were ready to devour the word" (Journal, 6:22). By evening, he had reached Dundee.

Forfar

Throughout the eighteenth century, Forfar existed as the center of the Scottish heavy linen industry, but the town did not really evidence any signs of expansion until after 1775. Then, new streets were constructed and old ones extended in almost every direction; the population doubled between 1755 and 1792. Also, new houses were built to accommodate the increase in the number of tradesmen. These dwellings tended to be of two storys, each with four apartments and a small garden. For some reason, the weavers preferred to occupy the lower level apartments, where they found a large window facing the street. The dwellings rented at a cost of £1 to £2 5s. per year, the rate determined by the distance of the building from the market-place (see Hamilton, Economic History, pp. 30, 383-384).

In his journals, Wesley noted but two fairly insignificant references to Forfar. He stated, on both occasions--Monday, 23 May 1763, and Thursday, 27 May 1790--that he rode through the town, although the latter entry contains the parenthetical observation

that it is "now a handsome and almost new Town. . ."
(Journal, 8:67). However, in May 1790, he did remain
long enough for the usual tea, conversation, and prayer
before moving on to Dundee.

Kinross

Two diary references indicate Wesley's presence in
Kinross: First, on Thursday, 20 May 1784, at which
time he paused there for morning tea; second, on
Monday, 17 May 1790, when he arrived at 10:45 A.M. and
departed forty-five minutes later. It appears strange,
considering Wesley's interest in Mary Queen of Scots
(see Chapter 2), that he never observed--or at least
never mentioned the observation of--Loch Leven Castle,
standing on an island in Loch Leven. Parts of the
structure date from as early as 1325, while the main
tower rises five storys. Queen Mary was imprisoned in
the Castle in June 1567, but managed to escape a year
later, when George Douglas rowed her away from the
island--but not before having locked all the Castle
gates from the outside and disservicing all of the
remaining vessels.

Auchterarder

According to the notations in Wesley's journals,
he left Brechin on Thursday, 27 May 1790, traveled
through Forfar and Cupar, and came to Auchterarder.
"Here we expected poor accommodations, but were
agreeably disappointed. Food, beds, and everything
else were as neat and clean as at Aberdeen or
Edinburgh" (Journal, 8:67). The next day, Friday, the
28th, he passed through Stirling and Kilsyth to
Glasgow. However, the journal and diary do not
parallel each other in this instance (there are other

such instances throughout the Curnock edition of the
journals). We would believe that Wesley spent Thursday
night at Auchterarder, and then went on to Glasgow on
Friday. On the other hand, the diary entry for 27 May
1790 reads as follows:

> 3 Prayed; 3.30 tea, chaise, Forfar, tea,
> conversed, prayer, chaise, Dunblane, tea
> conversed, chaise, sleep, chaise, Kilsyth,
> dinner conversed; 4.45 [P.M.] Glas[gow], at
> brother Richards's, tea, on business,
> letters; 7 [P.M.] 1 Sam. xxi, supper, prayer

Neither the diary entry for 27 May or the one for the
28th mentions Auchterarder; we must conclude,
therefore, that Wesley stopped at an inn there late
Thursday morning for food and a nap before proceeding
to Kilsyth, where he had dinner. He then went on to
Glasgow. Actually, considering Wesley's advanced age
(eighty-seven) and the number of towns through which he
passed during the course of a tour, we cannot blame him
for failing to recount accurately his activities when
he paused to note the events of several days passing in
his journal.

Monydie

Wesley's lone visit to Monydie came on Friday, 20
May 1774, when he rode over from Perth to attend the
burial of the mother-in-law of Mr. Fraser (see Chapter
3, under Perth). "Oh what a difference is there, he
exclaimed, "between the English and the Scotch method
of burial! The English does honour to human nature,
and even to the poor remains, that were once a temple
of the Holy Ghost! But when I see in Scotland a coffin
put into the earth, and covered up without a word
spoken, it reminds me of what was spoken concerning

Jehoiakim, 'He shall be buried with the burial of an ass!'" (Journal, 6:220)

Methven

Methven lies but a short distance west of Perth, and received only a single reference in Wesley's accounts of his journeys through Scotland. He spent a short time there on Monday, 27 April 1772, as he made his way from Perth north to Dunkeld.

Dunkeld

Dunkeld, sixteen miles north of Perth, gained prominence of a sort in the eighteenth century when it became the terminus for one of three major highways constructed by General George Wade (1673-1748). The second "Wade road," begun in 1728, ran from Inverness through the midst of the central Highlands by Kingussie, then on to Dalwhinnie, Blair Atholl, and finally Dunkeld. Of the total 102 miles of roads, the first forty were completed by the end of 1728, the next fifty-two in 1729, and the final ten miles by 1730 (Hamilton, Economic History, pp. 229, 230). Even prior to the planning and eventual construction of the Inverness-Dunkeld road, the major claim of the latter town was (and, in fact, still is) its Cathedral, situated on the north bank of the River Tay, amid a romantic Highland setting. Built over a period spanning the fourteenth to the sixteenth century, Dunkeld Cathedral housed a considerable quantity of art work, especially the interesting early-sixteenth-century wall paintings in the aisle under the tower.

Leaving Perth at 5:00 A.M., Wednesday, 25 April 1770, Wesley rode to Dunkeld, which he noticed to be "the first considerable town in the Highlands. We were

agreeably surprised; a pleasanter situation cannot
easily be imagined" (Journal, 5:363). Two years later,
he again journeyed northward from Perth, and on Monday,
27 April 1772, "came on to Dunkeld, once the capital of
the Caledonian kingdom, now a small town standing on
the bank of the Tay and at the foot of several rough,
high mountains. The air was sharp, yet the multitude
of people constrained me to preach abroad; and, I
trust, not in vain, for great was the power of God in
the midst of them" (Journal, 5:456).

Port Glasgow

Founded in 1668 as the port of Glasgow because the
River Clyde proved too shallow to allow sea-going
vessels to reach the city, Port Glasgow underwent
considerable change and expansion in the eighteenth
century. This growth paralleled the increase of the
Scottish tobacco trade, which obviously demanded larger
harbor and warehouse accommodations. Port Glasgow soon
absorbed the adjacent village of Newark, and in 1774,
the Glasgow town council permitted its satellite to
elect magistrates and to form its own council. Soon,
plans were drawn for lighting and paving the streets
and for providing an independent water system. The
funds for such services came from a tax of 2d. on each
pint of ale brewed (Hamilton, Economic History, p. 28).

John Wesley first preached at Port Glasgow on
Tuesday afternoon, 21 April 1772, describing it as "a
large town, two miles east of Greenock. Many gay
people were there, careless enough; but the greater
part seemed to hear with understanding" (Journal,
5:454). He returned there at 8:00 the following
morning (Wednesday, the 22nd), preaching in the Masons'
Lodge. "The house was crowded greatly; and I suppose

all the gentry of the town were a part of the congregation. Resolving not to shoot over their heads as I had done the day before, I spoke strongly of death and judgement, heaven and hell. This they seemed to comprehend; and there was no more laughing among them, or talking with each other; but all were quietly and deeply attentive" (Journal, 5:455).

Two more visits followed. On Monday, 16 May 1774, Wesley preached at the Scottish kirk--first at 7:00 A.M., and then again in the afternoon. "My subjects were Death and Judgement, and I spoke as home as I possibly could" (Journal, 6:19). Obviously, he had decided that Port Glasgow would be limited to a single sermon theme! Exactly when the next appearance came about is difficult to determine; the journal entry for Wednesday, 15 May 1776, reads, "I preached at Dundee to nearly as large a congregation as that at Port Glasgow" (Journal, 6:106). However, no journal entry between 7 May (when he left Carlisle and went on to Selkirk) and 15 May (his arrival at Dundee) contains a reference to Port Glasgow. Since he was in Glasgow on the 11th and 12th, and in Edinburgh on the 13th, we may assume that he preached at Port Glasgow on the 10th--either on the way to or back from Greenock (see immediately below).

Greenock

The growth of Greenock came about for reasons similar to the expansion of Port Glasgow, except that the former fared considerably better. Until early in the seventeenth century, its citizens led an uneventful existence as inhabitants of a serene fishing village; but then, Sir John Shaw, the landed proprietor, became anxious for his share of the expanding commerce of the River Clyde. Thus, in 1635, Sir John obtained a

charter that transformed Greenock into a burgh of
barony. Later, a harbor was built and then extended;
yet, the town entered the eighteenth century with a
population of barely one thousand persons. To develop
and maintain their harbor, the citizens of Greenock
volunteered to tax themselves--or, more accurately, to
tax the malt brewed within the town. By 1741, the
trade of the port had become significant; in 1751, the
harbor was extended and plans set forth for new
streets. The 1000 inhabitants had multiplied to 3858
in 1775, and by 1801 Greenock could boast of a
population of 17458! Perhaps the most noteworthy
statistic relating to the activity of the town directs
our attention to its role in the emergence of Scottish
foreign trade. In 1780, Greenock had the largest
number of ships in Scotland on its register, the
majority of which were engaged in trade with nations
abroad (Hamilton, Economic History, pp. 29, 287).

The mercantile mind and eye of Daniel Defoe could
easily perceive the economic potential of Greenock as
he came upon the town early in its development. ". . .
'tis not an ancient place, but seems to be grown up in
later years, only by being a good road for ships, and
where the ships ride that come into, and go out from
Glasgow, just as the ships for London do in the downs.
It has a castle to command the road and the town is
well built, and has many rich trading families in it.
It is the chief town on the west of Scotland for the
herring fishery; and the merchants of Glasgow who are
concerned in the fishery, employ the Greenock vessels
for the catching and curing the fish, and for several
parts of their other trades, as well as carrying them
afterwards abroad to market" (Defoe, Tour, p. 603).

When John Wesley first visited Greenock on Monday,

20 April 1772, he described it as "a seaport town, twenty miles west of Glasgow. It is built very much like Plymouth Dock, and has a safe and spacious harbour. The trade and inhabitants, and consequently the houses are increasing swiftly; and so is cursing, swearing, drunkenness, Sabbath-breaking, and all manner of wickedness. Our room is about thrice as large as that at Glasgow; but it would not near contain the congregation. I spoke exceeding plain, and not without hope that we may see some fruit, even among this hard-hearted generation." Remaining there overnight, he preached again on the following morning (Tuesday, the 21st) to a full room. The assembly "showed an excellent spirit; for after I had spoke a few words on the head, every one stood up at the singing." After spending most of the day at Port Glasgow, Wesley returned to Greenock in the evening for a sermon, "and God gave them a loud call, whether they will hear or whether they will forbear" (Journal, 5:454-455).

Returning to Greenock two years later, on Monday, 16 May 1774, Wesley preached in the evening to an "exceeding large" congregation. "I opened and enforced these awful words, 'Strait is the gate, and narrow is the way, that leadeth unto life.' I know not that ever I spoke so strongly. And some fruit of it quickly appeared, for the house, twice as large as that at Glasgow, was thoroughly filled at five in the morning [Tuesday, 17 May]" (Journal, 6:19). His last visit of record came on Friday, 10 May 1776. "It being their fast-day before the sacrament (ridiculously so called, for they do not fast at all, but take their three meals, just as on other days), the congregation was larger than when I was here before, and remarkably attentive" (Journal, 6:105). Again, he remained overnight and departed the next day for Glasgow.

Kilsyth

Defoe labeled Kilsyth, in Sterlingshire and approximately twelve miles northeast of Glasgow, as a "good plain country burgh, tolerably well built, but not large. . ." (Defoe, Tour, p. 610). Although Wesley, himself, paid little or no attention to the place, a considerable degree of evangelical activity went on in the town even before he began his regular series of journeys through Scotland. As early as 1740, James Robe, parish minister at Kilsyth, began to preach there on the doctrine of regeneration. He held a large revival service on 25 April 1741, and on 16 May converted upwards of thirty persons. The account of these events he set down in a volume entitled Narrative of the Extraordinary Work of the Spirit of God at Cambuslang, Kilsyth, Campsie, Kirkintilloch, Auchinloch, [etc.] in 1742 (1742; editions in 1790, 1840, 1843, and 1849). In about 1745, Robe wrote to a friend, "I was much pleased with what you wrote to me of the Messrs. Wesley. . . . I embrace fellowship with them, and pray that the Lord of the Vineyard will give them success. I have learned something new as to the exhorters [lay preachers]. From what you mention of them, I look upon them as so many licensed probationers, or useful public teachers; which is the case of our probationers. This provides us with an answer to objections, besides that of the extraordinary circumstances of the Established Church. . . .I beg you to salute the two brothers for me much in the Lord" (Benson, Apology, pp. 168-169). Thus, we observe Robe to have been one of the few Scots agreeable to the concept of lay preachers.

In his journal for Monday, 23 April 1753, Wesley noted that he "had a great desire to go round by Kilsyth, in order to see that venerable man, Mr. Robe, who was every day expecting (what his soul longed for), 'to depart and be with Christ.' But the continual rains had made it impracticable for us to add so many miles to our day's journey [from Glasgow to Edinburgh] . . ." (Journal, 4:64). According to information gathered from the diaries, he did not come to Kilsyth until Thursday afternoon, 27 May 1790; he remained there for several hours, enjoying dinner and conversation before departing for Glasgow.

Chapter Six

NORTH

Upon a simmer Sunday morn,
        When Nature's face is fair,
I walked forth to view the corn,
        An' snuff the caller air.
The rising sun, owre Galston muirs,
        Wi' glorious light was glintin;
The hares were hirplin down the furs,
        The lav'rocks they were chantin
                    Fu' sweet that day.
(Robert Burns, The Holy Fair, ll. 1-9)

Glamis

Wesley states, in his journal for Friday, 8 May 1761, that he rode from Aberdeen to Glamis, "about sixty-four measured miles, and on Saturday, the 9th, about sixty-six more to Edinburgh" (Journal, 4:452). Apparently, he did not preach at Glamis, but merely remained overnight; the next morning, he was quickly on his way again.

Montrose

Because of its location on the coast, Montrose existed as one of Scotland's key ports. For example, in 1789, some fifty-three vessels of 3543 tons were busily engaged in the coasting trade, bringing in coal from the Firth of Forth and carrying away sail-cloth, salmon, and agricultural produce (Hamilton, Economic History, p. 215). Daniel Defoe, sixty-five years earlier, saw the town as a "sea-port, and, in proportion to its number of inhabitants, has a considerable trade, and is tolerably well built, and capable of being made strong, only that it extends too far in length" (Defoe, Tour, p. 652). On the other hand, Samuel Johnson took little notice of the economic state of Montrose when he and Boswell toured the town before breakfast on Saturday, 21 August 1773. He "found it well built, airy, and clean. The townhouse is a handsome fabrick with a portico. We then went to view the English chapel, and found a small church, clean to a degree unknown in any other part of Scotland, with commodious galleries, and what was yet less expected, an organ" (Johnson, Journey to the Western Islands, p. 11).

The two travelers had arrived at Montrose at about 11:00 P.M. the previous evening (20 August), lodging at the Ship Inn, 107 High Street, presided over by an English landlord named William Driver. According to one report, the English chapel to which Johnson refers was burned down in 1857. Since the Established Church (Scottish) did not permit organs as early at 1773, the only places in Scotland where they might be found were in English chapels (Anglican)--and not all of them could afford the luxury of such an instrument (see Boswell's Journal of a Tour, ed. Pottle, p. 457).

Boswell casts some additional light on Johnson's observations through his own version of the visit to Montrose. "Before breakfast," he wrote, "we went and saw the town-hall, where is a good dancing-room, and other rooms for tea-drinking. The appearance of the town from it is very well; but many of the houses are built with their ends to the street, which looks awkward. When we came down from it, I met Mr. [G.

Adam] Gleg, a merchant here. He went with us to see
the English chapel. It is situated on a pretty dry
spot, and there is a fine walk to it. It is really an
elegant building, both within and without. The organ
is adorned with green and gold. Dr. Johnson gave a
shilling extraordinary to the clerk, saying, 'He
belongs to an honest church.' I put him in mind, that
episcopals were but <u>dissenters</u> here, they were only
<u>tolerated</u>. 'Sir, (said he) we are here, as Christians
in Turkey'" (Boswell, <u>Journal of a Tour</u>, p. 205).

The first mention of Montrose in Wesley's journal
occurs in the entry for Thursday, 30 April 1761, when
he rode through the town on his way from Dundee to
Stonehaven. Nine years later, at noon on Monday, 7 May
1770, he came for the specific purpose of delivering a
sermon, "but found no notice had been given. However,
I went down to the Green, and sung a hymn. People
presently flocked from all parts, and God gave me great
freedom of speech; so that I hope we did not meet in
vain" (<u>Journal</u>, 5:365). By 7:00 P.M., he had reached
Arbroath. Wesley's diary for Monday, 17 May 1784,
records his next visit: he arrived at 1:00 P.M. from
Bervie, took dinner at 2:00, and by 2:30 was in his
chaise and bound for Arbroath. The visit of Thursday,
25 May 1786, lasted longer, specifically because of a
heavy storm that delayed his journey south. After
arriving at 11:30 A.M., he had time for noon dinner and
a walk at 4:00 P.M. His final stop in Montrose, on
Thursday, 20 May 1790, lasted approximately ninety
minutes. On this occasion, he was proceeding north; he
arrived in the town at 6:30 A.M., tasted some tea, and
climbed back into his chaise at 8:00.

Brechin

Defoe described Brechin as an "ancient town with a castle finely situate; but the ancient grandeur of it not supported; the family of Penmure, to whom it belonged, having been in no extraordinary circumstances for some time past, and now their misfortunes being furnished, it is under forfeiture, and sold among the spoils of the late rebellion" (Defoe, Tour, p. 674). In the center of the town stands the fragment of mid-thirteenth-century ecclesiastical architecture known as the Maison Dieu Chapel. The ruins consist of a portion of the south wall of the chapel and a small extent of the east wall. Supposedly, William de Brechin founded this chapel in 1256, and it undoubtedly formed part of a hospital. Also, the town boasts of one of the two remaining round towers of the Irish type in Scotland; the other stands in Abernathy, Perthshire. The structure dates from about 1000, and was afterward attached to the thirteenth-century cathedral in Brechin.

Wesley first preached at Brechin at 1:00 P.M., Friday, 27 May 1763. "All were deeply attentive," he wrote. "Perhaps a few may not be forgetful hearers" (Journal, 5:14). When he returned the next year, on Friday, 1 June 1764, Christopher Hopper and his wife accompanied him. The party was received in the most friendly manner" by a Mr. Blair, a life-long resident of Brechin and a devoted friend of Methodism. In the afternoon, Wesley "preached on the side of a hill near the town, where we soon forgot the cold. I trust there will be not only a knowing but a loving people in this place" (Journal, 5:72). Thus, Brechin became a regular stop on Wesley's visits to County Angus. On Friday, 13 June 1766, he arrived there shortly before noon, afterward "preaching in the flesh-market, on the 'one thing needful.' It being the fair-day, the town was full of strangers, and perhaps some of them were found on Him they sought not" (Journal, 5:170).

Upon his next visit, Monday, 25 April 1768, he was unable to preach, having arrived from Perth late in the evening and finding it necessary to depart early the following morning for Aberdeen. However, after leaving Aberdeen on 1 May, he returned to Brechin at noon of the next day, Monday, the 2nd. "After sermon the provost desired to see me, and said 'Sir, my son had epileptic fits from his infancy:' Dr. Ogilvie prescribed for him many times, and at length told me he could do no more. I desired Mr. Blair last Monday to speak to you. On Tuesday morning, my son said to his mother he had just been dreaming that his fits were gone, and he was perfectly well. Soon after I gave him the drops you advised. He is perfectly well, and has not had one fit since'" (Journal, 5:258). Blair, we have already met, while "Dr. Ogilvie" was the minister of "the next parish" who apparently had considerable experience with epileptic cases (see Journal, 5:72-73).

Wesley came again to Brechin on Wednesday, 29 April 1772, at which time he preached in the town hall "to a congregation of all sorts--Seceders, Glassites, Non-jurors, and what not. Oh what excuse have ministers in Scotland for not declaring the whole counsel of God, where the bulk of the people not only endure, but love, plain dealing?" (Journal, 5:457) The last recorded instance of his work in the town bears the date of Wednesday, 26 May 1790. He arrived at 2:00 P.M. from Laurencekirk and, in the evening, began to preach in the Freeman's Lodge. However, "I was so faint and ill that I was obliged to shorten my

discourse" (Journal, 8:67). Apparently, the illness
was only temporary--and not surprising for a man of
eighty-seven; the next morning, Wesley arose at 3:00,
and by 3:00 was in his chaise and bound for Forfar.

Laurencekirk

The village of Laurencekirk, in Kincardineshire,
owed virtually its existence to the efforts of Francis
Garden, Lord Gardenstone (1721-1793), a Scottish jurist
who, in 1765, commenced the building of a new village
to replace that which had been steadily on the decline.
Lord Gardenstone planned a main street six furlongs in
length (1320 yards, by present definition), with space
on both side for the development of houses. His
Lordship also encouraged the settlement of weavers and
the layout of bleachfields for linen; thus, the
population increased from a mere fifty-four in 1762 to
approximately 500 by 1793. Also, in 1779, Laurencekirk
became a burgh of barony, which gave its citizens the
right to elect a municipal magistrate and four town
councillors (Hamilton, Economic History, p. 34).

Francis Garden also undertook, in Laurencekirk,
the building of a posting inn known as the Boar's Head
(presently labeled the Gardenstone Arms) and erected
and endowed an episcopal chapel, in the vestry of which
he placed a small library. Supposedly, he became so
elated with the inn that he regularly and eagerly read
the visitors' register; however, the managers withdrew
the volume after John Stuart (1751-1827), Professor of
Greek at Marischal College, Aberdeen, wrote the
following lines in it:

Frae sma' beginnings Rome of auld
Became a great imperial city.
'Twas peopled first, as were are tauld,

By bankrupts, vagabonds, banditti.
Quoth Thomas, Then the day may come,
When Laurencekirk shall equal Rome.

(Ramsay, <u>Reminiscences</u>, p. 129)

Adjacent to the north side of the Boar's Head Inn, Lord Gardenstone constructed a square building with a pyramidal roof; this one-room structure housed his larger and well-known library.

Boswell and Johnson came to Laurencekirk on Saturday, 21 August 1773. The former noted that "Lord Gardenstone, one of our judges, collected money to raise a monument to him [Thomas Ruddiman (1674-1757), master of the public school at Laurencekirk from 1695 to 1699] at this place, which I hope will be well executed. I know my father gave five guineas towards it. Lord Gardenstone is the proprietor of Laurence Kirk, and has encouraged the building of a manufacturing village, of which he is exceedingly fond, and has written a pamphlet upon it [<u>Letters to the Inhabitants of Laurencekirk</u>] as if he had founded Thebes; in which, however, there are many useful precepts strongly expressed. The village seemed irregularly built, some of the houses being of clay, some of brick, and some of brick and stone. Dr. Johnson observed they thatched well here" (Boswell, <u>Journal of a Tour</u>, p. 206). When Johnson insisted upon stopping at the Boar's Head, Boswell informed him that Lord Gardenstone had outfitted the place with "a collection of books, that travellers might have entertainment for the mind, as well as the body. He praised the design, but wished there had been more books, and those better chosen" (Boswell, <u>Journal of a Tour</u>, p. 207).

On Wednesday, 26 May 1790, John Wesley spent an

hour in the morning at Laurencekirk. ". . .from an inconsiderable village," he noted, "[it] is, by the care and power of Lord Gardenstoune, soon sprung up into a pleasant, neat, and flourishing town. His lordship has also erected a little library here, adjoining to a handsome and well-furnished inn. The country from hence to Brechin is as pleasant as a garden. Happy would Scotland be, if it had many such gentlemen and noblemen" (Journal, 8:66-67). We can only speculate as to whether, in his journal, Wesley was allowing himself the luxury of a pun ("The country . . .is as pleasant as a garden. . . .")!

Stonehaven

Stonehaven, in Kincardineshire and situated between Laurencekirk and Aberdeen, was, for John Wesley, mainly a place where he might rest temporarily as he traveled up and down the east coast of Scotland. Thus, on Friday, 2 May 1761, he came there from Montrose on his way from Aberdeen. On Monday, 22 May 1786, he arrived in Stonehaven at noon, had dinner, and by 1:15 was back in his chaise, again bound for Aberdeen. Three days later (Thursday, the 25th), he stopped in the town for tea at 6:00 A.M.; after a short walk, he headed his chaise in the direction of Montrose. Four years later, on Thursday, 20 May 1790, Wesley once more followed the same route, reaching Stonehaven at 12:45 P.M., taking some dinner, and then departing (at 1:30) for Aberdeen. On Wednesday, the 26th, he left Aberdeen at 3:30 A.M. and arrived in Stonehaven at 6:00; after the usual tea, he boarded his chaise and drove to Laurencekirk. There appears to be no evidence that Wesley preached in this town, or that a Methodist society existed there.

Bervie

Another of Wesley's Kincardineshire rest-stops, Bervie could claim, at the end of the eighteenth century, some contribution to the development of the Scottish linen industry. In 1790, the firm of Sim and Thom established a small mill in the town and installed a machine for spinning flax. The device, actually the first attempt to mechanize flax spinning, had been invented in 1787 by John Kendrew and Thomas Porthouse and initially installed in 1788 at a small mill near Leeds. In Bervie, the Kendrew and Porthouse machine produced yarn for the manufacture of thread (Hamilton, Economic History, pp. 154-155).

Wesley's maiden visit to Bervie appears to have been on Tuesday, 4 May 1784, as he made his way from Arbroath to Aberdeen. He remained there but an hour, arriving at 10:15 A.M. Almost two weeks later, Monday, the 17th, he reached the town at 9:30 A.M., took tea, and got back into his chaise at 10:30. On Thursday, 25 May 1786, Wesley informs us that he set out early (3:30 A.M.) from Aberdeen; "but when [at 7:00 A.M.] we came to Bervie, the inn was full; there was no room for man or beast, so we were constrained to go a double stage, to Montrose" (Journal, 7:164). Finally, on Thursday, 20 May 1790, after leaving Montrose at 6:30 A.M., he arrived in Bervie at 10:30; an hour later, he left for Stonehaven.

Newburgh

Lying fifteen miles north of Aberdeen, Newburgh, in the eighteenth century, was simply a small fishing village. However, John Wesley and his preachers must have labored effectively there, for the leader of the Methodists claimed, on 7 June 1782, that "the society swiftly increases. And not only men and women, but a considerable number of children, are either rejoicing in God or panting after Him" (Journal, 6:357). Wesley went there again on Sunday morning, 16 May 1784, noting that "Here is at present, according to its bigness, the liveliest society in the kingdom. I preached [on Matthew 22:4] here in a kind of Square, to a multitude of people; and the whole congregation appeared to be moved, and ready prepared for the Lord" (Journal, 6:508).

Essentially, Newburgh existed as one of the many small Scottish villages in which, as early as 1740, Methodist societies were founded, and then proceeded to prosper. Unfortunately, such villages could not always sustain their enthusiasm for Methodism, primarily because of Wesley's refusal to assign them permanent ministers and secondarily because of the clashes with Scottish prejudices. Thus, Scots were far from tolerant toward the steady stream of lay and itinerant preachers who came their way. In spite of Wesley's optimistic reflections, the size of Newburgh society was never really significant, although those who did belong held on with remarkable vigor and vitality. Yet, the village itself was but a poor fishing community--so poor that in the last decade of the eighteenth century, collections were taken in England on behalf of its inhabitants. One, an old woman known only as "Blind Meggy," lived alone in a single room; daily, she ventured forth to a neighbor, who would read to her a chapter from Scriptures. The old lady would then return to her home and meditate upon the words she had heard. On preaching day, she went round the village, ringing a large bell; then, she took her place in the chapel and raised the tunes (see Journal,

6:507-508, note 2).

     The Methodist chapel in Newburgh was merely a humble, thatched building, originally a small brewhouse. In fact, the widow of the brewer--himself a Methodist--had presented the brewhouse to the society upon her husband's death. Supposedly, the room was so small that the preacher could shake hands with those of the congregation seated in the front gallery! For his own quarters, the preacher had to make do with a small, thatched, single room, with a mud floor, situated next to the chapel. No doubt, the circumstances within Newburgh represented well the conditions under which Methodism functioned in the small towns and villages of Scotland during the mid and late eighteenth century (see Journal, 6:507-508, note 2).

Old Meldrum

     John Wesley first came to the small town of Old Meldrum, lying due west of Newburgh, on Friday morning, 8 June 1764. Here, he preached in the market-place at noon to "a large and serious congregation, among whom were the minister [of the kirk] and his wife. But I was more surprised to see a company of our friends from Aberdeen, several of whom had come on foot, twelve old Scotch miles, and intended to walk back thither the same day" (Journal, 5:74). Twelve years later he returned, preaching at 11:00 on Monday morning, 20 May 1776. Wesley's next visit to Old Meldrum came about on Thursday, 6 May 1784; upon his arrival at 10:00 A.M., he was met by a servant of Lady Banff's, who desired him to proceed immediately to Forglen House (see below, this chapter, under Forglen House). Finally, he visited the town on two occasions in May 1790--first, on Monday, the 24th, at 7:00 A.M., on his way from

Aberdeen to Forglen; then, the next day, taking tea
between 8:00 and 8:45 A.M., as he made the return trip
back to Aberdeen.

Monymusk

The estate of Sir Archibald Grant (1696-1778) at
Monymusk, Aberdeenshire, situated some twenty miles
northwest of Aberdeen, serves as a prime example of the
extent to which certain landowners in eighteenth-
century Scotland developed and improved their holdings.
In 1713, Sir Francis Grant purchased the estate from
the bankrupt Sir William Forbes; upon young Archibald's
marriage to Ann Hamilton of Pencaitland, Sir Francis
passed the estate on to his son. Immediately, the
latter began upon a life-long project of improving an
area known widely for its barrenness and poverty: "Not
one acre of arable estate enclosed nor any timber upon
it but a few elms, sycamore, and ash" (see Hamilton,
Economic History, p. 62). Thus, Sir Archibald set to
raising trees from seeds and from plants sent from
London and Holland: firs, alders, oaks, and elms.
Near the River Don, he planted the famous Paradise
Woods, and by 1754, estimated the extent of the
Monymusk plantations at two million trees (Hamilton,
Economic History, p. 66). According to the Reverend
William D. Macpherson, in his Church and Priory of
Monymusk, Lord Grant planted a total of forty-eight
million trees throughout his estate (see Wesley
Journal, 4:451, note 1).

By 1774, the property at Monymusk extended to
10,743 acres--a modest size by eighteenth-century
standards. The residence house--again in terms of the
standards of the period--was also considered modest,
the central portion built on the traditional "L" plan,

with wings added at different times between 1713 and Grant's death in 1778. When Sir Archibald received the estate from his father, the residence proved to be in a general state of disrepair--"six different roofs of various heights and directions, confusedly and inconveniently combined, and all rotten" (Hamilton, Economic History, p. 46). However, by 1731, the landowner had managed to improve conditions considerably; he could claim a house that consisted of a drawing-room, dining-room, six main bedrooms, a maid's room, servants' room, kitchen, brew-house, laundry, dairy, and cellar--the last four being out-buildings (Hamilton, Economic History, p. 46).

Sometime during the first week of May 1761, John Wesley received an invitation from Sir Archibald Grant, and on Thursday, the 7th, the leader of the Methodists rode from Aberdeen to Monymusk. "It lies in a fruitful and pleasant valley," he observed, "much of which is owing to Sir Archibald's improvements, who has ploughed up abundance of waste ground and planted some millions of trees. His stately old house is surrounded by gardens and rows of trees, with a clear river on one side. And about a mile from his house he had laid out a small valley into walks and gardens [Paradise Woods], on one side of which the river runs. On each side rises a steep mountain, one rocky and bare, the other covered with trees, row above row, to the very top" (Journal, 4:451-452). At six that evening he went to the church at Monymusk, noticing that it was crowded "with such persons as we did not look for so near the Highlands. But if we were surprised at their appearance, we were much more so at their singing. Thirty or forty sung an anthem after sermon, with such voices as well as judgement that I doubt whether they could have been excelled at any cathedral in England" (Journal, 4:452).

On Thursday, 7 June 1764, Wesley paid a second visit to Monymusk, which he recorded as lying "twelve computed miles from Aberdeen." By the term "computed miles" he was referring, of course, to the estimated distance, which always proved to be considerably less than the more precise measured miles. At any rate, he expressed surprise at seeing "how the country between [Monymusk and Aberdeen] is improved even within these three years. On every side, the wild, dreary moors are ploughed up, and covered with rising corn. All the ground near Sir Archibald's, in particular, is well cultivated as most in England." Little wonder that this should have been so, far Grant brought farming experts from England to teach his tenants the best of English agricultural methods. Wesley reached Monymusk by late afternoon, and at 7:00 P.M. delivered a sermon there. "The kirk was pretty well filled, though upon short notice. Certainly, this is a nation 'swift to hear and slow to speak,' though not 'slow to wrath'" (Journal, 5:74).

Two years later, on Tuesday, 10 June 1766, he again journeyed from Aberdeen to Sir Archibald Grant's estate. "The church was pretty well filled, and I spoke exceeding plain; yet the hearers did not appear to be any more affected than the stone walls" (Journal, 5:169-170). The next day, he returned to Aberdeen.

Inverurie

Inverurie, in Aberdeenshire, lies but a few miles southwest of Old Meldrum. On Wednesday, 22 May 1776, John Wesley rode southeast from Keith, remarking that the wind "turning north, we stepped at once from June

to January." Arriving in Inverurie at about 1:00 P.M.,
he preached in the town to "a plain, earnest, loving
people," and then pushed on for Aberdeen (Journal,
6:108). Three years later he came again, this time
arriving at 8:00 A.M., Friday, 4 June 1779, and then
preaching to a "considerable number of plain country
people, just like those we see at Yorkshire. My spirit
was much refreshed among them, observing several of
them in tears" (Journal, 6:236). After circling around
to Keith, Nairn, and Inverness, Wesley returned to
Inverurie on Saturday, 12 June, and preached at 1:00
P.M., to "a larger congregation than before, and was
again refreshed with the simplicity and earnestness of
the plain country people" (Journal, 6:239).

Huntly

Huntly, in Aberdeenshire, is situated in a small
vale of the River Bogie, and thus, prior to 1727, was
known as Strathbogie. In that year two old parishes
joined as one under the present name, in compliment to
Alexander Gordon (1678-1728), fifth Marquis of Huntly
and second Duke of Gordon. By the end of the
eighteenth century, according to the parish minister,
Huntly had "surprisingly increased. . .in population
and industry, insomuch that, when all around it, for
some distance, was formerly barren heath, swamps, or
marsh, there is now scarcely one uncultivated spot to
be seen" (see Hamilton, Economic History, p. 30).

In Huntly stands the remains of the old
Strathbogie Castle, one of the noblest baronial ruins
in Scotland, that at one time served as the seat of the
Gordon family. During most of the sixteenth and
seventeenth centuries, the Earls and Marquises of
Huntly stood as powerful supporters of the Catholic

cause in the counter-Reformation struggle. Thus, their castle was much involved in the various religious wars, and repeatedly underwent dismantling and reconstruction. Even when viewed in the present century, the heraldic enrichments of this structure appear as the most elaborate in Scotland; also, Huntly castle stands in a beautifully timbered park beside the rocky gorge of the Deveron.

John Wesley first rode into Huntly (which he preferred to identify by its former name of Strathbogie) on Tuesday, 12 June 1764, and noticed immediately that the town was "much improved by the linen-manufacture." He was traveling southeast from Keith, and observed that "All the country from Fochabers to Strathbogie has little houses scattered up and down; and not only the valleys, but the mountains themselves, are improved with the utmost care. There want only more trees to make them more pleasant than most of the mountains in England." Remaining overnight at an inn in Huntly, Wesley invited all the guests, "eleven or twelve in number," to join with him in prayer. "Indeed, so they did at every inn where we lodged [between Elgin and Aberdeen]; for, among all the sins they have imported from England, the Scots have not yet learned, at least not the common people, to scoff at sacred things" (Journal, 5:76-77).

Wesley next passed through Huntly on Friday, 4 June 1779, on his way from Inverness to Keith. No doubt he would have remained longer than he did were it not for the illness and fatigue of his traveling companion, Robert Carr Brackenbury. ". . .I desired him to go into the chaise, and rode forward to Keith" (Journal, 6:239). However, he returned to the town one week later, Friday, the 11th. "Here we were in a clean, convenient house, and had everything we wanted. All the family very willingly joined us in prayer. We then slept in peace" (Journal, 6:239).

Keith

Prior to the middle of the eighteenth century, Keith, in Banffshire, had all the appearances of a town in ruin and without promise of a future. However, in about 1750, James Ogilvy, sixth Earl of Findlater (1714-1770), perhaps the largest landholder in the county, developed and leased small lots located upon moorland above the River Isla and to the southeast of Keith. By 1793, the parish minister could describe Ogilvy's project as a development set out "according to a regular plan on which there now stands a large, regular, and tolerably thriving village, called New Keith." By the century's end, the new village could claim approximately 1075 inhabitants, the majority of whom were employed in the manufacture of linen. Earlier, Lord Findlater had amalgamated the old village and the fast-growing New Keith (Hamilton, Economic History, p. 34).

In a related development, undertaken soon after the planning of New Keith, James Duff, Earl of Fife, laid out a village on his land, on the north side of the Isla, and named it New Town of New Mill, to distinguish it from a nearby village already known as New Mill (see below). By 1793, New Town of New Mill (later to be known at Fife-Keith) held in excess of 330 persons; only in the nineteenth century, with the arrival of the railway, did the place become anything other than a small village. Nevertheless, from these two planned settlements--Old and New Keith on the right bank of the river and Fife-keith on the left--the present agricultural town of Keith developed (Hamilton, Economic History, p. 34).

On Tuesday, 12 June 1764, John Wesley, on his way from Elgin to Aberdeen, dined at Keith before moving on and taking lodging for the night at Huntly. When next he came to the town--this time on his way from Inverness to Aberdeen, Monday, 30 May 1770--he determined to stay at an inn that appeared dark and dirty, from the outside at least, "and promised us no great things. But we were agreeably disappointed. We found plenty of everything, and so dried ourselves at leisure" (Journal, 5:365). The wetness had resulted from a combination of rain and a rough crossing of the River Spey (see below). The next morning, he arose and rode on to Aberdeen.

As Wesley rode from Banff to Keith in mid-morning on Tuesday, 21 May 1776, he was impressed by the country between the two towns, labeling it "the best peopled of any I have seen in Scotland. This is chiefly, if not entirely, owing to the late Earl of Findlater. He was indefatigable in doing good, took pains to procure industrious men from all parts, and to provide such little settlements for them as enabled them to live with comfort" (Journal, 6:107). The day must have been excessively uncomfortable for late May in northern Scotland, and as Wesley rode south in the afternoon, "the heat overcame me, so that I was weary and faint before we came to Keith; but I no sooner stood up in the market-place than I forgot my weariness; such were the seriousness and attention of the whole congregation, though. . .numerous. . . ." Reverend Gordon, minister of the parish, invited him to supper and offered the hospitality of the kirk. Then, for the fist time since he had set foot north of the

Tweed, John Wesley found himself the owner of a piece of Scottish real estate. Apparently, a small Methodist society had formed in Keith; although it evidenced signs of increasing its numbers, there was danger that the owner of the preaching-house rented by the society would soon evict his tenants and then sell the building. "I saw but one way to secure it for them," reports Wesley, "which was to buy it myself. So (who would have though it?) I bought an estate, consisting of two houses, a yard, a garden, with three acres of good land. But he [the owner] told me flat, 'Sir, I will take no less for it than sixteen pounds ten shillings [presumably Scottish], to be paid, part now, part at Michaelmas, and the residue next May" (Journal, 6:108).

Also, on this busy day of 21 May, Reverend Gordon guided Wesley through the New Town of New Mill, which the latter termed "a great curiosity." he saw "a new town. . .containing, I suppose, a hundred houses, which is a town of beggars. This. . .was the professed, regular occupation of all the inhabitants. Early in spring, they all go out, and spread themselves all over the kingdom, and in autumn they return and do what is requisite for their wives and children" (Journal, 6:108). After the Earl of Fife had laid out and developed the New Town of New Mill, it became populated mainly by poor people who fixed their homes there essentially for the convenience of the land and the moss. According to one source, the town became a colony of paupers from various districts of the Highlands, "who, being indigent and supported by begging, or their own alertness, are allured there by the abundance of moss. During the summer months the poor, who are extremely numerous, range this and neighbouring parishes, and are a great encroachment upon what is truly the property of the native poor" (see Proceedings of the Wesley Historical Society, 4 [1904], 214, and 9 [1909], 155).

Wesley's next visit to Keith occurred on Saturday, 5 June 1779, at which time he again enjoyed the hospitality of Reverend Gordon, who invited him to his house for tea. That evening, Wesley went to the market-place, where four children, "after they had stood a while to consider, ventured to come near me; then a few men and women crept forward; till we had upwards of a hundred." At 9:00 the following morning, he addressed a crowd estimated at two hundred, and some of them seemed a little affected." After dinner with Reverend Gordon--"who behaved in the most courteous, yea, and affectionate manner"--he preached, at 3:00 P.M., in the parish kirk, "one of the largest I have seen in the kingdom, but very ruinous. It was thoroughly filled, and God was there in an uncommon manner. He sent forth His voice, yea, and that a mighty voice; so that I believe many of the stout-hearted trembled." Finally, in the evening, Wesley returned to the market-place and preached "on those awful words, 'Where their worm dieth not, and the fire is not quenched'" (Journal, 6:236-237). The next morning he departed for Grange Green, fully expecting to pass again through Keith on Friday, 11 June; however, he did not stop, but moved on directly to Huntly.

On Friday, 7 June 1782, while at Aberdeen, Wesley received, in his words, "a pleasing account of the work of God in the north. The flame begins to kindle even at poor, dull Keith. . ." (Journal, 6:357). Nevertheless, he did not actually visit the town during

the five or six days that he spent in and around
Aberdeenshire. Not until Friday, 7 May 1784, did
Wesley make his next and final visit to Keith, arriving
from Forglen at 6:15 P.M. "But I know not how we could
have got thither," he complained, "had not Lady Banff
sent me forward, through that miserable road, with four
stout horses" (Journal, 6:503). In the evening he
preached on Hebrews 9:27 and spoke to the Methodist
society; before leaving the next morning for Elgin, he
again preached (at 5:00 A.M.), this time on Acts 16:31.

Newmill

On Tuesday, 21 May 1776, Wesley preached at noon
in Newmill, "nine miles from Banff, to a large
congregation of plain, simple people" (Journal, 6:108).
This village is not to be confused with the Earl of
Fife's development near Keith, the New town of New Mill
(see directly above, under Keith); in fact, Lord Fife
had named his village as he did specifically to avoid
any confusion.

Banff

Even before the Union and the industrial
development of Scotland during the mid and late
eighteenth century, the small town of Banff, sixty
miles northwest of Aberdeen, was known as an important
seaport. From mid-century, ships trading with the
towns along the Moray Firth, and even from London,
docked there, while outging vessels transported salmon,
butter, cheese, meal, barley, oats, and cod. Incoming
vessels brought such goods as coal, flour, bricks,
tiles, spirits, wine, and the all-important salt,
suggesting bustling trade activity and a high standard
of living. Wesley described Banff as "one of the

neatest and most elegant towns that I have seen in
Scotland. It is pleasantly situated on the side of a
hill, sloping from the [North] sea, though close to it;
so that it is sheltered form the sharpest winds. The
streets are straight and broad. I believe it may be
esteemed the fifth, if not the fourth, town in the
kingdom" (Journal, 6:107).

Samuel Johnson arrived in Banff three years before
Wesley set down the description cited above, on the
evening of Wednesday, 25 August 1773. He remembered
"nothing that particularly claimed my attention. The
ancient towns of Scotland have generally an appearance
unusual to Englishmen. The houses, whether great or
small, are for the most part built of stones. Their
ends are now and then next the streets, and the
entrance into them is very often by a flight of steps,
which reaches up to the second story, the floor which
is level with the ground being entered only by stairs
descending within the house" (Journey to the Western
Islands, p. 19).

On Friday afternoon, 8 June 1764, John Wesley rode
from Old Meldrum to Banff, where he was scheduled to
deliver a sermon. However, "the stormy weather would
not permit" (Journal, 5:74), so he remained overnight
and set out for Nairn the next morning. Twelve years
later, on Monday, 20 May 1776, although he did not
reach the town until almost 7:00 P.M., Wesley went
"directly to the Parade, and proclaimed to a listening
multitude 'the grace of our Lord Jesus Christ.' All
behaved well but a few gentry, whom I rebuked openly;
and they stood corrected" (Journal, 6:107). Methodism
in Banff had begun early in 1775, when one of Wesley's
itinerants, Thomas Rutherford, journeyed there from
Keith. According to one source, the Parade to which

John Wesley referred also bore the name of <u>Battery Green</u>, and functioned as a regular outdoor preaching site. In addition, a house at the foot of Strait Park announces, by way of an inscription on the front, that Wesley lodged therein on his visits to Banff. At the north end of Strait Park, the Methodist society held its services, in a hall which, by the beginning of the present century, formed the upper story of a business establishment (see the <u>Methodist Recorder</u>, 25 August 1904).

After this sermon, Wesley accepted an invitation for supper at the home of a Mrs. Gordon, where he met "five or six as agreeable women as I have seen in the kingdom; and I know not when I have spent two or three hours with greater satisfaction." The following morning, Tuesday, 22 May, he prepared to preach at the Methodist meeting-house; however, the Episcopal minister at Banff offered him the use of his chapel. "It was quickly filled. After reading prayers, I preached on those words in the Second Lesson, 'What lack I yet?' and strongly applied them to those in particular who supposed themselves to be 'rich and increased in goods, and lacked nothing'" (<u>Journal</u>, 6:107). Of significance, at this juncture, is a letter dated 1 January 1777, from William and Isobel McPherson, members of the Banff Methodist society, to Robert Dall, one of Wesley's itinerant preachers serving Banffshire:

The society has been stationary ever since you left us. We are often neglected. Lately we had only one visit [from a Methodist preacher] in eight weeks. Mr. Wesley was here on the 20th May last, and preached on the Parade from 2 Cor viii. 9. He supped at

Lord Banff's and next night at Admiral
Gordon's Lady's house, with a great number of
great ones; and, at their request, he
preached in the English chapel to an elegant
and crowded congregation.

(Tyerman, Life of Wesley, 3:225)

Despite the appeal set forth in the above letter,
Wesley did not find the time to come again to Banff
until Friday, 14 May 1784. After arriving from Elgin
at 1:15 P.M., he read prayers and preached (on Romans
13:10) in the Episcopal chapel; by 3:30 he was back in
his chaise, bound for Forglen. He still believed Banff
to be "one of the neatest towns in the kingdom"
(Journal, 6:506).

Forglen House

Forglen House, a fifteenth-century dwelling, stood
on the bank of the Deveron River and served as the seat
of the Earls of Banff--a baronetey created in the
seventeenth century. John Wesley first came there on
Thursday, 6 May 1784; after an early stop at Old
Meldrum, he was met by a servant of Lady Banff, who
conveyed her mistress's request that he proceed
directly to Forglen. "In two hours [at 12:00 noon] we
reached an inn, which, the servant told us, was four
little [or Scottish] miles from her house. So we made
the best of our way, and got thither in exactly three
hours. All the family received us with the most
cordial affection. At seven I preached [on Proverbs
3:17] to a small congregation, all of whom were
seriously attentive, and some, I believe, deeply
affected" (Journal, 6:503). Mistress of Forglen House
at that time was Jean Ogilvy--nee Nisbet and originally
of Dirleton, Haddingtonshire--who, on 2 April 1749,

married Sir Alexander Ogilvy, seventh Lord Banff. She had been a widow since 1771.

The next day, Friday, 7 May, Wesley strolled about the grounds of Forglen House. "I know not when I have seen so pleasant a place," he commented. "One part of the house is an ancient castle, situated on the top of a little hill. At a small distance runs a clear river, with a beautiful wood on its banks. Close to it is a shady walk to the right, and another on the left hand. On two sides of the house there is abundance of wood; on the other, a wide prospect over fields and meadows." Later that morning, (the journal entry states 10:00, but the diary indicates noon) he preached "with much liberty of spirit on 'Love never faileth' [1 Corinthians 13:8]"; at 2:00 P.M., he departed for Keith, noting that "I know not how we could have got thither had not Lady Banff sent me forward, through that miserable road, with four stout horses" (Journal, 6:503).

A week later, Friday, 14 May, Wesley returned to Forglen House, arriving at 5:30 P.M., in time for tea. At seven he preached (on Job 22:21) in Lady Banff's dining room "to a very serious though genteel congregation; and afterwards spent a most agreeable evening with the lovely family" (Journal, 6:507). Wesley's final opportunity to partake of Lady Banff's hospitality occurred on Monday, 24 May 1790. After leaving Aberdeen at 4:00 A.M., he reached Forglen House at 11:15 A.M. "The face of the country is much changed for the better since I was here before. Agriculture increases on every side; so do manufactories, industry, and cleanliness." Unfortunately, he found Lady Banff "exceedingly ill; and I doubt whether she will be much better till she removes to her own country." Still,

Wesley spent "a very agreeable afternoon with the
lovely family, and preached [on Proverbs 3:17; see
above, 6 May 1784] to a serious congregation in the
evening [at 6:00]" (Journal, 8:66). The next morning
he returned to Aberdeen.

River Spey
     A rapid and generally unnavigable river, the Spey
flows approximately 110 miles northeast, from the
Inverness-shire highlands to Moray Firth. John Wesley
came to the Spey on at least three occasions during his
travels throughout Scotland, the first being on
Tuesday, 12 June 1764. He rode east from Elgin, in
Moray, and gazed upon "the most rapid river, next the
Rhine, that I ever saw. Though the water was not
breast-high to our horses, they could very hardly keep
their feet" (Journal, 5:76). It had only been a short
eighteen years since, in April 1746, William, Duke of
Cumberland, had marched his 8000 well fed and rested
regulars--with their eighteen pieces of artillery--
north from Aberdeen, across this torrent of the Spey
River, and on to the field at Culloden.
     Six years after his initial plunge, on Monday, 30
May 1770, Wesley again set out from Elgin, this time
riding through a driving rainstorm until he reached the
Spey, "the most impetuous river I ever saw. Finding
the large boat was in no haste to move, I stepped into
a small one, just going off. It whirled us over the
stream almost in a minute" (Journal, 6:365). Finally,
on Saturday morning, 8 May 1784, this time riding west,
from Keith toward Elgin, Wesley came to the bank of the
River Spey. "I suppose," he mused, "there are few such
rivers in Europe. The rapidity of it exceeds even that
of the Rhine; and it was now much swelled with melting

snow. However, we made shift to get over before ten, and about twelve reached Elgin" (<u>Journal</u>, 6:502-503).

Grange Green

Grange Green, near Forres, was the seat of Sir Lodovick Grant (d. 1790), fourth Baronet Grant. His grandfather, Sir James Grant, had been created the first baronet back in 1688, primarily as a reward for having served in the office of King's Advocate. The line extends, originally, from the Dalvey family, and thus is not to be confused with the Grants of <u>Monymusk</u> (see above). John Wesley knew not only Sir Lodovick, but his older brother, Sir Alexander, third Baronet Grant, who died in 1779.

"I have seldom seen a more agreeable place," exclaimed Wesley, when he visited Grange Green on Monday, 11 June 1764. "The house is an old castle which stands on a little hill, with a delightful prospect all four ways; and the hospitable master [Sir Alexander Grant] has left nothing undone to make it still more agreeable. He showed us all his improvements, which are very considerable in every branch of husbandry. In his gardens many things were more forward than at Aberdeen, yea, or Newcastle. And how is it that none but one Highland gentleman has discovered that we have a tree in Britain as easily raised as an ash, the wood of which is of full as fine a red as mahogany?--namely, the laburnum. I defy any mahogany to exceed the chairs of which he [Lord Grant] has lately made of this" (<u>Journal</u>, 5:76). The laburnum (<u>Laburnum amagyroides</u>), a small ornamental tree native to Europe, has sprays of yellow flowers in spring. The major furniture designers in Britain during the eighteenth century--Thomas Chippendale, Robert Adam,

George Hepplewhite, and Thomas Sheraton--preferred to work with walnut, oak, beechwood, or mahogany.

Fifteen years later, on Monday, 7 June 1779, Wesley came again to Grange Green, arriving at about noon and discovering "the house had changed its master since I was here before [probably May 1770]. . . . Mr. Grant (who then lived here in his brother's house) was now Sir Lodovick Grant; having succeeded to the title and estate of Sir Alexander, dying without issue. But his mind was not changed with his fortune. He received me with cordial affection, and insisted on my sending for Mrs. Smith and her little girl, whom I had left at Forres. We were all here as at home, in one of the most healthy and most pleasant situations in the kingdom; and I had the satisfaction to observe my daughter sensibly recovering her strength almost every hour. In the evening all the family were called in to prayers; to whom I first expounded a portion of Scripture. Thus ended this comfortable day. So had God provided for us in a strange land!" (Journal, 6:237).

Accompanying Wesley on this particular journey into Scotland were his step-daughter, Jane Vazeille Smith, and her younger daughter Jane. The former had married Wesley's friend, William Smith of Newcastle-upon-Tyne; because of her weak health, she made the trip with her daughter, in a chaise provided by her step-father. Of the two daughters of Jane and William Smith, the elder, Mary, later married John Stamp, one of John Wesley's preachers, who began his ministry in 1787. Jane, the younger daughter referred to above, married Christopher Sundius, a Swede who served in the British navy during the American Revolutionary War and later converted to Methodism. He eventually became one of the founders of the British and Foreign Bible Society (see Wesleyan Methodist Magazine, 83 [1904], 215).

Wesley spent two days with the Grants in May 1784, arriving at 5:00 P.M. on Saturday, the 8th. He found Sir Lodovick Grant "almost worn out. Never was a visit more seasonable. By free and friendly conversation his spirits were so raised that I am in hopes it will lengthen his life" (Journal, 6:504). For whatever reasons, Lord Grant managed to continue his tenure on earth until September 1790. The next day (9 May), Wesley preached at Grange Green to "a small company at noon on 'His commandments are not grievous [1 John 5:3].' As I was concluding Colonel Grant and his lady came in, for whose sake I began again, and lectured, as they call it, on the former part of the fifteenth chapter of St. Luke [15:7]. We had a large company in the afternoon [4:30], to whom I preached on 'judgement to come [Revelation 20:12].' And this subject seemed to affect them most" (Journal, 6:504). By 9:00 A.M. the following day, Wesley was off for Nairn and Inverness.

Fochabers

Samuel Johnson and James Boswell passed through Fochabers, in Moray, on Thursday, 26 August 1773, the latter noticing that the village was "a poor place, many of the houses being ruinous; but it is remarkable, they have in general orchards well stored with apple-trees" (Boswell, Tour to the Hebrides, p. 232). Wesley passed through the town first on Tuesday, 12 June 1764, on his way from Elgin to Aberdeen, observing, mainly, the surrounding countryside (see above, this chapter, under Huntly). Six years later, on 30 April 1770, he

came there again after a rough crossing of the River
Spey. "I waited at the inn at Fochabers (dark and
dirty enough in all reason), till our friends overtook
me with horses" (Journal, 5:365). He immediately rode
on for Keith.

Gordon Castle

North of Fochabers lay Gordon Castle, the seat of
Alexander, fourth Duke of Gordon (1745-1827), and his
wife, Jane Maxwell (1749-1812). The front of the
castle stretched approximately 560 feet in length, the
main body of the building being four stories high.
Surrounding the house was a park of some 13,000 acres.
Boswell thought the place had a "princely appearance"
(Tour to the Hebrides, p. 232), while Johnson
identified "an orchard, which in Scotland I had never
seen before, with some timber trees, and a plantation
of oaks" (Journey to the Western Islands, p. 22).

John Wesley, riding toward Banff on Friday
morning, 14 May 1784, "saw, at a distance, the Duke of
Gordon's new house, six hundred and fifty feet in
front. Well might the Indian ask, 'Are you white men
no bigger than we red men? Then why do you build such
lofty houses?'" (Journal, 6:506). The origin of the
quotation dates back to Wesley's mission to Georgia,
when, on Saturday, 3 July 1736, he dined with James
Oglethorpe and Chicali, leader of the Choctaws. "After
dinner, I asked the grey-headed old man [Chicali] what
he though he was made for. He said, 'He that is above
knows what He made us for. We know nothing. We are in
the dark. But white men know much. And yet white men
build great houses, as if they were to live for ever.
But white men cannot live for ever. In a little time
white men will be dust as well as I'" (Journal, 1:239).

Elgin

While in Elgin, Daniel Defoe observed "a great many rich inhabitants. . .for the gentlemen, as if this was the Edinburgh, or the court, for this part of the island, leave their Highland habitations in the winter and come and live here for the diversion of the place and plenty of provisions; and there is, on this account, a great variety of gentlemen for society, and that of all parties and of all opinions. This makes Elgin a very agreeable place to live in, not withstanding its distance, being above 450 measured miles from London, and more, if we must go by Edinburgh" (Defoe, _Tour_, p. 659). To Samuel Johnson, Elgin seemed "a place of little trade, and thinly inhabited. The episcopal cities of Scotland, I believe, generally fell with their churches. . . ." As he walked down the High Street, his discriminating eye beheld "the houses [that] jut over the lowest story, like the old buildings of timber in London, but with greater prominence; so that there is sometimes a walk for a considerable length under a cloister, or portico, which is now indeed frequently broken, because the new houses have another form, but seems to have been uniformly continued in the old city" (Johnson, _Journey to the Western Islands_, p. 21).

The chief attraction of the town, Elgin Cathedral, stood as perhaps the grandest of all Scottish churches. All that remains today, however, consists of a nave with double aisles and north and south porches; twin western towers with a fine portal window between; transepts, above which, at one time, rose a great central tower; the choir, with aisles and presbytery; and a detached octagonal chapter-house. Founded in 1224, the Cathedral was built along the high and rich

style of the thirteenth century; in 1390, it suffered
extensively from fire, and considerable reconstruction
followed almost immediately--including work on the
chapter-house, completed sometime during the fifteenth
century. Directly opposite Elgin Cathedral stands a
small remnant of the townhouse of the Bishops of Moray.
Coats of arms on the building include those of Bishop
Patrick Hepburn (1535-1573) and Robert Reid, Abbot of
Kinross and Bishop of Orkney (1541-1548).

"The ruins of the cathedral of Elgin," commented
Samuel Johnson, "afforded us another proof of the waste
of reformation. There is enough yet remaining to show,
that it was once magnificent. Its whole plot is easily
traced. On the north side of the choir, the chapter-
house, which is roofed with an arch of stone, remains
entire; and on the south side, another mass of
building, which we could not enter, is preserved by the
care of the family of Gordon; but the body of the
church is a mass of fragments." Johnson then outlined
the history of the structure, lamenting that during
"the intestine tumults of the barbarous ages," Elgin
Cathedral had "been laid waste by the irruption of a
highland chief [the so-called "Wolf of Badenoch"], whom
the bishop had offended; but it was gradually restored
to the state, of which the traces may be now discerned,
and was at last not destroyed by the tumultuous
violence of Knox, but more shamefully suffered to
dilapidate by deliberate robbery and frigid
indifference." Nevertheless, he urged his English
readers not to "make much haste to despise our
neighbours. Our own cathedrals are mouldering by
unregarded dilapidation. It seems to be part of the
despicable philosophy of the time to despise monuments
of sacred magnificence, and we are in danger of doing

that deliberately, which the Scots did not do but in the unsettled state of an imperfect constitution" (Johnson, Journey to the Western Islands, pp. 20-21).

When John Wesley first came to Elgin on Tuesday, 12 June 1764, he set his eyes upon "the ruins of a noble cathedral, the largest that I remember to have seen in the kingdom" (Journal, 5:76). However, he lingered there only briefly before crossing the River Spey and moving on to Keith and Huntly. Six years later, on Monday, 30 April 1770, he came by the same route, passing through Elgin on his way from Nairn to Keith and then to Aberdeen. On Saturday, 8 May 1784, Wesley arrived in the old cathedral town at noon and remained for approximately two hours. "Here I was received by a daughter of good [Reverend] Mr. Plenderleith, late of Edinburgh, with whom having spent an agreeable hour [1:00-2:00 P.M.], I hastened towards Forres" (Journal, 6:504).

Four days later, he came back. "A church being offered me at Elgin, in the evening [6:00] I had a multitude of hearers, whom I strongly exhorted [from Isaiah 55:6] to 'seek the Lord while He may be found.'" The following day, Thursday, 13 May, he viewed the "poor remains of the once-magnificent cathedral. By what ruins are left, the workmanship appears to have been exquisitely fine. What barbarians must they have been who hastened the destruction of this beautiful pile by taking off the lead of the roof!" He has reference to the removal of the lead in February 1568, by order of the Privy Council of Scotland, to pay the soldiers. Unfortunately, the vessel carrying the weighty material sank before it reached its destination in Holland. At 6:00 that evening, Wesley preached in Elgin on Matthew 16:26: "The church was again well filled. . .by those who seemed to feel much more than the night before. In consequence, the morning [Friday, 14 May, at 5:00] congregation was more than doubled; and deep attention sat on every face. I do not despair of good being done even here, provided the preachers be 'sons of thunder'" (Journal, 6:506).

Dalwhinnie, Dalmigavie

On Wednesday evening, 25 April 1770, Wesley--on his way from Scone to Inverness--came to Dalwhinnie, "the dearest inn I have met with in North Britain. In the morning [26 April] we were informed so much snow had fallen in the night that we could get no farther. And, indeed, three young women, attempting to cross the mountain in Blair, were swallowed up in the snow. However, we resolved, with God's help, to go as far as we could. But about noon we were at a full stop; the snow, driving together on the top of the mountain, had quite blocked up the road. We dismounted, and striking out of the road warily, sometimes to the left, sometimes to the right, with many stumbles, but no hurt, we got on to Dalmigavie, and before sunset to Inverness" (Journal, 5:363-364).

Inverness

When Daniel Defoe came upon Inverness early in the eighteenth century, he described it as "a pleasant, clean, and well built town. There are some merchants in it, and some good share of trade. It consists of two parishes, and two large, handsome streets, but no public buildings of any note, except. . .the old castle and the bridge" (Defoe, Tour, p. 662). Inverness Castle had been built either by Malcolm or David I, blown up in 1746 by Charles Edward (the Young

Pretender), and eventually razed in 1834. The common tendency is to confuse this site with that of Macbeth's castle, which was actually destroyed in the eleventh century by Malcolm Canmore, the son and avenger of Duncan.

Johnson and Boswell arrived in Inverness on Saturday, 27 August 1773. On the following day, they toured what Johnson identified as "the castle of Macbeth, the walls of which are yet standing. It was no very capacious edifice, but stands upon a rock so high and steep, that I think it was once not accessible, but by the help of ladders, or a bridge. Over against it, on another hill, was a fort built by Cromwell, now totally demolished; for no faction of Scotland loved the name of Cromwell, or had any desire to continue his memory" (Johnson, Journey to the Western Islands, p. 23). Situated on the right bank of the River Ness, downstream from the town, Cromwell fort had been destroyed during the Restoration, although the site remains visible even to this day. Johnson also made reference to "a kirk, in which only the Erse language is used. There is likewise an English chapel, but meanly built, where. . .we saw a very decent congregation" (Johnson, Journey to the Western Islands, p. 24).

Actually, the condition of the chapel had resulted from its having been a place of worship for a non-juring congregation of the Episcopal Church in Scotland. It was really a room in a house on Baron Taylor's Lane, owned by the widow of the Reverend John Stewart (d. 1770), a priest of the Episcopal Church in Scotland. Upon Mr. Stewart's death, William Falconer, Bishop of Moray, appointed the Reverend William Mackenzie to succeed him; however, a majority of the

congregation, dissatisfied with the appointment, rented
a room in Mrs. Stewart's house and secured the services
of a qualified clergyman, the Reverend Mr. Tate,
chaplain to the garrison at Fort George. Mackenzie's
successor in 1779, the Reverend Andrew Macfarlane,
united the two factions and built a more conventional
chapel, St. John's, in Church Street, opposite the
Gaelic Church (Scots Presbyterian). That structure was
eventually replaced by a second St. John's, also in
Church Street, but in a different location (see
Boswell's Journal of a Tour, ed. Pottle and Bennett,
pp. 461-462).

Boswell, also, described the English chapel at
Inverness as "mean," adding that the "altar was a bare
fir table, with a coarse stool for kneeling on, covered
with a piece of thick sail-cloth doubled, by way of
cushion. The congregation was small. Mr. Tait, the
clergyman, read prayers very well, though with much of
the Scotch accent. He preached on 'Love your
Enemies.'" After service, the two travelers walked to
Inverness Castle, where Boswell had "a romantick
satisfaction in seeing Dr. Johnson actually in it [both
believing that this was Macbeth's Castle]. It
perfectly corresponds with Shakespeare's description,
which Sir Joshua Reynolds has so happily illustrated,
in one of his notes on our immortal poet:

> 'This castle hath a pleasant seat; the air
> 'Nimbly and sweetly recommends itself
> 'Unto our gentle sense.' &c.

Just as we came out of it, a raven perched on one of
the chimney-tops, and croaked. Then I repeated

> '----The raven himself is hoarse,
> 'That croaks the fatal entrance of Duncan
> 'Under my battlements?'"

(Boswell, _Journal of a Tour_, p. 241)

John Wesley reached Inverness at 8:00 A.M., Sunday, 10 June 1764, intending to conduct an open-air service. Unfortunately, he could not "preach abroad because of the rain, nor could I hear of any convenient room, so that I was afraid my coming hither would be in vain, all ways seeming to be blocked up. At ten I went to the kirk. After service Mr. Fraser, one of the ministers, invited us to dinner, and then to drink tea. As we were drinking tea he asked at what hour I would please to preach. I said, 'At half-hour past five.' The high kirk was filled in a very short time, and I have seldom found greater liberty of spirit. The other minister came afterwards to our inn, and showed the most cordial affection. Were it only for this day, I should not have regretted the riding a hundred miles" (_Journal_, 5:74-75).

On the following morning (11 June), "a gentleman, who lives three miles from the town," invited Wesley to his house and assured him that the minister of the parish kirk would be most happy to have him preach there. The leader of the Methodists had to decline the offer, since he was due in Aberdeen on Wednesday, the 13th. Thus, he preached again at the high kirk, observing that it "was fuller now than before, and I could not but observe the remarkable behaviour of the whole congregation after service. Neither man, woman, nor child spoke one word all the way down the main street. Indeed, the seriousness of the people is the less surprising when it is considered that for at least a hundred years this town has had such a succession of pious ministers as very few in Great Britain have known." Before departing later that morning, Wesley took note of the general condition of Inverness: "The

main streets are broad and straight; the houses mostly
old, but not very bad nor very good. It stands in a
pleasant and fruitful country, and has all things
needful for life and godliness. The people in general
speak remarkably good English, and are of a friendly,
courteous behaviour" (Journal, 5:75).

Wesley's next visit to Inverness occurred on
Thursday, 26 April 1770; he had come from Perth, by way
of Dunkeld, Dalwhinnie, and Dalmigavie, and arrived
shortly before sunset. Here he found two of his
preachers, Benjamin and William Chappel, "who had been
here three months, [and] were waiting for a vessel to
return to London. They had met a few people every
night to sing and pray together; and their behaviour,
suitable to their profession, had removed much
prejudice." Benjamin Chappel, who formed the first
Methodist society at Inverness, had been, originally, a
wheelwright; from London he emigrated to Prince Edward
Island, and then to Charlotte Town. On Friday, the
27th, Wesley breakfasted with the senior minister of
Inverness, a Mr. M'Kenzie, "a pious and friendly man.
At six in the evening I began preaching in the church,
and with very uncommon liberty of spirit. At seven in
the morning [Saturday, the 28th] I preached in the
library, a large commodious room; but it would not
contain the congregation: many were constrained to go
away." The next morning, Sunday, 29 April, at 7:00,
"the benches being removed, the library contained us
tolerably well; and I am persuaded God shook the hearts
of many outside Christians. I preached in the church
at five in the afternoon. Mr. Helton [John Hilton, at
this time still one of Wesley's itinerants] designed to
preach abroad at seven; but the ministers desired he
would preach in the church, which he did, to a large

and attentive congregation. Many followed us from the church to our lodgings, with whom I spent some time in prayer, and then advised them, as many as could, to meet together and spend an hour every evening in prayer and useful conversations" (Journal, 5:364).

When Wesley next appeared in Inverness on Tuesday afternoon, 8 June 1779, he found that decided changes had taken place during the past nine years. "Good Mr. M'Kenzie had been for some years removed to Abraham's bosom. Mr. Fraser, his colleague, a pious man of the old stamp, was likewise gone to rest. The three present ministers are of another kind; so that I have no more place in the kirk; and the wind and rain would not permit me to preach on the Green. However, our house was large, though gloomy enough. Being now informed (which I did not suspect before), that the town was uncommonly given to drunkenness, I used the utmost plainness of speech; and I believe not without effect. I then spent some time with the society, increased from twelve to between fifty and sixty. Many of these knew in whom they had believed, and many were going on to perfection; so that all the pains which have been taken to stop the work of God here have hitherto been in vain" (Journal, 6:238). The rain continued into the following day (9 June), and thus Wesley again preached tin the Methodist meeting-house, where "again I delivered my own soul, to a larger congregation than before." On Thursday morning, "we had an affectionate parting, perhaps to meet no more. I am glad, however, that I have made three journeys to Inverness. It has not been lost labour" (Journal, 6:238).

Nevertheless, one more visit remained. At 9:00 A.M., Monday, 10 May 1784, Wesley left Elgin for

Inverness; in the chaise with him were George Whitfield and Mrs. Duncan M'Allum, while Duncan M'Allum had been sent ahead to give notice of Wesley's arrival. George Whitfield (not to be confused with the great Methodist field-preacher who had died in 1770) served Methodism in various capacities, particularly as a traveling companion to its founder and leader. In 1789, Wesley appointed him to succeed John Atlay as book steward, an office he retained until 1803. As for Duncan M'Allum, he existed as one of those self-taught scholars who comprised the Methodist itinerancy in the eighteenth century. After having been converted early in life, he acquired a knowledge of Latin, Greek, Hebrew, and Syriac, in addition to a considerable body of information in civil and ecclesiastical history, as well as several branches of physical and mental science. In March 1775, Wesley appointed M'Allum to the ministry and kept him in Scotland, where he labored until his death in 1834. According to several sources, he would preach as often as four times on a given Sunday, twice in English and twice in Gaelic, and thus became the best known and most highly esteemed of all Wesleyan ministers in Scotland (see Wesleyan Methodist Magazine, 13 [1834], 717).

After an unduly long and tiring journey, Wesley and his companions arrived in Inverness at 5:15 P.M.; at 6:45, he preached on Psalms 33:1 "to a far larger congregation than I had seen here since I preached in the kirk. And surely the labour was not in vain, for God sent a message to many hearts." On the following day, Tuesday, 11 May, "Notwithstanding the long discontinuance of morning preaching, we had a large congregation at five," the sermon text being based upon Luke 20:35. Wesley then breakfasted with the three daughters of Reverend M'Kenzie, afterward taking a walk "over the bridge into one of the pleasantest countries I have seen. It runs along by the side of the clear river, and is well cultivated and well wooded. And here first we heard abundance of birds, welcoming the return of spring." That evening, at 6:30, he preached on 1 Samuel 20:3; the "congregation was larger this evening than the last, and great part of them attended in the morning [at 5:00, 12 May, the text being Revelation 14:1]. We had then a solemn parting, as we could hardly expect to meet again in the present world" (Journal, 6:505).

Nairn

Johnson and Boswell reached Nairn on Friday, 27 August 1773, in time for breakfast. "Though a country town and a royal burgh," states Boswell, "it is a miserable place" (Boswell, Journey of a Tour, p. 233). John Wesley had come to the town along the Moray Firth some nine years earlier--having left Banff on Saturday morning, 9 June 1764, and arriving in Nairn by evening. However, he left us with no impression of the place, either positive or negative. Six years later, on Monday, 30 April 1770, he set out from Inverness on his way to Aberdeen. "A little before we reached Nairn we were met by a messenger from the minister, Mr. Dunbar; who desired I would breakfast with him, and give them a sermon in his church" (Journal, 5:364-365). Apparently, both breakfast and sermon were carried off with dispatch, for Wesley then hastened toward Elgin.

On Tuesday, 8 June 1779, the leader of the Methodists "found another hearty welcome from Mr. Dunbar, the minister of Nairn. A little after ten [A.M.] I preached at his kirk, which was full from end to end. I have seldom seen a Scotch congregation so sensibly affected. Indeed it seemed that God smote the rocks, and brake the hearts of stone in pieces" (Journal, 6:238). Wesley's final recorded visit to Nairn seems to have been on Monday, 10 May 1784, as he rode from Elgin to Inverness. He arrived at 10:30 A.M., walked about for a time, and then boarded his chaise.

Fort George

Fort George, in Inverness-shire, came into being in 1747 after the Rebellion of 1745 as one of a series of fortifications intended to keep the turbulent Highlands under control. Since the facility could accommodate in excess of 3000 troops, it stood as one of the most considerable fortresses in Great Britain. In fact, its appearance today has changed little from that of the eighteenth century, and as late as the 1960's served as the depot of the Queen's Own Highlander's and the Gordon Highlanders.

Although both James Boswell and Samuel Johnson visited Fort George on Saturday, 28 August 1773, neither seemed able to provide any real account of the place. The good Doctor's excuse was that he could not "delineate it scientifically, and a loose and popular description is of use only when the imagination is to be amused. There was every where an appearance of the utmost neatness and regularity. But my suffrage is of little value, because this and Fort Augustus are the only garrisons that I ever saw" (Johnson, Journey to the Western Islands, p. 23). As for Boswell, he was apparently too wrapped up in the atmosphere of the fort to allow for sharp focus upon its physical qualities. For example, at 3:00 P.M., "the drum beat for dinner.

I, for a little while, fancied myself a military man, and it pleased me" (Boswell, Journal of a Tour, p. 238). No doubt Boswell had not forgotten his unsuccessful attempt of ten years earlier to secure a commission in the Guards (see Boswell's London Journal, 1762-1763, ed. Frederick A. Pottle [New York: McGraw-Hill Book Company, 1950], pp. 47, 69-70).

John Wesley had never been inclined toward the military, except as a prime audience for his sermons. Thus, he rode over to Fort George from Inverness on Friday, 27 April 1770. In general terms, he viewed the installation as "a very regular fortification, capable of containing four thousand men." As usual, Wesley tended to overestimate numbers. In any event, as he prepared to leave, "the commanding officer sent word I was welcome to preach. But it was a little too late: I had but just time to ride back to Inverness" (Journal, 5:364).

APPENDICES

A. Historical Summary
B. John Wesley's Scottish Itinerary
C. A Selection of Books on Scotland, 1699-1790
D. List of Works Cited and Consulted

Appendix A

HISTORICAL SUMMARY

The dates set forth below identify, for the benefit of the reader making his way through the details of the preceding chapters, those events during the eighteenth century that are considered important to the life of John Wesley, the development of English Methodism, and the history of Scotland.

1703. Birth of John Wesley

1705. Creation of the commission to draft a Treaty of Union between England and Scotland

1706. Treaty of Union drafted

1707. Union between England and Scotland; Scotland allowed forty-five members in the Parliament at Westminster

Birth of Charles Wesley

Birth of Selina Shirley, Countess of Huntingdon

1708. James Edward, the Old Pretender, sails for Scotland; turns back to France without landing

Scottish Privy Council abolished

Widespread discontent in Scotland with the Union

Society for the Propagation of Christian Knowledge (S.P.C.K.) founded; primarily designed to dispel the ignorance in the Highlands

1709. Reverend Greenshields opens an Episcopal meeting-house in Edinburgh

Treason laws made uniform throughout Great Britain

1711. Act legalizing "patronage": a local laird given
          the right to install his own minister in a
          kirk; the congregation allowed no say in the
          matter
       Newly created Scottish peers no longer given the
          privilege of seats in the House of Lords
1712. Act of Toleration: Episcopalians can worship in
          their own way, provided that they swear not
          to support the Stuarts
1713. Malt tax extended to Scotland
1714. Death of Queen Anne
       George I, King of England
       John Wesley enters Charterhouse School, London
1715. Jacobite uprising; James Edward proclaimed James
          VIII at Aberdeen, Dunkeld, Dundee, and
          Inverness; battle of Sheriffmuir
       Public "middens" forbidden in Glasgow streets
       The Glasgow Courant begins publication
       Disarming Act
1716. James Edward leaves Scotland
       Eighty-nine Scottish rebels taken from Edinburgh
          to Carlisle, there to be tried by English
          juries
1718. Act rendering all Episcopal clergymen who
          performed divine worship without having taken
          the prescribed oaths liable to six months'
          imprisonment; every religious assembly of
          nine or more persons (exclusive of the
          household) declared to be a meeting-house
1719. Spanish troops land on Inverness-shire coast;
          battle of Glenshiel
       First ship built on the River Clyde, at
          Greenhaven, sails for America
1720. John Wesley enters Christ Church College, Oxford

Beginning of the "Improving Movement" in Scottish agriculture

First public concerts in Edinburgh

Catholic seminary opened in Glenlivet, Banffshire

1722. Birth of Charles Edward, the Young Pretender

1723. Founding of the Honourable Society of Improvers in the Knowledge of Agriculture

1724. Increase of the Malt Tax in Scotland by 6d. per barrel

1725. Ordination of John Wesley as deacon in Christ Church Cathedral, Oxford

Malt Tax riots in Glasgow and Edinburgh

General George Wade begins construction of military road system in the Highlands ("Wade roads")

1726. John Wesley elected Fellow of Lincoln College, Oxford

1727. Death of George I

George II, King of England

M.A. degree conferred upon John Wesley

Royal Bank of Scotland founded

Commissioners and Trustees for Improving Fisheries and Manufactures established

Last capital sentence for witchcraft in Scotland

Act to regulate linen and hemp manufacture

Iron works built at Invergarry

1728. Allan Ramsay establishes, in Edinburgh, the first circulating library in Scotland

First theatrical performance in Glasgow

1729. Founding of the Oxford Methodists (the Holy Club)

1730. Bank of Scotland institutes system of accepting deposits

1733. Ebenezer Erskine, of Stirling, denounces
      limitation of the Scottish congregations to
      choose their own ministers; beginning of the
      Secessionist movement (Associate Presbytery
      of the Church of Scotland)

1735. John and Charles Wesley embark, in the Simmonds,
      for Savannah, Georgia

1736. Porteous Riot, Edinburgh
      Invergarry iron works bankrupt
      Completion of the Wade roads

1738. John Wesley returns from Georgia; his conversion
      at Aldersgate, in London; visits Zinzendorf
      and the Moravians

1739. London Methodists purchase the King's Foundry,
      in Upper Moorfields
      John Wesley conducts, in Bristol, his first
      open-air meeting
      Founding of the first Methodist society, in
      Bristol
      The Black Watch (Royal Highland Regiment) formed

1740. John Wesley splits with the Moravians
      Members of the Associate Presbytery formally
      excluded from the ministry of the established
      Kirk

1741. George Whitefield's first visit to Scotland;
      meets with Ralph Erskine at Dunfermline;
      confers with the Associate Presbytery
      Quarrel between John Wesley and George
              Whitefield
      John Murray begins to organize Jacobite
              associations
      The Glasgow Journal issues its first number

1742. John Wesley and George Whitefield heal their
      differences

George Whitefield's second visit to Scotland; famous revival at Cambuslang, Lanarkshire, where penitents seized with hysteria and convulsions

Thomas Maxfield becomes the first regular Wesleyan Methodist lay preacher

1743. Associate Presbytery denounces Whitefield; labels his previous visits "among the sins of Scotland"

1744. First Methodist Conference

Charles Edward escapes from Rome; reaches Paris

Louis XV of France plans, then abandons, a French invasion of Scotland

1745. Jacobite uprising; Charles Edward lands in Scotland

Battle of Prestonpans

1746. Battle of Culloden

Charles Edward sails for France

British Linen Company founded

Aberdeen Journal begins publication

Episcopalians compelled to swear allegiance to the House of Hanover

John Wesley organizes the Methodist societies into circuits

1747. Disarming Act attempts to abolish the clan system

Associate Presbytery divided into Anti-Burgher (Nonjuror) and Burgher factions

John Wesley opens his school at Kingswood

George Whitefield on a six-week tour of Scotland; Synods of Glasgow, Lothian, and Perth pass resolutions intended to exclude him from churches

Lady Huntingdon appoints Whitefield as one of

          her domestic chaplains

          First public concerts in Aberdeen

1749.   Sulfuric acid works opened at Prestonpans

          Aberdeen Banking Company founded

          Culloden anniversary riot in Edinburgh

1750.   Fulton Silk Factory, Paisley, established

          Glasgow Arms Bank founded

          Ship Bank, Glasgow, founded

1751.   John Wesley marries Mrs. Molly Vazeille

          George Whitefield in Scotland

          First Turnpike Act for Scotland passed

1752.   Act gives the government control over estates of
          Scottish chiefs who had joined the Young
          Pretender during the 1745 rebellion

          Aberdeen Banking Company closes

1753.   George Whitefield visits Scotland; in August, a
          playhouse at Glasgow, against which he had
          declaimed, was pulled down

1754.   St. Andrews Club founded

1755.   The Foulis Academy of the Fine Arts opened at
          Glasgow

1757.   George Whitefield in Scotland; attends General
          Assembly of the Kirk of Scotland, at which
          time Alexander Carlyle, D.D., is prosecuted
          for attending a performance in John Home's
          tragedy of <u>Douglas</u>

          Molly Vazeille leaves John Wesley

1760.   Death of George II

          George III, King of England

          Carron Iron Works opened

1761.   Sarah Crosby leaves London for Derby and becomes
          the first female Wesleyan Methodist preacher

          Thistle Bank, Glasgow, founded

          Founding, in Brighton, of Lady Huntingdon's

Methodist Connexion

Relief Church of Scotland founded by Thomas Gillespie, of Carnock

1763. James Small invents the swing plow.

1765. First signposts and mile-posts appear on Scottish roads

1766. Death of James Edward, the Old Pretender

1769. James Watt secures patent for his steam engine

1770. Death of George Whitefield

Deepening of the River Clyde begun

1775. American Revolution

"Emancipation" of Scottish colliers; no longer must they be attached for life to the mines in which they labor

1777. Anti-Catholic riots in Edinburgh

1778. Forth and Clyde Canal opened

1779. First effective cotton mill in Scotland established at Rothesay

Countess of Huntingdon's Connexion separates from the Church of England

1781. Death of Molly Vazeille

James Watt Produces his rotary engine

1782. Glasgow Chamber of Commerce founded

Ineligibility of Scottish peers to sit in the House of Lords declared illegal

1783. The Glasgow Advertiser begins publication

1784. Estates of Scottish chiefs restored

Highland and Agricultural Society formed

Andrew Meikle invents his threshing machine

1785. Edinburgh Chamber of Commerce founded

Thompson's Bank, Glasgow, founded

1787. First Glasgow Directory published

The Gordon Highlanders Regiment formed

1788. Death of Charles Edward, the Young Pretender

        Death of Charles Wesley
        First paid police force in Glasgow
1790.   Chair of Agriculture established at Edinburgh
           University
        Opening of Forth and Clyde Canal
1791.   Death of Selina Shirley, Countess of Huntingdon
        Death of John Wesley

Appendix B

JOHN WESLEY'S SCOTTISH ITINERARY: 1751-1790

Since Chapters 3 through 6 have been organized, generally, in geographical order, readers may wish to perceive some sense of the overall chronology of John Wesley's visits to Scotland. Thus, they can easily determine the intervals between the journeys, the length of each, and, perhaps most important, the extent and emphasis of each--or, where he spent most of his time. In all, Wesley spent 425 days in Scotland; of these, he devoted 206 complete days to the three major cities: 93 in Edinburgh, 58 in Aberdeen, and 55 in Glasgow. Or, from another point of view, we may conclude that Methodism's founder and leader directed more than 48% of his efforts in Scotland toward those three principal cities. Finally, in addition to the aforementioned areas, the itinerary outlined below will reveal further conclusions of equal importance, such as the specific months of the year that Wesley set aside for his journeys to Scotland and the degrees to which age did or did not affect his movements back and forth over rugged country. Yet, whatever answers such information provides, there never exists any reasonable doubt that John Wesley's efforts north of the River Tweed stand as a singular tribute to the strength of his faith and the intensity of his energy.

1751 (age 48)

April

   Wednesday, 24. Old Camus, Prestonpans, Musselburgh

Thursday, 25. Edinburgh, Musselburgh

1753 (age 50)

April

  Monday, 16. Dumfries, Thornhill
  Tuesday, 17. Leadhills, Lesmahagow, Glasgow
  Wednesday, 18. Glasgow
  Thursday, 19. Glasgow
  Friday, 20. Glasgow
  Saturday, 21. Glasgow
  Sunday, 22. Glasgow
  Monday, 23. Kirk o' Shotts, Edinburgh, Tranent

1757 (age 54)

May

  Tuesday, 31. Dumfries, Thornhill, Leadhills

June

  Wednesday, 1. Glasgow
  Thursday, 2. Glasgow
  Friday, 3. Glasgow
  Saturday, 4. Glasgow
  Sunday, 5. Glasgow
  Monday, 6. Kirk o' Shotts, Musselburgh
  Tuesday, 7. Musselburgh
  Wednesday, 8. Dunbar

1759 (age 56)

May

  Monday, 21. Ruthwell, Dumfries
  Tuesday, 22. Thornhill, Leadhills, Lesmahagow
  Wednesday, 23. Glasgow
  Thursday, 24. Glasgow
  Friday, 25. Glasgow
  Saturday, 26. Glasgow

Sunday, 27. Glasgow
Monday, 28. Edinburgh, Musselburgh
Tuesday, 29. Musselburgh
Wednesday, 30. Dunbar
Thursday, 31. Dunbar

                   1761 (age 58)
April
Monday, 27. Moffat
Tuesday, 28. Edinburgh
Wednesday, 29. Edinburgh
Thursday, 30. Queensferry, Dundee

May
Friday, 1. Montrose, Stonehaven
Saturday, 2. Aberdeen
Sunday, 3. Aberdeen
Monday, 4. Aberdeen
Tuesday, 5. Aberdeen
Wednesday, 6. Aberdeen
Thursday, 7. Monymusk
Friday, 8. Glamis
Saturday, 9. Edinburgh
Sunday, 10. Edinburgh
Monday, 11. Edinburgh, Musselburgh
Tuesday, 12. Musselburgh, Haddington, North Berwick,
              Dunbar
Wednesday, 13. Dunbar

                   1763 (age 60)
May
Saturday, 21. Edinburgh
Sunday, 22. Edinburgh
Monday, 23. Forfar

Tuesday, 24. Aberdeen

Wednesday, 25. Aberdeen

Thursday, 26. Aberdeen

Friday, 27. Brechin, Broughty Castle

Saturday, 28. Kinghorn Ferry, Leith

Sunday, 29. Edinburgh

Monday, 30. Dunbar

1764 (age 61)

May

Thursday, 24. Dunbar

Friday, 25. Haddington, Musselburgh

Saturday, 26. Edinburgh

Sunday, 27. Edinburgh

Monday, 28. Edinburgh

Tuesday, 29. Edinburgh

Wednesday, 30. Edinburgh

Thursday, 31. Dundee

June

Friday, 1. Brechin

Saturday, 2. Aberdeen

Sunday, 3. Aberdeen

Monday, 4. Aberdeen

Tuesday, 5. Aberdeen

Wednesday, 6. Aberdeen

Thursday, 7. Monymusk, Grange Green

Friday, 8. Old Meldrum, Banff

Saturday, 9. Nairn

Sunday, 10. Inverness

Monday, 11. Inverness, Nairn, Grange Green

Tuesday, 12. Elgin, Fochabers, Keith, Huntly

Wednesday, 13. Aberdeen

Thursday, 14. Aberdeen

Friday, 15. Dundee, Cupar

Saturday, 16. Kinghorn Ferry, Edinburgh
Sunday, 17. Edinburgh

1765 (age 62)

April

Tuesday, 23. Dunbar, Edinburgh
Wednesday, 24. Edinburgh
Thursday, 25. Edinburgh
Friday, 26. Musselburgh, Edinburgh
Saturday, 27. Glasgow
Sunday, 28. Glasgow
Monday, 29. Kilmarnock, Ayr, Maybole, Girvan
Tuesday, 30. Ballantrae, Stranraer, Port Patrick

1766 (age 63)

May

Friday, 23. Old Camus, Cockburnspath, Dunbar
Saturday, 24. Prestonpans
Sunday, 25. Edinburgh
Monday, 26. Edinburgh
Tuesday, 27. Edinburgh
Wednesday, 28. Leith, Edinbrugh
Thursday, 29. Edinburgh
Friday, 30. Edinburgh
Saturday, 31. Edinburgh

June

Sunday, 1. Edinburgh
Monday, 2. Dundee
Tuesday, 3. Dundee
Wednesday, 4. Dundee
Thursday, 5. Dundee
Friday, 6. Aberdeen
Saturday, 7. Aberdeen
Sunday, 8. Aberdeen

Monday, 9.   Aberdeen
Tuesday, 10.   Monymusk
Wednesday, 11.   Aberdeen
Thursday, 12.   Aberdeen
Friday, 13.   Brechin, Dundee
Saturday, 14.   Kinghorn Ferry, Edinburgh
Sunday, 15.   Edinburgh
Monday, 16.   Edinburgh
Tuesday, 16.   Edinburgh
Wednesday, 18.   Glasgow
Thursday, 19.   Glasgow
Friday, 20.   Glasgow
Saturday, 21.   Glasgow
Sunday, 22.   Glasgow
Monday, 23.   Thornhill
Tuesday, 24.   Dunfries

1767 (age 64)

March
  Thursday, 26.   Ruthwell
  Friday, 27.   Dumfries, Gatehouse-of-Fleet
  Saturday, 28.   Port Patrick
July
  Wednesday, 29.   Stranraer
  Thursday, 30.   Ayr
  Friday, 31.   Glasgow
August
  Saturday, 1.   Glasgow, Edinburgh
  Sunday, 2.   Edinburgh
  Monday, 3.   Edinburgh
  Tuesday, 4.   Dunbar

1768 (age 65)

April
  Monday, 18. Dumfries, Drumlanrig
  Tuesday, 19. Glasgow
  Wednesday, 20. Glasgow
  Thursday, 21. Glasgow
  Friday, 22. Glasgow
  Saturday, 23. Perth
  Sunday, 24. Perth
  Monday, 25. Perth, Brechin
  Tuesday, 26. Aberdeen
  Wednesday, 27. Aberdeen
  Thursday, 28. Aberdeen
  Friday, 29. Aberdeen
  Saturday, 30. Aberdeen
May
  Sunday, 1. Aberdeen
  Monday, 2. Brechin
  Tuesday, 3. Dundee
  Wednesday, 4. Dundee
  Thursday, 5. Perth, Scone
  Friday, 6. Perth
  Saturday, 7. Edinburgh
  Sunday, 8. Edinburgh
  Monday, 9. Edinburgh
  Tuesday, 10. Edinburgh
  Wednesday, 11. Edinburgh
  Thursday, 12. Edinburgh
  Friday, 13. Edinburgh
  Saturday, 14. Edinburgh
  Sunday, 15. Edinburgh
  Monday, 16. Dunbar
  Tuesday, 17. Dunbar

1770 (age 67)

April

Sunday, 15. Dumfries
Monday, 16. Leadhills, Lesmahagow
Tuesday, 17. Glasgow
Wednesday, 18. Glasgow
Thursday, 19. Glasgow
Friday, 20. Edinburgh
Saturday, 21. Perth
Sunday, 22. Perth
Monday, 23. Perth, Scone, Perth
Tuesday, 24. Perth
Wednesday, 25. Dunkeld, Castle Blair, Dalwhinnie
Thursday, 26. Dalmigavie, Inverness
Friday, 27. Inverness
Saturday, 28. Inverness, Fort George, Inverness
Sunday, 29. Inverness
Monday, 30. Nairn, Elgin, Fochabers, Keith

May

Tuesday, 1. Aberdeen
Wednesday, 2. Aberdeen
Thursday, 3. Aberdeen
Friday, 4. Aberdeen
Saturday, 5. Aberdeen
Sunday, 6. Aberdeen
Monday, 7. Montrose, Arbroath
Tuesday, 8. Arbroath
Wednesday, 9. Dundee
Thursday, 10. Dundee
Friday, 11. Edinburgh
Saturday, 12. Edinburgh
Sunday, 13. Edinburgh
Monday, 14. Edinburgh
Tuesday, 15. Edinburgh
Wednesday, 16. Edinburgh

Thursday, 17. Edinburgh, Musselburgh, Dundee
Friday, 18. Haddington, Dunbar

1772 (age 69)

April

Wednesday, 15. Selkirk
Thursday, 16. Edinburgh
Friday, 17. Edinburgh
Saturday, 18. Glasgow
Sunday, 19. Glasgow
Monday, 20. Greenock
Tuesday, 21. Greenock, Port Glasgow, Greenock
Wednesday, 22. Port Glasgow, Glasgow
Thursday, 23. Glasgow
Friday, 24. Glasgow, Edinburgh
Saturday, 25. Edinburgh, Perth
Sunday, 26. Perth
Monday, 27. Perth, Methven, Dunkeld
Tuesday, 28. Dunkeld, Perth
Wednesday, 29. Brechin
Thursday, 30. Brechin, Aberdeen

May

Friday, 1. Aberdeen
Saturday, 2. Aberdeen
Sunday, 3. Aberdeen
Monday, 4. Aberdeen
Tuesday, 5. Arbroath
Wednesday, 6. Arbroath
Thursday, 7. Dundee
Friday, 8. Dundee
Saturday, 9. Edinburgh
Sunday, 10. Edinburgh
Monday, 11. Edinburgh
Tuesday, 12. Ormiston

Wednesday, 13. Leith, Edinburgh
Thursday, 14. Edinburgh
Friday, 15. Edinburgh
Saturday, 16. Edinburgh
Sunday, 17. Edinburgh
Monday, 18. Edinburgh, Leith
Tuesday, 19. Leith, Edinburgh
Wednesday, 20. Edinburgh, Dunbar
Thursday, 21. The Bass, Tantallon Castle
Friday, 22. Dun Hill

1774 (age 71)

May

Tuesday, 10. Selkirk
Wednesday, 11. Edinburgh
Thursday, 12. Glasgow
Friday, 13. Glasgow
Saturday, 14. Glasgow
Sunday, 15. Glasgow
Moday, 16. Glasgow, Port Glasgow, Greenock
Tuesday, 17. Greenock, Glasgow
Wednesday, 18. Edinburgh
Thursday, 19. Perth
Friday, 20. Monydie
Saturday, 21. Perth
Sunday, 22. Perth
Monday, 23. Rait, Dundee
Tuesday, 24. Arbroath
Wednesday, 25. Aberdeen
Thursday, 26. Aberdeen
Friday, 27. Aberdeen
Saturday, 28. Aberdeen
Sunday, 29. Aberdeen
Monday, 30. Arbroath

Tuesday, 31. East Haven, Dundee

June

Wednesday, 1. Edinburgh

Thursday, 2. Edinburgh

Friday, 3. Edinburgh

Saturday, 4. Edinburgh

Sunday, 5. Ormiston

Monday, 6. Edinburgh

Tuesday, 7. Edinburgh

Wednesday, 8. Dunbar

1776 (age 73)

May

Tuesday, 7. Selkirk

Wednesday, 8. Edinburgh

Thursday, 9. Glasgow

Friday, 10. Greenock

Saturday, 11. Glasgow

Sunday, 12. Glasgow

Monday, 13. Edinburgh

Tuesday, 14. Perth

Wednesday, 15. Dundee

Thursday, 16. Arbroath

Friday, 17. Aberdeen

Saturday, 18. Aberdeen

Sunday, 19. Aberdeen

Monday, 20. Old Meldrum, Banff

Tuesday, 21. Banff, Newmill, Keith

Wednesday, 22. Inverness, Aberdeen

Thursday, 23. Aberdeen

Friday, 24. Arbroath

Saturday, 25. West Haven, Dundee

Sunday, 26. Dundee

Monday, 27. St. Andrews

Tuesday, 28. Edinburgh
Wednesday, 29. Edinburgh
Thursday, 30. Edinburgh
Friday, 31. Dunbar

1779 (age 76)

May

Wednesday, 17. Dunbar
Thursday, 18. Edinburgh
Friday, 19. Joppa, Edinburgh
Saturday, 20. Edinburgh
Sunday, 21. Edinburgh
Monday, 22. Edinburgh
Tuesday, 23. Roslin Castle, Dunbar
Wednesday, 24. Dunbar

1782 (age 79)

May

Wednesday, 29. Dunbar
Thursday, 30. Edinburgh
Friday, 31. Edinburgh, Saughton Hall

June

Saturday, 1. Edinburgh
Sunday, 2. Edinburgh
Monday, 3. Dundee
Tuesday, 4. Arbroath
Wednesday, 5. Aberdeen
Thursday, 6. Aberdeen
Friday, 7. Keith, Fraserburgh, Newburgh, Aberdeen
Saturday, 8. Aberdeen
Sunday, 9. Aberdeen
Monday, 10. Arbroath
Tuesday, 11. Dundee
Wednesday, 12. Edinburgh

Thursday, 13. Edinburgh
Friday, 14. Kelso
Saturday, 15. Kelso

1784 (age 81)

April

Friday, 23. Selkirk
Saturday, 24. Edinburgh
Sunday, 25. Edinburgh, Gardiner's Hall, Edinburgh
Monday, 26. Glasgow
Tuesday, 27. Glasgow
Wednesday, 28. Glasgow
Thursday, 29. Glasgow, Edinburgh
Friday, 30. Edinburgh, Queensferry, Perth

May

Saturday, 1. Perth, Dundee
Sunday, 2. Dundee
Monday, 3. Dundee, Arbroath
Tuesday, 4. Bervie, Stonehaven, Aberdeen
Wednesday, 5. Aberdeen
Thursday, 6. Aberdeen, Old Meldrum, Forglen
Friday, 7. Forglen, Keith
Saturday, 8. Keith, Elgin, Dalvey
Sunday, 9. Dalvey
Monday, 10. Dalvey, Nairn, Inverness
Tuesday, 11. Inverness
Wednesday, 12. Inverness, Dalvey, Elgin
Thursday, 13. Elgin
Friday, 14. Elgin, Banff, Forglen
Saturday, 15. Forglen, Aberdeen
Sunday, 16. Newburgh, Aberdeen
Monday, 17. Bervie, Montrose, Arbroath
Tuesday, 18. Arbroath, Dundee
Wednesday, 19. Dundee, Melville house

Thursday, 20. Kinross, Queensferry, Edinburgh
Friday, 21. Edinburgh, Leith, Edinburgh
Saturday, 22. Edinburgh
Sunday, 23. Edinburgh
Monday, 24. Edinburgh, Haddington, Dunbar
Tuesday, 25. Dunbar
Wednesday, 26. Dunbar, Berwick-upon-Tweed
                (Northumberland)
Thursday, 27. Berwick-upon-Tweed, Kelso, Roxburghe
               (Floors) Castle, Kelso

1786 (age 83)

May
Saturday, 13. Glasgow
Sunday, 14. Glasgow
Monday, 15. Glasgow
Tuesday, 16. Glasgow
Wednesday, 17. Glasgow, Edinburgh
Thursday, 18. Edinburgh
Friday, 19. Leith, Dundee
Saturday, 20. Dundee, Arbroath
Sunday, 21. Arbroath
Monday, 22. Montrose, Bervie, Stonehaven, Aberdeen
Tuesday, 23. Aberdeen
Wednesday, 24. Aberdeen
Thursday, 25. Stonehaven, Montrose, Arbroath
Friday, 26. Arbroath, Dundee
Saturday, 27. New Inn, Kinghorn, Leith, Edinburgh
Sunday, 28. Edinburgh
Monday, 29. Edinburgh
Tuesday, 30. Haddington, Dunbar

1788 (age 85)

May

  Tuesday, 13. Dumfries

  Wednesday, 14. Dumfries

  Thursday, 15. Moffat, Ellenfoot, Douglas Mills

  Friday, 16. Hamilton, Glasgow

  Saturday, 17. Glasgow

  Sunday, 18. Glasgow

  Monday, 19. Livingstone, Edinburgh

  Tuesday, 20. Edinburgh

  Wednesday, 21. Edinburgh

  Thursday, 22. Dalkeith, Dunbar

1790 (age 87)

May

  Thursday, 13. Tranent, Edinburgh

  Friday, 14. Edinburgh

  Saturday, 15. Edinburgh

  Sunday, 16. Edinburgh

  Monday, 17. Queensferry, Kinross, Melville House

  Tuesday, 18. Dundee

  Wednesday, 19. Arbroath

  Thursday, 20. Montrose, Bervie, Stonehaven, Aberdeen

  Friday, 21. Aberdeen

  Saturday, 22. Aberdeen

  Sunday, 23. Aberdeen

  Monday, 24. Old Meldrum, Forglen

  Tuesday, 25. Old Meldrum, Aberdeen

  Wednesday, 26. Stonehaven, Laurencekirk, Brechin

  Thursday, 27. Forfar, Dunblane, Kilsyth,
                 Auchterarder, Glasgow

  Friday, 28. Glasgow

  Saturday, 29. Glasgow

  Sunday, 30. Glasgow

  Monday, 31. Hamilton, Douglas Mills, Elvinfoot,
                 Moffat, Dumfries

June
  Tuesday, 1. Dumfries

Appendix C

A SELECTION OF BOOKS ON SCOTLAND PUBLISHED
BETWEEN 1699 AND 1790

The following list presents to the reader a
selection of works that Wesley could easily have read
or consulted in preparation for his various journeys
into Scotland. Or, from another point of view, the
list simply constitutes a selection of volumes on
Scotland published slightly before and throughout John
Wesley's lifetime.*

1. Description and Travel
    "An Account of a Journey from Lancashire into
        Scotland." The Gentleman's Magazine, April
        1766.
    Adair, John (d. 1722). The Description of the Sea
        Coast and Islands of Scotland, with Large and
        Exact Maps for the use of Seamen. Edinburgh,
        1703. The first part only; second part never
        published.
    Brand, John (1668-1738). A Brief Description of
        Orkney, Zetland, Pightland, Firth, and
        Caithness, with a Short Journey of the
        Author's Voyage Thither. Edinburgh, 1701;
        London, 1703.
    Buchan, Alexander. A Description of St. Kilda, the
        Most Remote Western Isle of Scotland.
        Edinburgh, 1727; further editions 1741, 1752,
        1774.
    Burt, Captain Edward (d. 1755). Letters from a

Gentleman in the North of Scotland Containing the Description of a Capital Town and an Account of the Highlands. 2 vols. London, 1754; Dublin, 1755; London, 1759. The "capital town" = Inverness.

Campbell, John (1708-1755). A Full and Particular Description of the Highlands of Scotland, Its Situation and Produce, the Management and Customs of the Natives. London, 1752.

Cordiner, Rev. Charles (1746-1794). Antiquities and Scenery of the North of Scotland, in a Series of Letters to Thomas Pennant. London, 1780; 2nd ed., 1790. Cordiner served as Episcopal minister of St. Andrew's Chapel, Banff.

Douglas, Francis (1710-1790). A General Description of the East Coast of Scotland, from Edinburgh to Cullen. Paisely, 1782. Includes accounts of the Universities of St. Andrews and Aberdeen, as well as of trade and manufacturing in the large towns.

English, John. Travels through Scotland. London, 1762. An uncomplimentary and prejudiced account.

Forbes, Rev. Robert (1708-1775). Journals of the Episcopal Visitation of the Dioceses of Ross and Caithness, and of Ross and Argyll, 1762 and 1770. London, 1770. Forbes served as bishop of Ross and Caithness.

Gilpin, Rev. William (1724-1804). Observations Relating Chiefly to Picturesque Beauty, Particularly in the Highlands of Scotland. 2 vols. London, 1789.

Gordon, Alexander (1692-1754). Itinerarium

Septentrionale: or, a Journey through Most of
the Counties of Scotland, and Those in the
North of England. London, 1726; expanded ed.
1732; Latin translation in 1731.

Hanway, Mrs. Mary Anne. A Journey to the Highlands
of Scotland, with Remarkds on Dr. Johnson's
Tour. London, 1775; further ed. 1777.

Haydock, Roger (1644-1696). A Collection of the
Christian Writings, Labours, Travels, and
Sufferings of That Faithful and Approved
Minister of Jesus Christ, Roger Haydock, ed.
John Field. London, 1700. Haydock traveled
to Scotland and Ireland in 1680.

Journals of an English Medical Officer Who Attended
the Duke of Cumberland's Army As Far North As
Inverness during the Rebellion. London, 1746.

A Journey through Part of England and Scotland
Along with the Army of the Duke of Cumberland,
by a Volunteer. London, 1746.

A Journey to Scotland, Giving a Character of That
Country, the People and Their Manners, by an
English Gentleman. London, 1699.

Kirk, Thomas. A Modern Account of Scotland by an
English Gentleman. London, 1679; 2nd ed.,
London, 1699. Contemporary reviewers appear
doubtful of Kirk's facts.

Knox, John (1720-1790). A Tour through the
Highlands of Scotland and the Hebride Isles in
MDCCLXXXVI. London, 1787.

Loch, David (d. 1780). A Tour through Most of the
Trading Towns and Villages of Scotland.
Edinburgh, 1778.

Lunardi, Vincenzo (1759-1806). An Account of Five
Aerial Voyages in Scotland. London, 1786.

Macky, John (d. 1736). A Journey through Scotland. London, 1723; further eds. 1724, 1729.

Martin, Martin (d. 1719). A Description of the Western Isles of Scotland, with a Brief Description of the Isles of Orkney and Shetland.

_____. A Late Voyage to St. Kilda, the Remotest of the Hebrides. London, 1698; further eds. 1716, 1749, 1753, 1774.

Mission de Valbourg, Henri (1650-1722). Memoirs and Observations in His Travels over England, with Some Account of Scotland and Ireland, Translated from the French by John Ozell. London, 1719. Ozell died in 1743; French ed. 1698.

Morer, Rev. Thomas. A Short Account of Scotland. London, 1702; further eds. 1706, 1715.

Newte, Thomas. A Tour in England and Scotland in 1785. London, 1788; 2nd ed. 1791. Also ascribed to William Thomson (1746-1817), who edited and enlarged the work.

Pococke, Bishop Richard (1704-1765). Travels in Scotland. London, 1747. Further eds. 1750, 1760.

Shaw, Rev. Stebbing (1762-1802). A Tour in 1787 from London to the Western Highlands of Scotland, Including Excursions to the Lakes of Westmorland and Cumberland. London, 1788.

Sullivan, Sir Richard Joseph (1752-1806). Observations Made during a Tour through Parts of England, Scotland, and Wales in a Series of Letters. London, 1780; 2 vols., 1785; Dublin, 1785.

Taylor, Joseph. A Journey to Edenborough in

Scotland. London, 1705.

Thomson, William. See under Newte, Thomas.

Topham, Edward (1751-1820). Letters from Edinburgh, 1774 and 1775, Containing Some Observations on the Diversions, Customs, Manners, and Laws of the Scotch Nation. Edinburgh, 1776; 2 vols., Dublin, 1780.

A Tour in England and Scotland in 1784 by an English Gentleman. London, 1788.

A Voyage to Shetland, the Orkneys and the Western Isles of Scotland. London, 1751.

2. History and Biography

Anderson, James (1662-1728). Collections Relating to the History of Mary Queen of Scotland. 4 vols. Edinburgh, 1727-1728.

_____. An Historical Essay, Shewing That the Crown and Kingdom of Scotland Is Imperial and Independent. Edinburgh, 1705.

Crookshank, William (1712-1769). The History of the State and Sufferings of the Church of Scotland, from the Restoration to the Revolution. 2 vols. London, 1749; Edinburgh, 1751, 1762; Glasgow, 1787.

Dalrymple, Sir David, Lord Hailes (1726-1792). Annals of Scotland, from Malcolm III to the Accession of the House of Stewart. 2 vols. Edinburgh, 1776-1779.

_____. Miscellaneous Remarks on the Evidence against Mary Queen of Scots. London, 1784.

_____. Remarks on the History of Scotland. Edinburgh, 1773.

Goodall, Walter (1706-1766). An Examination of the

Letters, Said To Be Written by Mary, Queen of
Scots to James, Earl of Bothwell, Shewing That
They Are Forgeries. 2 vols. Edinburgh, 1754.
_____. An Introduction to the History
and Antiquities of Scotland, Translated from
the Original Latin. London, 1769.

Grose, Francis (1731-1791). The Antiquities of
Scotland. 2 vols. London, 1789-1791.

Guthrie, William (1708-1770). A General History of
Scotland, from the Earliest Accounts to the
Present Time. 10 vols. London, 1767-1768.

Howie, John (1735-1793). Biographia Scotiana: or,
a Brief Historical Account of the Lives,
Characters and Memorable Transactions of the
Most Eminent Scots Worthies. Glasgow, 1775; 2
parts, Glasgow, 1781-1782.

Lockhart, George (1673-1757). Memoirs Concerning
the Affairs of Scotland, from Queen Anne's
Accession to the Commencement of the Union.
London, 1714; enl. ed., London, 1714.

Maitland, William (1693-1757). The History of
Edinburgh, from Its Foundation to the Present
Time. Edinburgh, 1753.

Pinkerton, John (1758-1826). An Enquiry into the
History of Scotland Preceding the Reign of
Malcolm III, or the Year 1056. London, 1789.

Ridpath, George (1717-1772). The Border History of
England and Scotland. London, 1776.

Robertson, William (1721-1793). The History of
Scotland during the Reigns of Queen Mary and
of King James VI, till His Accession to the
Crown of England. 2 vols., London, 1759; 11
eds. through 1791.
_____. Memorial Relating to the

University of Edinburgh. London, 1768.

Salmon, Nathaniel (1675-1742). A Short View of the Families of the Scottish Nobility. London, 1759.

Stuart, Gilbert (1742-1786). The History of Scotland from the Establishment of the Reformation till the Death of Queen Mary. 2vols. London, 1782.

_____. The History of the Establishment of the Reformation of Religion in Scotland. London, 1780.

Tytler, William (1711-1792). An Historical and Critical Enquiry into the Evidence Produced by the Earls of Murray and Morton against Mary Queen of Scots. London, 1762; four eds. through 1790.

Whitaker, John (1735-1808). Mary Queen of Scots Vindicated. 3 vols. London, 1787.

*For Works by Defoe, Boswell, and Johnson, see Appendix D.

Appendix D

LIST OF WORKS CITED AND CONSULTED

The following titles served as sources for the preparation of and writing of this study:

Allibone, Samuel Austin. A Critical Dictionary of English Literature and British and American Authors. 3 vols. Philadelphia: J.B. Lippincott, 1858.

Arnot, Hugo. The History of Edinburgh. Edinburgh, 1788.

Bell, Colin, and Rose Bell. City Fathers. Town Planning in Britain from Roman Times to 1900. New York: Frederick A. Praeger, Publishers, 1969.

Benson, Joseph. An Apology for the Methodists. London, 1801.

Brady, Frank, and Frederick A. Pottle (eds.). Boswell in Search of a Wife, 1766-1769. London: William Heinemann, Ltd., 1957.

Bunting, John, Thomas Jackson, et al. Wesleyan Methodist Magazine, 3rd ser. London: Wesleyan Conference Office, 1822--.

Butler, Dugald. John Wesley and George Whitefield in Scotland. London, 1898.

Chapman, R. W. (ed.). Boswell's Life of Johnson. London: Oxford University Press, 1960.

_____. Johnson's "Journey to the Western Islands of Scotland" and Boswell's "Journal of a Tour to the Hebrides with Samuel Johnson, LL.D." London: Oxford University Press, 1930.

Childe, V. Gordon, and W. Douglas Simpson. <u>Illustrated</u>
     <u>Guide to Ancient Monuments in the Ownership or</u>
     <u>Guardianship of the Ministry of Works. Volume VI:</u>
     <u>Scotland</u>. Edinburgh: Her Majesty's Stationery
     Office, 1961.

Churchill, Winston S. <u>A History of the English</u>
     <u>Speaking Peoples. Volume II</u>. New York: Dodd,
     Mead, and Company, 1966.

Clark, Adam. <u>The Miscellaneous Works of Adam Clarke</u>.
     13 vols. London: Printed for T. Tegg and Son,
     1836-1837.

Cleland, James. <u>Statistical and Population Tables</u>
     <u>Relative to the City of Glasgow</u>. Glasgow, 1828.

Cunningham, John. <u>The Church History of Scotland</u>. 2
     vols. Edinburgh: James Thin, 1882.

Curnock, Nehemiah (ed.). <u>The Journal of the Rev. John</u>
     <u>Wesley, A.M.</u> 8 vols. London: Charles H. Kelly,
     1909-1916.

Currie, Robert, Alan Gilbert, and Lee Horsley.
     <u>Churches and Churchgoers. Patterns of Church</u>
     <u>Growth in the British Isles Since 1700</u>. Oxford:
     Clarendon Press, 1977.

Daw, A. R. "John Wesley in Scotland: The Bicentenary
     of Methodism." <u>Scots Magazine</u>, 29 (1938), 127-
     132.

Defoe, Daniel. <u>A Tour through the Whole Island of</u>
     <u>Great Britain</u>, ed. Pat Rogers. Harmondsworth:
     Penguin Books, 1971.

<u>Dictionary of National Biography</u>.

Fletcher, C. R. L. <u>An Introductory History of England</u>.
     London: John Murray, 1916.

Geyl, Peter. <u>Orange and Stuart, 1641-1672</u>, trans.
     Arnold Pomerans. New York: Charles Scribner's
     Sons, 1969.

Hamilton, Elizabeth. William's Mary, a Biography of
    Mary II. New York: Taplinger Publishing Company,
    1972.

Hamilton, Henry. An Economic History of Scotland in
    the Eighteenth Century. Oxford: Clarendon Press,
    1963.

Harrison, G. Elsie. Son to Susanna. The Private Life
    of John Wesley. Nashville: Cokesbury Press,
    1938.

Hetherington, W. M. History of the Church of Scotland.
    New York: Robert Carter, 1859.

Innes, Sir Thomas. The Tartans of the Clans and
    Families of Scotland, 8th ed. London: Johnston
    and Bacon Publishers, 1971.

Jackson, Thomas (ed.). The Works of the Rev. John
    Wesley, A.M., 3rd ed. 14 vols. London: Wesleyan
    Conference Office, 1872.

Jeffery, David Lyle. A Burning and a Shining Light.
    English Spirituality in the Age of Wesley. Grand
    Rapids, Michigan: William B. Eerdmans Publishing
    Company, 1987.

Jones, Thomas Snell. The Life of the Viscountess
    Glenorchy, with Extracts from Her Diary and
    Correspondence. Edinburgh, 1822.

Johnson, Edgar. Sir Walter Scott: The Great Unknown,
    2 vols. New York: The Macmillan Company, 1970.

Kyd, J. G. Scottish Population Statistics. Scottish
    Historical Society, 3rd ser., Volume 9.
    Edinburgh: Scottish Historical Society, 1952.

Lecky, William Edward Hartpole. A History of England
    in the Eighteenth Century, 3rd ed., rev. 8 vols.
    London: Longmans, Green, and Company 1883-1890.

Lockhart, John Gibson. Memoirs of the Life of Sir
    Walter Scott. 7 vols. Edinburgh: Robert Cadell,
    1837.

Lunn, Arnold. John Wesley. New York: The Dial Press,
     1929.

Mackie, R. L. A Short History of Scotland, ed. Gordon
     Donaldson. New York: Frederick A. Praeger,
     Publisher, 1963.

Maclean, Fitzroy. A Concise History of Scotland. New
     York: The Viking Press, 1970.

Methodist Recorder, 25 August 1904, p. 320.

Moore, Henry. The Life of the Reverend John Wesley. 2
     vols. London, 1825.

Osborn, George (ed.). The Poetical Works of John and
     Charles Wesley. 13 vols. London: Wesleyan
     Methodist Conference Office, 1868-1872.

Petrie, Charles. The Jacobite Movement. The Last
     Phase, 1716-1807. London: Eyre and Spottiswoode,
     1950.

Pottle, Frederick A. (ed.). Boswell's London Journal.
     New York: McGraw-Hill Book Company, 1950.

_____, and Charles H. Bennett (eds.).
     Boswell's Journal of a Tour to the Hebrides with
     Samuel Johnson, LL.D., 1773. London: William
     Heinemann, Ltd., 1963.

The Private Correspondence of Horace Walpole, Earl of
     Orford. London: Printed for Rodwell and Martin,
     Bond Street, 1820, 3:441.

Proceedings of the Wesley Historical Society, 4 (1904);
     9 (1909).

Ramsay, Edward Bannerman Burnett. Reminiscences of
     Scottish Life and Character. Edinburgh, 1858.

Reed, Joseph W., and Frederick A. Pottle (eds.).
     Boswell: Laird of Auchinleck. New York and
     London: McGraw Hill Book Company, 1977.

Reid, W. Standford. Trumpeter of God. A Biography of
     John Knox. New York: Charles Scribner's Sons,
     1974.

Rogal, Samuel J.   John and Charles Wesley.   Boston:
     G. K. Hall/Twayne Publishers, 1983.

Ryskamp, Charles, and Frederick A. Pottle (eds.).
     Boswell: The Ominous Years, 1774-1776.   London:
     William Heinemann, Ltd., 1963.

Scotland, James.   Modern Scotland.   A Short History
     from 1707 to the Present Day.   London: G. Bell
     and Sons, Ltd., 1953.

Scots Magazine, 1750-1800.

Smollett, Tobias George.   The Expedition of Humphry
     Clinker, ed. Andre Parreaux.   Boston: Houghton
     Mifflin and Company, 1968.

Southey, Robert.   The Life of Wesley and the Rise and
     Progress of Methodism.   London: George Bell and
     Sons, 1901.

Story, George, and Joseph Benson (eds.).   The Methodist
     Magazine.   24 vols.   London: The Methodist Book
     Concern, 1798-1821.

Telford, John (ed.).   The Letters of the Rev. John
     Wesley, A.M.   8 vols.   London: The Epworth Press,
     1931.

_____.   The Life of the Rev. John
     Wesley, A.M.   London: Wesleyan Methodist Book
     Room, 1900.

Thomson, George Malcolm.   The Crime of Mary Stuart.
     New York: E. P. Dutton and Co., Inc., 1967.

Tobin, Terence.   Plays by Scots, 1660-1800.   Iowa City:
     University of Iowa Press, 1974.

Trevelyan, George Macaulay.   England under Queen Anne:
     Ramillies and the Union with Scotland.   London:
     Collins/The Fontana Library, 1965.

_____.   Illustrated English Social
     History.   Volume Three: The Eighteenth Century.
     Harmondsworth: Penguin Books, Ltd., 1964.

Tyerman, Luke. The Life of the Rev. George Whitefield.
     London: Hodder, and Stoughton, 1876-1877.
_____. The Life and Times of the
     Reverend John Wesley, M.A. New York: Harper and
     Brother, 1872.
Walker, Ralph S. (ed.). The Correspondence of James
     Boswell and John Johnston of Grange. New York:
     McGraw-Hill Book Company, n.d.
Walker, Williston. A History of the Christian Church,
     3rd ed. New York: Charles Scribner's Sons, 1970.
Wesley, John and George Story (eds.). The Arminian
     Magazine. 20 vols. London: John Atlay,
     1778-1797.
Wimsatt, William K., and Frederick A. Pottle (eds.).
     Boswell for the Defence, 1769-1774. London:
     William Heinemann Ltd., 1960.
The Works of the Reverend George Whitefield, M.A.
     London: 1771-1772.
Youngston, A. J. The Making of Classical Edinburgh,
     1750-1840. Edinburgh: At the University Press,
     1966.

INDEX OF BIBLICAL REFERENCES

GENERAL INDEX

STUDIES IN THE HISTORY OF MISSIONS